Incarnational
AGENTS

A GUIDE TO DEVELOPMENTAL MINISTRY

BY JOHN R. CHEYNE

New Hope
Birmingham, Alabama

New Hope
P. O. Box 12065
Birmingham, Alabama 35202-2065

Dewey Decimal Classification: 261.8
Subject Headings: CHURCH AND SOCIAL PROBLEMS
                  CHURCH WORK
                  MISSION ACTION
                  HUNGER
                  POVERTY

Cover design by Barry Graham

ISBN: 1-56309-168-2
N963117•0796•5M1

"There is a wound in the Creation, and it groans
and travails until now, and I don't know why;
therefore I follow Francis, and ask to be given some part in the
healing of it. It is the only way in which
I can give meaning to my life, and indeed meaning
to life upon the earth."

—Alan Paton

This book is warmly dedicated to the many Incarnational Agents who serve our Lord by sharing their lives to enable others to have life . . . and that more abundantly.

CONTENTS

FOREWORD

Human suffering in our world confronts us daily. Statistics reflect the growing numbers of impoverished peoples, the hungry, the homeless, the refugee, and those whose security has been destroyed by war and conflict. Those who have lost the basic quality of life may represent a larger percentage of our world or they may simply have kept pace with the exploding population. But our awareness of their needs has been enhanced by modern media and travel.

There was a time when an occasional newspaper or magazine article would prick our conscience regarding the needs of people in some remote corner of the world. Now our senses are inundated with graphic portrayals of starving children in the Horn of Africa, earthquake victims in India, villages in Bangladesh devastated by typhoons. The threat of war among global powers has been replaced with hundreds of local conflicts. Political contention and ethnic hatred have embroiled helpless citizens in senseless wars.

So what? Can anything be done about the AIDS epidemic in Africa or

the tide of refugees displaced from their homes and deprived of liveli-
hood in war-torn nations? Can anything be done to reforest the moun-
tains, purify contaminated water, restore productivity to arid soil, and
equip the illiterate with income-generating skills? Many would say,
"No." The problems are too massive, the needs too great, the resources
too small. Others would point out the millions of dollars in governmental and charitable aid being wasted and misapplied, absorbed in administration and delivery costs while the poor continue to suffer.

But John Cheyne sees a solution. Not a theoretical solution born in the
isolated offices of ivory-tower administrators, but a practical solution
discovered through 40 years of living and working in the midst of hurting people. That solution is expressed in the title of this book,
Incarnational Agents. Those involved in relief and development ministry
must also identify with and live among the sufferers. We cannot effectively transform a community of hurting people without being there and
serving next to the need. We must become a partner with them in effect-
ing relief, not a patron who creates dependency or provides immediate
aid but no long-term solution.

Appointed as a Southern Baptist missionary to Rhodesia in 1954,
John, and his wife, Marie, worked in evangelism and administration in
what is now Zimbabwe and later helped open Southern Baptist missions
work in Ethiopia. There they gave leadership to designing and organizing rural development projects. He concluded his 24 years of experience
overseas in the broader administrative role of field representative for
Eastern Africa.

From 1978 to 1990 John served as an associate, and then as a consultant on relief ministries on the Foreign Mission Board's staff. He later
became associate director of the research and planning office where he
related to the programs of human needs on a global basis. This involved
hunger relief, health care, social work, agriculture, disaster response, and
crisis management coordination.

He has written two previous books, scores of articles, and 27 position
papers and manuals. His practical involvement and global exposure in
surveys, training conferences, and strategy planning, in addition to field
experience, have equipped him with the unique insights reflected in this

book. On behalf of the Foreign Mission Board of the Southern Baptist Convention, he organized and developed the disaster response procedures, manual, and training that in 1992 allowed the FMB to respond to a major flood in Bangladesh, a cholera epidemic in South America, ministry among Kurds in Iraq, and famine relief in Africa, all at the same time. In the last 15 years he has been responsible for channeling more than $100 million in donations for hunger and relief so that 100 percent of these funds could be applied to projects overseas.

Incarnational Agents moves beyond the usual spiritual apartheid of evangelism and social ministry as an either/or proposition. It presents a holistic approach to suffering that is biblical, practical, realistic, and workable. John tells how to appraise the situation and to see beyond the obvious by classifying needs and engaging in survey, research, and feasibility studies. A dimension often missing from other books and manuals that major on the technical is the cross-cultural sensitivity born out of the author's own experience overseas. One of the greatest benefits of this book is the insightful understanding of cross-cultural communication, contextualized values, relationships, group dynamics, and decision making. This insight and understanding is essential to the incarnational approach. We also gain a comprehensive perspective on the process of strategic planning in determining methodologies, utilizing resources, implementing objectives, and evaluating results.

This book will be a valuable textbook, planning guide, and project manual for any individual or agency responding to suffering and human needs. Not only should it become a primary resource for every missions organization, but it should find widespread use among governmental and international secular agencies involved in relief around the world.

Jerry Rankin, President
Foreign Mission Board, SBC

PREFACE

One of the first things one recognizes in the process of attempting to write is the fact that very little, if anything, is actually original today. Over the past 16 years I have been very much involved in providing guidance for the work of human needs for the Foreign Mission Board of the Southern Baptist Convention. Prior to that time, my wife and I served for 24 years in Africa in the field of evangelism and administration.

During those two periods of time, I have been greatly impressed with teachers, authors, and proponents involved in caring ministries who have written, taught, and been involved in various aspects of responding to human need. I have learned from them and am deeply indebted for all I have been able to glean from their efforts. In as many cases as possible, I have given credit to those who are either quoted, or whose material has been modified by my own use and experience in the field. There may be instances where I have failed to remember sources from lectures, etc., or have inadvertently left off proper acknowledgment of the source. If so, I will be happy to make such acknowledgment and subsequent corrections. I do recognize that once we have begun to use materials, modify them, and initiate them in practical applications, ownership tends to become blurred. If this has happened, I apologize to the ones who may have planted the thoughts, and hereby recognize my indebtedness to all with whom I have come in contact during these years and who have provided the inspiration and information thus used.

I owe a special word of thanks and appreciation to Clark Scanlon, my immediate supervisor at the Foreign Mission Board, who made it possible for me to spend the necessary time in developing this manuscript. Ramona Beam and Elaine Rideout made invaluable contributions in proofreading the text. I am also indebted to Marie, my lovely wife, who spent many lonely hours at home while I was in the process of traveling overseas and involved in various aspects of human need ministries.

INTRODUCTION

The gaunt face of a starving child. The windswept desert plain of a drought-stricken part of Africa. The plight of 145 million street children in the megacities across the world. Mothers scavenging amid mushrooming mounds of garbage. Shanties teetering on the edge of lowland marshes outside of city centers. These and other images, coupled with major movie stars making emotional appeals to save the children or feed the starving, flash daily across our television screens.

Most of those who have lived and worked in the developing world, and who have experienced these human tragedies first-hand, have tried to do something about it. Yet, the enormity of hunger and hurt has not abated. One of the reasons may be that people have been lulled into thinking that by merely handing out food or by providing emergency aid they may remove the problems. Obviously, however, it is much easier and even more dramatic to provide temporary help for urgent needs than it is to solve the underlying problems which create the need.

Experts in the secular world are constantly coming together to discuss what they should do about the problems of the poorest of the poor. International leaders espousing a "new world order" now propose to grant empowerment to the poorest through bilateral agreements to support the developing nations. Through financial arrangements with world banks, new aid programs, investments by multinational corporations and trade agreements between the rich and the poor nations, idealistic plans are now being fashioned in the counsel rooms of the international forums. Tragically for the poor nations, those holding the power and making the decisions are the ones who inevitably benefit the most. As Richard Nixon said in 1968, "Let us remember that the main purpose of foreign aid is not to help other nations but to help ourselves." Much of US foreign aid has been used for political leverage rather than for the purpose of meeting human need.

Some kinds of developmental projects can and do help. No matter how we describe the tragedy of human hurt, however, it will take more than humanistic development or even aid programs to solve the real dilemma of the human condition. Beyond quick-fix proposals, massive food distribution in crisis situations, or highly structured government projects, there is a growing and uniquely Christian concept to deal with problems of human hurt which has been called "transformational ministries."

Fundamental to this approach is the understanding that material progress without spiritual transformation is most often made at the expense of those most desperately in need.

Humanistic developmental plans often fail when those implementing and receiving the benefits of the plans are self-limited by human greed, power politics, graft, or just plain lethargy. Real transformation calls for wholeness. As Wayne Bragg says, "It is a change from a level of human existence that is less than that envisioned by our Creator, to one in which man is fully human and free to move to a state of wholeness in harmony with God and with every aspect of his environment."[1]

Trained national Christians, development workers, and missionary personnel are in a unique position to deal with some of these problems. By understanding the culture and knowing the language they can employ grassroots approaches in which transformed people fully participate in the processes of self-realization and enablement. Such approaches allow for the maximum of local involvement and are designed to enable indigenous peoples to replicate the processes without constant dependency on outside assistance. In this way those involved with transformational ministry do more than just meet the immediate or crisis need. Transformation moves into and then beyond the immediate need to discover and minister to the underlying problems—spiritual, physical, or emotional—which create the need.

There are some foundational principles in transformational ministries which must be understood if they are to be effective. Those who desire a new world order, which, idealistically, is capable of solving the enormous problems of human hurt, must first:

- have an honest respect of human life and traditional values in terms of God's eternal purpose and biblical revelation for those being served;
- so incarnationalize the gospel that all people everywhere may first see it and experience it in action, then embrace it by faith;
- recognize that only Christ can create the change necessary within individuals and through which participation in the transformation can be successful;
- be sensitive and responsive to every dimension of the human condition of those with whom they would share Christ, meeting people at the point of their deepest need and where they can best comprehend the message of love;
- ensure that those enabling processes or programs of work allow for the fullest local participation and the application of transforming experiences both spiritually and physically;
- initiate those holistic approaches for dealing with human hurt which are carried out in the context of the essential purpose for missionary presence. These must be interdependent and interrelated to all else they do;
- provide self-sustaining opportunities for those in need to move

toward personal empowerment in the areas of their greatest potential and unique abilities;

• provide for ways to escape from the injustices, inequities, and importunities which bind them in political, social, and spiritual bondage.

Individual missionaries, missions agencies, international relief agencies, or even world governmental bodies have not solved the world's hunger problems. They probably will not be able, in our lifetime, to remove the tragedy of the ghetto, the street children, or the ravages of drought and famine. As those who love the Lord go about sharing the Word of the gospel, however, they can demonstrate the dynamic power of Christ to change men and women spiritually and to transform them physically.

We have no shame in declaring that the motivation behind our capacity to minister and care is at once the love of Christ and His saving grace in and through transformed lives.

This book represents an attempt to provide those who would be incarnational agents in meeting human need some basic helps in understanding efficient and effective ways to respond to those needs in the context of the Great Commission which calls us to "go ye into all the world, and preach the Gospel to every creature," and the Great Commandment, which says, "thou shalt love thy neighbor as thyself."

Notes

¹Tom Sine, *The Church in Response to Human Need*, "Beyond Development," 71.

CHAPTER 1

BIBLICAL FOUNDATIONS . . . FOR A HOLISTIC APPROACH IN MISSIONS

The Old Testament Worldview—The Genesis of Holism

These days missiologists have come to talk a lot about holistic missions. If indeed the implications of a holistic approach in missions are to be understood, it will be important to understand the biblical basis for the holistic concept. This chapter is not written for the purpose of providing a series of proof texts which point out the obvious in the Scriptures; i.e., that the Bible is full of references showing God's concern for the poor, the needy, the oppressed, the hungry, or the hurting. It is rather to contextualize a few of those references in regard to the theological implications which give rise to the demand for a holistic approach in meeting human needs while sharing the good news.

The opening salvos of Scripture suggest immediately that humanity has a responsibility toward all of God's creation. In Genesis, chapter 1, humanity is told to use all that God has created, blessed, and called good. In the next chapter God invokes the responsibility to guard and keep it. In the beginning people had a twofold obligation in their relationship with God—the vertical, with God Himself, as the individual walks in harmony with the Creator, and the horizontal, as the individual has responsibility and concern for everything in the surrounding world. Almost immediately we see that relationship broken.

Man's sin separates him from the Creator and forges an enmity between the created and the Creator. Not only does a break exist between humanity and God, there is also a breakdown between man and man; he becomes a killer to be hunted as a fugitive and a vagabond. Further, there is a rift between humanity and the environment; man is cast from the garden and becomes a tiller of the soil which has been cursed to bring forth thorns and thistles. Man, we discover, must not only be reconciled with God, but also be reconciled with other people, and even be reconciled with the environment!

In this context, Cain asks the question, "Am I my brother's keeper?" But this is not his question alone, it is an eternal question that never really goes away. From that time on, it continues to echo through the halls of history until we hear it on the lips of a lawyer who comes to Jesus wanting to know how to be saved. The context is very important here. In His response, Jesus points him to the law and the Great Commandment. In the first part of the commandment the Lord tells him, "Love the Lord thy God with all thy heart, and with all thy soul, and with all thy strength, and with all thy mind," and the second part demands you must "love thy neighbor as thyself." Again the vertical and the horizontal are evident. The implications are clear; i.e., there is an intrinsic relationship between person and God, between the individual and other people, and between person and all that God has created. The point is not whether one is saved by loving one's neighbor, but rather whether one can really claim to love God with a whole heart when there is no apparent evidence of the incarnate love which manifests itself in loving one's neighbor. Matthew 25 carries this a bit further. The "inasmuch as you did it (or did it not) . . . unto me" passages imply that the only valid credibility for claiming that

Christ dwells in the believer is the fact that those lives emulate Christ's life. Going back to Cain's question, it would therefore seem to suggest that to whatever extent one fails to be his brother's (or sister's) keeper, he participates in becoming his brother's killer.

An Intrinsic Interrelationship

This worldview of an intrinsic interdependent relationship between the Creator, the creature, and all of creation is consistent throughout the Bible. In the Old Testament it is perhaps best illustrated in the Book of Job. Job is left stripped of every physical thing that had meaning to him—his possessions, his family, his health, his dignity, his sense of self-worth—even to the point of total despair for his life. In this context, his wife asks him a very interesting question. She says, "Do you still hold on to your integrity? Curse God and die." (Job 2:9) The use of the word integrity is most significant at this point, for what she really appears to be asking relates to Job's understanding and belief that all of his life has been fully integrated in God. He cannot separate the physical from the spiritual. His home, cattle, camels, donkeys, farm, family, and physical well-being have all been totally integrated in the will and purpose of God in his life. No one part of life can be dealt with outside the framework of the interaction of God in the whole of his life.

He doesn't divide his life into spiritual and physical components. To him, all of life had a spiritual significance, and all of it related to God's involvement with him and God's perfect will for him. Now the essence of the question is, 'Do you still hold on to the idea that God is concerned or involved in your livestock, your buildings, your money—the physical things of life?' Job knew God was vitally concerned! As a matter of fact, this concern was the key to the meaning of life itself. All of his life was integrated in God, hence, his integrity had to do with worldview, not just his moral righteousness.

The Poor and the Law–The Land and the People

The same principle of integration in Job's life is demonstrated when the three friends come to talk with him. In chapter 22,

Eliphaz charges that the real reason for Job's suffering was related to his attitude toward the poor and needy. It had, he said, to do with his failure to cover the naked, give drink to the thirsty, his withholding bread from the hungry, acting unjustly regarding the division of his land, and not caring for the widows and orphans. In other words, drawing his conclusions from the law as illustrated in Leviticus 19:9-10 and 25:35, Eliphaz alleges Job failed to act responsibly with all that he had received from God.

God had therefore, implies Eliphaz, "withdrawn from every part of Job's life."

Now, of course, Job goes on to deny this charge, crying, "If I have denied justice to my menservants . . . . If I have denied the desires of the poor . . . . If I have kept my bread to myself, not sharing it with the fatherless . . . . If I have seen anyone perishing for lack of clothing, or a needy man without a garment . . . then let briers come up instead of wheat, and weeds instead of barley. Oh, let me be weighed in a just balance." He finally cries, "Oh, that God may know my integrity!" (Job 31:5-6) There's that word again. Job seems to be saying, "No, none of that is true, my record is right with the Lord! I have related every part of my life holistically, both to the vertical relationship with my Lord, and the horizontal relationship to my fellow man." Job cannot separate the two. They are intrinsically interdependent.

Worship–Its Relationship to Justice and Judgment
Isaiah gives another insight into the biblical understanding of the interdependent relationship between one's capacity or desire for true worship and one's responsibility toward others. This is not just an argument concerning the importance of faith and works, but rather that justice, love, and concern for the poor and needy are seen as part of the act of worship. In chapter 58, Isaiah brings up the subject of the people's mechanical, legalistic presumption of true worship as revealed in their acts of fasting and prayer. The worshipers have asked, in effect, "How come God doesn't respond when we fundamentally follow all the rules?" God's word through His prophet suggests that they need to take another look at the real

meaning of worship and justice. In the middle of your fasting, Isaiah says, "You do as you please and exploit all your workers." Later, he exclaims, "Is this the kind of fast that God chooses?"

He then answers his own question: "Is it not to divide your bread with the hungry, and bring the homeless poor into your house? When you see the naked that you cover him, and that you hide not yourself from the needs of your own flesh and blood? Then shall your light break forth as the morning, and your healing shall spring forth speedily; your righteousness shall go before you and the glory of the Lord shall be your rear guard" (Isa. 58:7-8).

The prophet clearly emphasizes that there is no way one can give expression to a pure worship experience, even in fasting and praying, while, at the same time, one is acting unjustly toward others, or failing to respond to their basic physical needs. James amplifies the same truth when he exclaims, "External religious worship that is pure and unblemished in the sight of God the Father is this: to visit and help and care for the orphans and widows in their affliction and need, and to keep one's self unspotted from the world" (James 1:27).

The Great Commission and the Great Commandment– Where Do They Meet?
Few, if any, would really argue as to whether the church has a biblical mandate to be concerned with the physical dimensions of human need. For many, however, it becomes a matter of the priority of pure evangelism over that of physical concerns. The problem to be faced is that of harmonizing the evangelistic expectations of the Great Commission to go into all the world making disciples with the ministry message of the Great Commandment which requires disciples to wholly love God and their neighbor. Are both valid? Are both equally binding? If so, should one have priority over the other? How does one manage to fulfill the fundamental concern to win this world to the Lord Jesus Christ, when so much of it has such a desperate physical need? Or how, in the midst of such immeasurable human hurt, do incarnational agents keep from getting bogged down in social work or

humanitarian concerns, when so many are lost and will go to an eternity without Christ if we fail to win them?

The real issue is not one of either/or, it is the question of how one can scripturally reconcile or integrate both the evangelistic mandate and the ministry mandate without compromising one or the other.

The Ministry and Message of Reconciliation

The relationship between ministry and message is most clearly expressed by Paul in his second letter to Corinth, when he says, "Now all those things are from God, who reconciled us to Himself through Christ, and gave us the ministry (*diakonus*) of reconciliation, namely, that God was in Christ reconciling the world to Himself, not counting their trespasses against them, and He has committed to us the message (*logos*) of reconciliation . . . be ye reconciled to God" (2 Cor. 5:18-20).

Whatever position or whatever particular theological understanding the Christian worker may have, to be scriptural, they must be consistent with the underlying biblical responsibility to integrate both the ministry and message of reconciliation. For it is within the reconciling work of our Lord that ministry and message come together.

The ultimate purpose or motivation behind any valid scriptural ministry must be that of bringing individuals into a full and abundant relationship with Jesus Christ as Lord and Savior—to be fully reconciled with Him. The term *fully reconciled* should be understood to mean more than just the initial salvation experience and discovery of new life in Christ—the message of reconciliation. It also refers to the capacity to grow and to express a mature Christian faith in relationship to God, fellow human beings, and the circumstances of life itself—the ministry of reconciliation. Anything less than this is not the whole gospel to the whole person.

Jesus came, not only to give us life, but that we might have life "more abundantly." A singular emphasis upon what Peter Wagner calls "proclamation evangelism," in his book, *Church Growth and the Whole Gospel,* without an honest sensitivity and compassion for people, may well lay the Christian agent vulnerable to the charge that such eschatology is more concerned with a "pie-in-the-sky-by-and-by" kind of ticket-punching theology, than with an honest concern and sensitivity to the present reality of the human condition. This kind of theology relates to only one sphere of life—that which introduces persons to God. It fails to relate to all of life—the spiritual birth and all that follows in every sphere of life and spiritual relationship as we grow into God's likeness. In practice, what normally happens is the creation of a dichotomy both theologically in faith and functionally in practice.[1]

One of the causes of the dichotomy and subsequent tension is the inevitable tendency to categorize the two mandates, polarizing and prioritizing them. Thus, there tends to be a duality in carrying out the gospel mandates which makes everything that is not considered pure evangelism part of the means to an end.

On the one hand, the evangelist may say, "God has called me to preach, not to do social work." On the other hand, the social worker may say, "God has equipped me to serve, let the preachers do the preaching." Each may feel that his or her role is the most important or that it stands alone.

Some Honest Concerns and Differences
Some fear the rebirth of a "rice Christian" kind of social gospel which often used food as a poorly disguised reward for joining the church. They also fear the potential for the rise of a neosocial gospel, or liberation theology which would undermine a fundamental and essential evangelistic emphasis. Others, like Peter Wagner, seem to reflect a similar concern and emphasize that losing the primacy of evangelism may have negative consequences for church growth by creating a tension between what he calls primary "spiritual" issues and secondary matters "of the flesh." He would, therefore, redefine evangelism on three levels:[2]

1. Presence Evangelism: the fulfilling of the "cultural" (ministry) mandate or evangelizing the structures of society. It stresses presence as sufficient evangelism. Witness is summed up in lifestyle—goodness, love, or acts of mercy. Living the good life is therefore considered evangelism.

2. **Proclamation Evangelism:** announcing the good news. Some hold that to evangelize does not demand that one be concerned with the actual results of proclamation, but simply to carry out the responsibility of making the proclamation.

3. **Persuasion Evangelism:** evangelism that results in men and women accepting the gospel, believing in Jesus, and becoming incorporated into churches as responsible members.

The Mission of the Church

Many strong evangelicals would describe the Great Commission and the call to witness given in Acts 1:8 as being the "mission of the church," and would, therefore, tend to define missions solely in terms of what Wagner calls proclamation evangelism. Traditionally, the role of the missionary has been that of an itinerant preacher giving full priority to the proclamation of the Word. Philip Crowe at the Islington Conference in 1968 is quoted as telling the story of R. N. Cust, a missionary of the last century, who argued that money for missions was "collected for the purpose of converting a soul, not sharpening an intellect." He drew the line when it came to using missions funds for the support of "a pious industrial superintendent, or an evangelical tile manufacturer, or a low church breeder of cattle or raiser of turnips." (This would be rather heavy for some of our modern missionary veterinarians!) Of course, schools, hospitals, and benevolent ministries have always had their place in missions, but to this day they are often considered as either auxiliary or secondary to the primary purpose of missionary presence on the field.

Statements from the World Council of Churches have, in the past, moved almost in the opposite direction of Cust and his persuasion. The 1967 publication of the World Council titled, "The Church for Others," developed the thesis that: "God is at work in the historical process, that the purpose of His mission, the 'missio Dei,' is the establishment of shalom in the sense of social harmony, and that this shalom (which it suggested was identical with the kingdom of God) is exemplified in the emancipation of colored races, the concern for the humanization of industrial relations, various attempts at rural development, the quest for business and professional ethics, and the concern for intellectual honesty and integrity."

Close to this are the reflections of liberation theology, especially as enunciated by Gustavo Gutierrez in his book, *The Theology of Liberation.* In the context of an honest concern for individuals to have the right to give expression for self-fulfillment and liberation from those things which would limit or impede their exercise of personal freedom, he presents social and political liberation in such a way that one could almost interpret it as his definition of salvation. Rather than emphasizing evangelism, he points toward political action and social reformation as being the vital direction in which the church should be moving. The kingdom of God would seem to be equated with the building up of the social order and salvation part of the historical process of liberating humanity from political and social injustice. Unfortunately such terms as holistic and incarnational missions are sometimes identified solely with those who hold a liberal theological position in other matters of faith. In some cases, such identification could imply that all evangelicals are therefore bigoted and unconcerned with issues such as justice, freedom, and social action. When evangelicals fail to emphasize the importance of these matters, they then appear to imply these are, in fact, only peripheral issues, of little primary concern to the church.

Some go to the Scriptures using an identical passage in an attempt to prove the correctness of their opposing positions. When the passage in question is ambiguous, such as Luke 4:18-19, where the Lord quotes from Isaiah, it makes it even more difficult. Jesus says: "The Spirit of the Lord is upon Me, because He hath anointed Me to preach the gospel to the poor. He hath sent Me to heal the broken-hearted, to preach deliverance to the captives, and recovering of sight to the blind, to set at liberty them that are bruised, to preach the acceptable year of the Lord."

One man picks up the Book, and says, "See, this authenticates both social ministries and social action." Another man declares that the Lord is really speaking about those who are spiritually poor, broken, blind, or captive of Satan; therefore, this is speaking of the evangelistic mandate. The real point is that the Lord did not clarify or differentiate!

In the seventh chapter of Luke, our Lord's response to John the Baptist gives further room for comparison. When John asks, "Are you the one who was to come, or shall we look for another?" Jesus does not refer to the prophecies of the past, the signs fulfilled surrounding His birth, doctrinal proof-texts or even the voice of the Father at the time of His baptism, but rather exclaims: "Go back and report to John what you have seen and heard: the blind receive sight, the lame walk, those who have leprosy are cured, the deaf hear, the dead are raised, and the good news is preached to the poor" (Luke 7:22).

As so often happened, Jesus rested His case for authenticity on the manifestation of the Father through His ministry in the context or circumstances regarding human need. Does this then mean that the most authentic way of spreading the gospel is in the arena of good works? Of course not! As we shall see, however, it does present a strong argument for sharing Christ contextually with a strong sensitivity and consideration for those factors that will most fully reveal Christ through both the ministry and the message of the evangel. Many of the world's poorest, hungriest, and most unreached people may still be asking the question of the most ardent kind of evangelist, "Are you the Christ kind of person, or do we wait for another?"

An Evangelical Theology of Liberation

Humanity is in bondage. John affirms this, "Whoever commits and practices sin is the slave of sin" (John 8:34). Or, as Paul puts it, we are "by nature, children of wrath" (Eph. 2:3). Again he says, "Do you not know that when you present yourselves to someone as slaves for obedience, you are slaves of the one who you obey, either of sin resulting in death, or of obedience resulting in righteousness"

(Rom. 6:16). In Romans, chapter 1, he suggests further that when "God gave them up," they became also subject to the worst the world and the flesh had to offer. Humanity's bondage, therefore, is primarily symptomatic of the wider effect of sin and separation from God. The effect of this sin, however, is twofold.

The first is a self-inflicted, willful separation from God and spiritual freedom which keeps one from knowing and enjoying the abundant life offered in Christ. The second is the result of insatiable self-interest which has just as effectively enslaved others either by denying them the opportunity to hear the gospel message which proclaims, "If the Son liberates you, you shall be free indeed," or by a callous lack of concern for them. This often moves to the crass exploitation of the poor, ignorant, weak, and needy, thus creating a deeper level of spiritual, physical, social, and political enslavement. Obviously, this is not only contrary to the Christian message, but unfortunately, it actually appears to be symptomatic of some who portray themselves as being evangelicals.

It is clear that the world shall not be freed from the bondage of sin by dealing only with the physical symptoms. The whole gospel is not finished when the possibility of a new life in Christ is proclaimed, however. The babe in Christ, who has reached out to accept this new life, may truly desire to be saved. Yet, the new believer may never experience or be able to give expression to the life he or she would possess, unless also freed from those things which cause physical, intellectual, cultural, economical, political, or social enslavement.

How then shall the role of evangelicals be defined? If the incarnational agent is to be true to the spirit of our Lord, the gospel must first of all become incarnate in the life of the proclaimer. Freedom or liberation is not summarized wholly in the initial act of repentance. Someone has said, "Only that is really free which is in harmony with the nature of its being." Man is a spiritual being, but also a physical one. Christians may not be *of* this world, but they are *in* this world. It seems evident, therefore, that a person's freedom is derived from the act of faith in Christ as Lord, in which the new believer is released through the incarnational power of the Spirit to become what God intended. A person is always in the process of becoming. As Nietzsche said, "Freedom is the capacity to become what we truly are." Or as John indicated, "As He (Christ) is so are we in this world." The gift of the Gospel, therefore, is freedom to be what we were born again in Christ to become.

Conversely, humanity's slavery results from personal efforts to find a center for life apart from God. Man's freedom as well as his being is rooted and grounded in the fact that God is. As creature to the Creator, as one made in the image of God, man's existence is a dependent existence. We are really alive only in relation to God. Freedom and selfhood are expressions of this fundamental relationship of one's existence.

Contextualizing Missions—Toward a People-Centered Approach

As used here, the term "contextualizing" simply means that the impact of the immediate circumstances of a person's existence determines the particular manner of sharing God's love.

The individual does not live in a vacuum, but is part and parcel of cultural circumstances. An individual can only understand this freedom in the context of personal circumstance. Conversely, if missionaries and others are to present the opportunity for spiritual freedom to people who have never heard, that message must be filtered through the context of those cultural circumstances which they may know and experience as bondage. The gospel message has meaning to them only in relationship to their capacity to interpret spiritual truth, to apply that truth, and to give expression to the implications of it as part of the body of Christ. To whatever degree they are blinded spiritually by superstition, ignorance, demonic powers, or whatever, they cannot be totally free until Christ is fully revealed to them and manifested through them. Their capacity to grasp the message proclaimed may be so inhibited by the physical and spiritual circumstances of their environment that they may never translate the truth of the gospel into meaningful reality. One of the great tragedies relating to human deprivation centers on the fact that often the cause of their privation is the result of the sins of those who have the most, and sometimes even of those who are the supporters and proclaimers of the gospel.

Let me cite a personal experience. On a trip to Recife, Brazil, I was escorted by a local pastor whose church was located in one of the worst slum areas, called an invasion area. It was very close to one of the largest industrial compounds in the city. We walked about a mile from the church and finally came to the end of the wall surrounding the industrial plant. Just beyond the wall there was a corridor about 150 yards wide. The corridor followed the outer edge of the wall and back about a mile. At that point, a huge hole was created to allow for the sewage of the plant to flow freely out into the corridor, where it wound its way to the place where we stood. Some 60,000 people had "invaded" the corridor to build their shanties amidst the filth of the sewage and the collective debris of the residents who had no facilities or other forms of sanitation.

The pastor led me into the heart of the ghetto and finally stopped in front of a tiny shack which stood about five feet from top to bottom and from front to back. It was mostly cardboard, with a bit of sackcloth for the doorway. There was no floor other than the muddy slime from the sewer. He called out and a young woman, hardly old enough to be a mother, crawled out with two small children. This was home for them. The father had long since left. The mother was illiterate, unemployable, destitute, and all alone. My first impulse was to tell her about the love of Christ. Then I tried to imagine how that would sound from her vantage point. I could imagine her responding, "What makes you think so? If God loves me, why must I live like this?"

Explaining that God loved her in Christ would not have been adequate without some down-to-earth demonstration of that love. The message of the proclamation would first of all be filtered by her perception of the proclaimer, as well as by the years of broken promises, personal loss, heartbreak, unheard pleas, and unanswered prayers to a series of "saints," all of whom seemed to have deaf ears and blind eyes. It then would have to be translated in symbols which had concrete meaning to her—which could convey the message, "God loves you," "I love you," or even that "there is a God." Fortunately, our trip was for the purpose of telling her that the church had found a place for her to live, and that she could start immediately in a vocational training and literacy course while her children were fed and until she could find work.

If the gospel message is to be understood and interpreted into meaningful expressions of the life of Christ, it must be free to deal not only with the spiritual reality of eternal life, but also with the finite physical realities of poverty, ignorance, disease, political oppression, exploitation, guilt, and despair. It is conceivable that a hungry mother watching her child die may never fully grasp, in that context, what we mean when we say that Jesus is the "bread of life," or "Jesus loves you." On the other hand, people imprisoned by poverty and superstition may all too eagerly reach out for the hope offered for spiritual release, only to become disillusioned, if and when we fail to translate the spiritual truth into a tangible expression of compassion related to those circumstances.

Obviously, there is a constant tension. Lacking any evidence of compassion toward them, so-called rice Christians may easily be bought and brought into the church, only to fall away when the bowl is no longer extended. At the same time, genuine compassion cannot afford to turn away for fear of being misunderstood. Our Lord's feeding of the five thousand was misinterpreted, but He still went on to feed four thousand more on another occasion. He took the risk, considering it was more important to express agape kind of compassion in the crisis of human hurt, than to guard against the potential for misunderstanding.

One wonders how Zacchaeus managed the handing out of half of his goods to the poor without creating an inappropriate response or continuing expectation from them. Difficult as it might have been, Jesus applauded his response as being in perfect harmony with the manifestation of his newfound faith.

Dichotomy in Ministry–A Type of Spiritual Apartheid!

Many have tended either to separate evangelism and social responsibility, or in the other extreme, to interpret evangelism largely in terms of social action. In some cases, this has led to establishment of denominational relief agencies—a kind of spiritual apartheid or separate development.

From the functional viewpoint, another impact has been the establishment of a multiplied number of parachurch agencies dealing with relief and development. There are now said to be well over 10,000 in the United States alone, not counting the nongovernmental organizations (NGOs). The resulting effect of this has been twofold. First, there has been a blurring of the lines of responsibility between the church's role in dealing with human hurt and that of humanitarian, nonsectarian agencies. Since both vie for government funding, and therefore are subject to government regulations, church leaders cannot always insist upon personnel who share a Christian lifestyle witness. For instance, if government aid funds (such as PL 480, Title 2) are used, the denominational agency cannot require that national workers must be born-again Christians. They may have to hire qualified Muslims, Hindus, or whatever, over devoted Christian laymen. Thus, evangelism becomes a separate and distinct part of their work.

One of the natural results has been the amplification of the dichotomy between ministry and message. The NGOs, being charged with the responsibility of humanitarian concerns, came into existence as separate and parallel units even though programs were, in many ways, coordinated with the work of other missions groups. Cleo F. Shook identifies some of the reasons why this dichotomy arose:[3]

1. The social gospel versus the *true* gospel debate, and eventual division.
2. The proliferation of missions groups:
   a. competing for the same funds.
   b. more narrowly defining/justifying their existence, their work over against others.

3. The course of history itself. As the world expanded, it shrank. Life everywhere became transcultural, at home and abroad. The resulting mixture of cultures gave rise to "don'ts" that supposedly identified the believer and spoke of "being in the world, but not of it!"
4. Problems in public, secular education, and the resulting development of Christian schools and a type of insular, isolationist thinking.
5. Problems in denominations—splits and split/splits, basically theologically-oriented (liberal versus conservative).
6. Among conservatives, differences, often oriented according to lifestyle, economic level, education, and geographic location.
7. Eschatological pressures—souls were saved before the judgment snatched people out of the work, but they were not shown how to live in the world with its problems.

This dichotomy, even though it accepts both mandates as important and valid, sees them as distinct and separate. By the very nature of their distinctiveness, however, they create a mind-set which both prioritizes and tends to place the ministry mandate in an inferior or a merely supportive role.

Evangelicals have been slow to accept the place of the ministry mandate as part of the primary mission of the church.

This kind of spiritual apartheid may evolve into the classifying of missionaries according to the relative value of their job assignment to the time spent in direct evangelism. Evangelists must be

DICHOTOMY (Separate Development)	
THE EVANGELISTIC MANDATE	THE MINISTRY MANDATE
Essential	Optional
Primary	Secondary
Intrinsic	Auxiliary
Spiritual	Physical
Proclamation Centered	Service Centered
Clergy Oriented	Lay Oriented
On "Cutting Edge"	Supportive
Primary Witness	Secondary Witness

extremely careful, however, that in the zeal to proclaim the Word, they do not create a cloud of doubt as to the level of our sense of Christian compassion. The wrong signals may proclaim a different message than they think! The dichotomy is most often perceived as on the previous page.

The 1974 Lausanne Covenant spoke to this issue and related it to the biblical concept of reconciliation, saying: "Although reconciliation with man is not reconciliation with God, nor is social action evangelism, nor is political liberation salvation, nevertheless we affirm that evangelism and social-political involvement are both part of our Christian duty. For both are necessary expressions of our doctrines of God and man, our love for our neighbor, and our obedience to Jesus Christ. The message of salvation implies also a message of judgment upon every form of alienation, oppression, and discrimination, and we should not be afraid to denounce evil and injustice wherever they exist. When people receive Christ, they are born again into His kingdom and must seek not only to exhibit but also to spread its righteousness in the midst of an unrighteous world. The salvation we claim should be transforming us in the totality of our personal and social responsibilities. Faith without works is dead."

Program-Centered Approaches–Spiritual Fragmentation
In many cases, what is sometimes thought of as being a holistic approach is merely a continuation or elaboration of the historic involvement of missions in benevolent ministries. Almost all denominations recognize that there has always been a place for these ministries, and that the church truly has a responsibility for carrying out the ministry mandate. However, in practice such ministries are still treated as being secondary to the essential purpose of missions.

While accepting the place of various "functional" ministries within the scope of the overall missions mandate, these ministries are more often seen as a means to an end, rather than having a justification all on their own, or of being part of the whole message of reconciliation. Taking exception to this concept Carl Henry says, "The primary reason for social involvement ought not to be an indirect ploy, but rather a straightforward demonstration of God's justice in the world."[4]

Wagner, on the other hand, suggests, "My view is that granting priority to evangelism will help, rather than retard the implementation of the social mandate."

As is evident in both of these statements, the concept of a holistic approach is not the issue, but rather the relative justification for both approaches. Covering the whole of the need with various functional segments of ministry does not guarantee that the ministry itself will be holistic. A holistic approach must involve a synergy of relationships in which every aspect of ministry and message is functioning in total harmony with the purpose of God for the life of those who are the objects of the ministry.

The whole is more than the sum of the parts. The emphasis in a functional approach is often primarily program centered, rather than people centered, a kind of spiritual fragmentation. The sense of primary and secondary is still there, especially at budget time. Evangelism, as a program, is then seen as the only essential or intrinsic function, while various other ministries are allowed to have their legitimate place. Each separate function may be in tension with each of the other phases of ministry as they vie for prominence in the program. What appears to be a unified ministry is in fact a fragmented environment for competition and/or comparison. It may be diagrammed as follows:

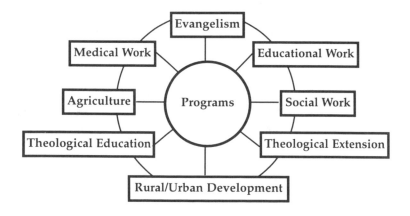

Contextualizing–A Holistic Approach!
One of the great problems in understanding the concept of a holistic approach is the tendency to stereotype those who work in disciplines other than our own. If the evangelist, doctor, social worker, or other specialist is primarily concerned about people, however, the focus of their efforts will be determined by the total condition or circumstance of the persons whom they would serve. It is not suggested that the evangelist stop being an evangelist or necessarily spend a significant amount of time in ministry-centered activities. Nor should every specialist become a preacher. Becoming servant, the evangelist and the other specialists must discover how best to initiate and carry through the total work of reconciliation between people and God, people and people, and people and their environment.

This is part of what Paul meant when he said, "I have become all things to all men that by some means I might win some."

Characteristics of a Holistic Approach
1. There is a clear definition and understanding of the overriding purpose of the church—the reconciliation of individuals to God through Jesus Christ. Do not forget, however, that individuals have been separated not only from the Father through sin, they have been separated from one another, creating inequalities and barriers. They have also been separated from the perfect environment which God created. Because of this separation, they now have a lack of understanding and care about the world in which they live and breathe.
2. Each aspect of the ministry and message of reconciliation is interdependent on each other part to complete the whole. The evangelist must be as sensitive to the physical condition of those to whom he would minister, as the doctor or agriculturist is to the spiritual condition of those whom they would heal or feed.
3. It is people centered—not program centered. Any program tends to become primary to the one heading it. Whether that program is a program of preaching, teaching, healing, or developing,

there is a tendency to lose the perspective of the whole circumstance in which people live.

4. Each phase of the work is contextually oriented, e.g., is sensitive to the whole of human circumstances in which it would attempt to communicate and apply the gospel. A mother holding her starving child may not be able to comprehend the message of the evangelist who proclaims, "God loves you!" but then fails to feed the child. A mother watching a caring and loving nurse ministering to her baby throughout the night may not understand the motivating power is the love of Christ, unless someone takes time to explain why she would care. It is not a question of which is more important. They stand together!

5. It speaks to and ministers in and through the whole circumstance of life without ulterior or secondary motivation. It is not a means to an end. If one's only motivation for caring is to deliver one's message, the message may not be wholly authentic. As Christians we care because that is the nature of Christ within us. If we do not care, "How can we say that the love of Christ dwells in us?" (1 John 3:16-17). Even our Lord said to the disciples, "Believe me when I say that I am in the Father and the Father is in me. If not, believe me because of the things I do" (John 14:11).

6. The whole message of the gospel is communicated through channels in which God's love can most clearly be interpreted, understood, and applied toward God's redemptive purpose. Understanding the gospel message may very well come at the point where we most clearly communicate the nature of God.

Holistic or Whole(istic)

Some have been confused as to the difference between holistic and what has erroneously been called wholistic. When we look at the concept of wholeness, it may simply refer to the sum total of the parts. It does not necessarily assume the interrelationship or interdependency of those parts in completing the whole. One way of illustrating this might be shown in the difference between a working watch and one taken apart with all its various parts and pieces.

One may have a whole watch lying on the table, but it has little value until each of the pieces is joined and functioning. We recognize, of course, it is the complete working together and mutual interdependency of those parts that make it a watch—not just the parts. Without this it is merely a montage of disconnected pieces.

Unfortunately, missions can often follow a similar pattern. All the various parts may be present, but they do not necessarily present the whole gospel to the whole person, and, in fact, the various parts may be in tension with one another rather than functioning as vital parts of the whole.

In a small booklet, Tetsunao Yamamori refers to the holistic concept as a symbiotic relationship and defines it as "two or more concerns or two or more forms of ministry, which, though functionally separate, are inseparable in relationship and essential for the ongoing of total life." He borrows his idea from the term *symbiosis*, taken from the field of biology. The term is made up of the Greek prefix-*sym*, meaning interdependence, and a Greek morpheme-*bios*, meaning life. Together they depict the harmonious living together of two functionally dissimilar organisms in a way beneficial to each other. It is described as a relationship which is obligatory in some sense, one partner being unable to live without the other, or each depending heavily upon the other.

If this symbiotic relationship is applied to the work of the local church or mission, it implies that the context will determine the specific emphasis or approach to individuals based upon the contextual reality in which they are found. In this way evangelism is seen in the context of total ministry; i.e., all ministry, whether that of the preacher, the doctor, the dentist, the social worker, or whoever, has as its essential purpose the liberation of people to the freedom found only in a full relationship to Jesus Christ as Lord and Savior. Obviously, these circumstances are interwoven and dynamic, but like a pattern must be considered as part of the whole piece of cloth.

This might best be illustrated by drawing a series of concentric circles. Each circle represents either a bridge or a barrier to witness and ministry. The person is always at the center. As one attempts to reach this person, one is confronted with a series of cultural and physical circumstances which may inhibit or even make communication of the gospel message impossible. Whether in human needs ministries or evangelistic ministries, success may depend on an awareness and sensitivity to those circumstances.

We do not see the evangelistic mandate and the ministry mandate as being identical or contradistinctive, rather we see them as an integral part of missions in the work of reconciling men and women to Jesus Christ. Neither the evangel nor the specialist in other disciplines must presume to function holistically without being fully sensitive to the whole circumstance of a person's life. Neither can they minister fully and ignore the reality of those circumstances which affect the whole of life in community. Therefore, they must deal with individuals in context. They may very well effect their most powerful witness as they stop by the side of the road to pick up and care for the fallen stranger, even though their primary function remains in their particular area of specialization.

Their own lifestyle and personal circumstance may be the message with the greatest impact and loudest voice—either for good or bad.

In a survey conducted by the social concern track at Lausanne over an eight-month period, 68 human needs projects, representing all five continents, were evaluated. In the summary, it was stated that the most important finding was that evangelism takes place best when the target community is treated not as a project, but as a people who have dignity and deserve respect. It also indicated that almost all groups surveyed engaged in these projects in response to the demands of the gospel rather than as a means to an end relating to an opportunity for evangelism. Finally, it revealed that a combination of evangelism and social action brought clear changes in the values and attitudes in communities; "marriages were strengthened, people accepted themselves as created by God and thus of great value; deep respect grew for the Word of God; and there was an increase in their sense of self-

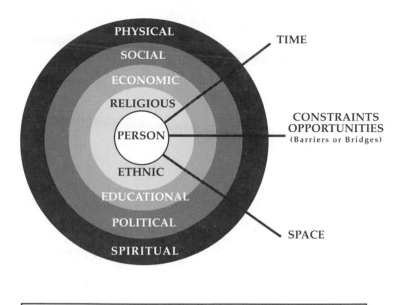

The context of each situation presents an opportunity or a constraint (a bridge or a barrier) toward ministering to the whole person. Ministry must be based on the unique problems to be confronted, the quality and thoroughness of a situational study, and the specific time and space factors. The strategic planner must take all factors into consideration before a holistic approach can be attained.

dependence to increase their development." Almost all groups mentioned an increase in church attendance and the growth of new churches through their work.

From the vantage point of the evangelical's sense of purpose, the goal in any given project is to help people discover their true worth in the eyes of God as the object of His love. They do this when they also discover a sense of self-reliance and spiritual dignity rather than just becoming objects of charity.

Notes

[1]Wagner, Peter. *Church Growth and the Whole Gospel*, 55-56.
[2]Ibid., 55-56.
[3]Shook, Cleo. *The Ministry of Development in Evangelical Perspective*, 86.
[4]Henry, Carl. *A Plea for Evangelical Demonstration*, 112.

CHAPTER 2

NEEDS AND SATISFIERS . . . CLASSIFYING AND CONSIDERING VALUES

Classifying Ministry Approaches

One of the greatest problems in ministering cross-culturally is the strong tendency toward a bias in favor of one's own culture. This becomes particularly insidious at the point of rejecting without serious thought that which one does not understand. The rejection of another's culture and religion devalues not only the society, but the individual in that society. The problem is made worse because the foreigner tends to take on the personal responsibility of deciding what needs to be torn down or fixed. He or she is at least as often wrong as right. A lack of cultural understanding and a bias toward one's own culture will lead one into confusion, so that one has trouble sorting out what is bad from what is merely different. The most obvious example of this was the tendency of the foreigner to judge the practice of polygamy as a purely pagan practice, without understanding the intrinsic moral standards of the primitive society regarding marriage and the spiritual bond it stood for within their cultural structures. Failing to see through the eyes of the members of society, one will fail to assign the right meanings to the problems perceived, and therefore may assign them values derived from one's particular orientation. The foreigner may also fail to distinguish between that which is trivial, and that which is significant in terms of the values given within the culture in which he or she is dealing. As a result, a well-meaning worker may undermine the very foundations of the society without even realizing it. Failing to appreciate the other society and its values, one will usually fail to provide for socially acceptable or appropriate substitutes for that which has been dismissed as being worthless or of little value. One may also fail to notice or simply ignore some of the truly valuable aspects of the culture being served, and uncritically assume that one's own customs and values are of necessity superior.

President Kaunda of Zambia made a point of this in a speech when he said, "There is an aggressive self-confidence about the Western mind, to whose questing so many of the problems and mysteries of the world have succumbed. Europeans, therefore, find it difficult to imagine a better way of doing things than their own.

"They observe the difference between the methods and aims of our present Government and those of its colonial predecessor and conclude that where they deviate they must be inferior."[1]

Unfortunate is the developmental or transformational worker whose predisposition toward his or her own culture and prejudice toward another's manifests itself in a position of presumed superiority. This attitude, according to Van der Post[2], revealed that, "The rejection of Africa in all dimensions was complete as it could possibly be." This type of rejection becomes obvious and clear when the project leader or project designer presumes to move ahead without the proper interrelatedness and participation of the people to whom he or she would minister. This rejection is of especially serious consequences to the extent that it affects the potential for spiritual leadership.

Closely related to this type of ethnocentric attitude is the relationship it provokes—paternalism. *Webster's* defines paternalism as "a system under which authority treats those under its control in a fatherly way especially in regulating their conduct and supplying their needs." Having a sense of Christian compassion and adequate funds available to meet some of the most urgent needs tend to encourage an attitude of rushing into a situation to help, prior to considering the value of the people themselves in working through the problems, providing the resources, and developing adequate solutions.

As Mayer indicates, perhaps one of the most onerous aspects of paternalism is the basic lack of trust it exhibits. It seems to question not only the local people's ability to grasp hold of concepts or even the gospel, but also questions the work of the Holy Spirit to transform those lives. Paternalism quite often manifests itself in the guise of compassion. In such instances, hospitals, orphanages, schools, clinics, or various types of developmental programs are seen as so many masquerading inducements to allegiance, whatever actual benefit may accrue from them.

One of the most difficult areas related to cross-cultural communication has to do with isolationism. This is particularly true in terms of the kind of involvement required to be effective in transformational project work. In the biblical sense, too often the missionary or transformational worker simply does not "sit where they sit," but rather attempts to minister from outside the camp. Thus, the mission or mission station tends to become too much like an inverted pyramid, a huge service organization dominating a single congregation or community. This inevitably creates the idea that to be a Christian is to receive aid from institutions rather than to live a Spirit-filled life. Knowing and understanding the local culture is virtually impossible without participating in that culture.

From Relief to Transformation—Classifying Concepts
Correct responses to human needs demand a tremendous understanding not only of the biblical foundations which motivate the Christian to care, but also social, cultural, political, and emotional dimensions of the problems with which people may be confronted at a given time.

In dealing with problems of human need, it is important to differentiate between acute problems brought about by crises such as earthquakes and floods, and complex circumstances producing a pattern of prolonged human need.

Defining Some Terms

Relief: Generally refers to the response to "that short-term crisis of such magnitude that the essential needs of the victims cannot be fulfilled without the intervention of outside assistance." However, responses to crises should be designed to enable the victims to return to a normal pattern of life as quickly as possible. Many disaster situations will expose the long-term needs of a community and may call for the kind of long-term planning that will enable the communities affected to escape from the circumstances which brought them there. The relief phase of a response should rarely, if ever, go beyond six months. By that time it is important to consider long-term strategies to help the total situation become restabilized.

Development: Refers to "those enabling processes and programs which are characterized as self-sustaining and participatory and deal with the underlying causes of human hurt." Most secular development programs tend to focus on the overall economic ills of a country, moving from the top leadership down through the infrastructure of the various bureaucracies. As a background to the major development movements over the past several decades, one might refer to Tom Sine's excellent summation "Development: Its Secular Past and Its Uncertain Future," found in *The Church in Response to Human Need*, 9-35.

Transformation: One moves from secular development to spiritual and social transformation when those response processes are so integrated and implemented as to deal with the whole of life of the individual. The person then has an opportunity not only to meet urgent physical needs but may also come to understand, embrace, and live the spiritual dimensions of life offered only in Christ Jesus.

Some Principles in Determining the Classification of Human Need Responses

Social scientists normally differentiate between the classification of needs and satisfiers. Most are familiar with Maslow's hierarchy of needs. In the study of various cultures, however, one first of all has to understand that need is not satisfied the same way in every culture. For instance, one society will satisfy its need for fulfillment in terms of status, rank, job, house, wealth, or even freedom to escape to a wilderness retreat. In another society, that need may be satisfied by the size of family, the possession of the tribal spirit, the adornments of bones, colors, or characteristic tattoos. If the planner is to understand how to approach planning in reference to meeting human needs, it will be important to predetermine a system of classification of needs and their satisfiers. It will help if one uses the following conditions:

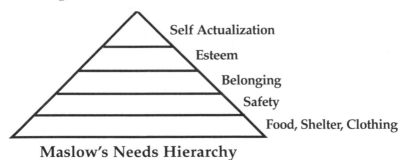

Maslow's Needs Hierarchy

1. The classification must be understood by those who use it.
2. The classification must be limited enough to be specific, yet broad enough to include any of the fundamental needs felt by the culture being addressed.
3. The classification must allow for a clear understanding between the needs and the way in which the local culture finds satisfaction regarding those needs. An old man in the Zambezi Valley wore a heavy wool army coat during the hottest months of the year. He did not need the coat to keep warm, but he did need it to fulfill his need for recognition of having served in the army. The temperature was not his concern.

4. The classification must not only indicate specific ways of satisfying the need, but also indicate areas where there may not now be an immediate satisfier. This is particularly true in the spiritual realm. The need for reconciliation with God will not be met through existing forms of religion in non-Christian cultures, but that which is presented as an alternate may not satisfy unless the planner understands fully how faith and religion are expressed and understood in that culture.

5. The classification must be capable of revealing the relative inadequacies of propositions recommended as the way of meeting and satisfying the needs addressed. It should act as a catalyst to develop other approaches in keeping with the perception of those whose needs are being addressed.

Prior to deciding exactly what to do in solving a need, it is important to know and to understand two things. First, what value does the target audience place on the proposed response to their need, and how will their attitude affect the outcome? Second, what impact will the immediate circumstances (political, social, physical, etc.) have on the situation?

Beyond Apparent Needs to Potential Opportunities

People may be satisfied with less than the best. The interrelationship between needs, satisfiers, physical things, and spiritual matters is dynamic.

One of the intrinsic problems with the old rice-Christian approach was the assumption that either the rice or the required acceptance of an alien religion gave the level of satisfaction needed. A humanistic response to human need can never substitute for the whole need of men and women because it is one dimensional. In the same way, if the only aspect of human need which is met is a relatively minor part of the whole human problem, i.e., the physical part, it may be correspondingly difficult to presume that one has in any way ministered to the broader spiritual needs.

In the process of attempting to meet human needs, one may discover that the real need was not actually satisfied, but only seemingly so. Sometimes meeting a need gives a false sense of satisfaction to those receiving it, in that the immediate concern is taken away. More often than not, however, the subsequent withdrawal of the commodity or other element leaves the group more vulnerable than before and creates an even greater dissatisfaction. Many who have been lured into joining a church with the hope that their perceived need would be satisfied have later turned violently against the group they joined when their expectations were not fulfilled.

In Somalia, shortly after a major drought had devastated the nation, scores of relief agencies rushed into the country to provide the urgent relief needed at the moment. Weeks went into months and months into years in the process of continuing relief efforts. Farmers who had attempted to eke out a living in the arid country decided they no longer needed to attempt to grow crops because the food was now being provided free without labor. With the market depressed, local shop owners lost everything because they had no food stuffs to sell. Even the military sent their soldiers to the relief camps for food rather than provide food for themselves. Farms dried up, tools were discarded, and the country became a "basket case." The process not only created dependency, it destroyed something even greater, the sense of self-reliance and self-worth vital to the recovery of the country.

People are often willing to accept a substitute for the real satisfier. This is true both biblically and physically. A prostitute will accept a companion as a substitute for love. A lost person will accept an idol as a substitute for the living God. The poor will accept charity as a substitute for subsistence. The illiterate will accept indoctrination as a substitute for understanding. A puppet leader will accept the status symbol as a substitute for self-identity. It is important for the planner to understand just what is being offered in the process of responding to apparent human needs.

There is a sad, but beautiful story told by Billie Davis, a professor of sociology and social psychology at Evangel College in Springfield,

Missouri. She grew up in a migrant family moving from one state to another, following the seasons for harvesting. She said, "As a migrant child I learned some important things about how to help needy people—and how not to help them." One of the first things she learned was that poverty was not her worst problem. Rather, it was the sense of not belonging. She had no sense of personhood or self-esteem as a child. Once, during the Depression, when they were literally starving, many people took pity on them. A Christian man in a nearby town owned a bakery and expressed compassion for the migrants. So he loaded all his day-old bread on the back of a delivery truck and drove through the migrant village and threw the bread off the back of the truck. Billie, like the other children, would run to pick up the bread out of the dirt and take it home to the family. She says, however, "How I hated that bakery! I despised the man who stood there and threw me the bread. I despised him because I had to trade my dignity, myself, for a loaf of bread."

Following a major earthquake in Italy, I was asked to work with the missionaries and the national leaders to develop an adequate response to the awesome need experienced by the survivors. We traveled throughout the southern part of the country visiting dozens of small towns and villages. In the process I made an amazing discovery. Outside many of the towns there were literally piles of burning clothes. These were from parcels sent from the United States and Europe, donated to "meet the urgent needs" of the victims. One might think, "How ungrateful of them to burn the clothes that were given as gifts from concerned people." The donors, however, failed to understand both the real need and the perception of those receiving the help. In the first place, their most urgent need was not for clothing. Secondly, the clothes were almost completely inappropriate— bright-colored dresses and blouses, short skirts, lingerie, high-heeled shoes, and a hodgepodge of other attire in various forms and shapes. The people most affected were conservative mountain folks. Daily dress for them usually consisted of what others might consider drab or dull. Their favorite colors seemed to be dark brown or black! Now the giving satisfied the need of the givers to do something good, but was perceived by the recipients as insensitive and to some, even insulting.

Self-Reliance Must Be at the Center of Developmental or Transformational Ministries

People need relationships. They need to know that they are special in the eyes of God and of their fellow man. The problems we see on the outside are merely symptoms of the unmet needs of inner lives. If we are to hope for holistic change in people, the missionary or church member must not be perceived as the rich and benevolent suppliers of the down-and-out, but rather as authentic representatives of the Christ person as they attempt to enable people to be all that they are capable of becoming through Christ.

An old man in the Zambezi Valley came to know the Lord in the context of multiple ministries to meet human needs. When asked what he really wanted most, he indicated that he wanted to learn how to read. Apparently, he had never been to school, never attended a class, but recognized that it was possible to read the Word of God from a book. Following several months of study in a literacy class, his dream came true. Later, when the missionary was visiting the area, he talked to the old man who was now filled with questions about the Book he had been reading, the Bible. To the amazement of the missionary, he began quoting lengthy passages from the Old Testament, and then comparing them with similar passages in the New Testament—all from memory. The man had almost total photographic recall! Within a short time he was like a walking commentary on the Scriptures. He had been set free to a new dimension of life he had never before known. It would have been easy to have let him be an observer of others in the church, but the Lord had endowed him with the potential of being a leader in the church. He was just waiting to be set free.

Dependent relations frustrate the potential for the satisfaction of human needs. It is only when people assume leadership roles in their own domain, their space and their time, that transformation can be generated or self-reliance can be experienced. Self-reliance, in the sense of Christian missions, refers to the capacity for interdependence with the community and participation in realizing solutions to their needs. Even Christ allows men and women to participate in the act of bringing salvation to the lost. Self-reliance will, of necessity, promote participation in local decision-making, creativity toward resolution of problems, political and social self-determination, a redistribution of wealth, and a recognition and tolerance for diversity. "His divine power has given us everything we need for life and godliness through our knowledge of Him Who called us by His own glory and goodness. Through these He has given us His very great and precious promises, so that through them you may participate in the divine nature" (2 Peter 1:3-4*f*).

Top Down or Bottom Up?
Dependency moves from the top to the bottom. It always flows downward from the macro to the micro and from the international vantage point to the local scene. It also moves from the social sector to the individual domain. Intergovernmental programs of development have usually been based on the trickle-down theory, assuming that if one could invest sufficient funds in the infrastructure, the benefits would ultimately flow down to the individuals through increased manufacturing, production, and sales. Relationships which develop self-reliance, however, have an exponential effect when they flow from the bottom upward. Local self-reliance actually promotes and encourages regional self-reliance. In the same way, personal growth and social development result from participation and involvement in the process of problem solving. It is through this kind of process that real needs are satisfied rather than through the acceptance of programs, projects, or activities generated outside their sphere of influence and decision-making.

Reconciling External Promotion with Internal Initiatives
One of the greatest challenges for any transformational or developmental planner is to achieve an appropriate balance between the role of the catalyst on the one hand, and the capacity of the recipient on the other hand, regarding the spontaneous activities of local groups to know their needs and initiate appropriate responses to those needs. The local group will never have any impact if the planners do

not nurture and empower them to act freely and fully in every facet of the response. Much of the initial phases of planning by the expatriate need to be spent in planning for local initiatives and autonomy. This kind of planning should target the mobilizing of existing groups and communities to transform their survival strategies into life options which they can articulate through their own language, symbols, ideas, and ideals.

In contrast with holistic development, the prevailing humanistic economic rationale places its primary focus upon the accumulation of wealth and/or things as the indicator of real development and the panacea which can cure the ills of the developing world. Transformational development focuses upon individuals and their capacity to achieve an acceptable quality of life. The planner sometimes makes the mistake of assuming that bringing people up from an existing way of conducting their lifestyle to one more in keeping with a Western lifestyle and introducing modern industry and technology will also give them the kind of satisfaction which improves their actual quality of life. Quality of life cannot be measured by the accumulation of things.

Various types of indicators have been developed in an attempt to measure quality of life standards. Unfortunately, most of the scales which have been designed to measure relative quality of life measure inputs rather than results. Hence, a country or a people may be considered to have a quality of life which measures favorably, when considered against the quality of life measured in another country by the same scale, even though the majority of the people in that country still suffers.

A valid measurement must include the possibility of access and/or the fact of confrontation and freedom of various choices. Measurement, which is inclusive of an entire country, will inevitably fail to make the necessary accommodation for the poorest of the poor and/or those whose physical circumstances and life situations deny them the opportunity to what may be the average or mean value for the country as a whole. Quality of life is inevitably tied to human value systems; therefore, any valid measurement must take this into consideration.

Value systems form one of the most important elements in the understanding needed in cross-cultural communications. These, in turn, are vitally linked to beliefs and attitude systems. In scope, these systems include such qualities as usefulness, goodness, aesthetics, need satisfaction ability, and those things which produce pleasure. Effective intercultural communication demands a clear understanding of local and individual cultural values. These have been defined as primary, secondary, or tertiary values, depending on the location of particular values in a culture's hierarchy of values.[3]

VALUE CLASSIFICATION SYSTEM[4]				
Value	Primary	Secondary	Tertiary	Negligible
Individuality	W	B	E	M
Motherhood	BE	MW	—	—
Hierarchy	WEMA	B	—	—
Masculinity	BMEWA	—	—	—
Gratefulness	EA	MB	W	—
Peace	E	B	WA	M
Money	WAB	M	E	—
Modesty	E	BAM	—	W
Punctuality	W	B	ME	A
Saviorism	W	M	—	EBA
Karma	E	—	—	MWBA
Firstness	W	B	—	EAM
Aggressiveness	WB	M	AE	—
Collective Responsibility	EAM	B	—	W
Respect for Elders	EAM	B	—	W
Respect for Youth	W	MABE	—	—
Hospitality to Guests	EA	B	MW	—
Inherited Property	E	—	MWAB	—
Preservation of Environment	E	BA	W	M
Color of Skin	EWB	M	—	A
Sacredness of Farm Land	E	A	—	BMW
Equality of Women	W	EB	A	M
Human Dignity	WB	EAM	—	—
Efficiency	W	B	EM	—
Patriotism	BMAE	W	—	—
Religion	WBMAE	—	—	—
Authoritarianism	EMA	WB	—	—
Education	WB	EAM	—	—
Frankness	W	BEMA	—	—

Legend: W=Western cultures, E=Eastern cultures, B=Black cultures, A=African cultures, M=Muslim cultures

Quality of Life and Human Values
The physical quality of life index (PQLI) is a concept developed

by the US Overseas Development Council. It is a composite index calculated by averaging four indices: per capita income; life expectancy; infant mortality; and literacy. Equal weight is given to each of the indicators. Each index is rated on a scale from 1 to 100. It should be noted that this is generally applied to countries as a whole and does not attempt to discriminate between urban/rural, slum/upper class, etc. Many other attempts at measuring quality of life include other indices such as mortality rates, gross national product, etc. If real needs are to be satisfied, they must be satisfied on the basis of an acceptable quality of life on the part of those for whom programs are targeted. It is understood that the community or individuals within the community may not fully understand the difference between what is now considered an acceptable quality of life, and what may become a higher standard once exposed to other possibilities. This is particularly true in the spiritual realm.

Some basic weaknesses of the present system of measurement:
Present indicators tend to measure averages of general economic or physical welfare and performance of an entire nation. They do not give any indication of the relative quality of life in local communities and/or underdeveloped sections of the country. Since they indicate the overall averages of the various income groupings, there is no way to differentiate between the rich and the poor, the urban or rural, the ghetto or the high-class residential zones. Nor does the PQLI indicate anything about the distribution of wealth/facilities or the relative position of any particular segment of society. In most Third World countries 90 percent of the wealth is normally controlled by less than 10 percent of the population. Hence, the per capita income may be $2,000, while the mean income is $150. The PQLI measures production, not consumption.

An accurate quality of life measurement must consider relationships between a series of interdependent factors including the following:

Spiritual	Medical
Social	Physiological
Psychological	Cultural
Nutritional	Environmental

In turn, each of these factors will be perceived in terms of a time and space continuum as they relate to the local culture and its understanding and interpretation of needs and satisfiers.

Other factors which influence quality of life greatly, such as the following, are not always considered:

Longevity	Political freedoms
General health	Literacy
Density of population	Mortality (especially of children)
Incidence of drug use	Size of families
Alcoholism	Number per room in homes
Level of economic well-being	

Questions which must be raised:
1. How can these relationships be measured adequately on a local level so as to be applicable?
2. What conditions have to be satisfied to determine if an acceptable level of development is/has been successful in terms of satisfying local value systems?

Some fallacies about quality of life indices:
GNP/per capita income is not a measurement of total welfare and cannot measure such intangibles as "happiness, justice, security, freedom, leisure, social harmony, opportunity, length of life, etc."

Criteria for a composite indicator:
1. It should not assume that there is only one pattern of development.
2. It should avoid standards that reflect only the values of specific societies.

3. It should measure results, not inputs.
4. It should be able to reflect the distribution of social benefits: economic, physical, spiritual, etc.
5. It should be simple to construct and easy to comprehend.
6. It should lend itself to international comparison.
7. In attempting to interpret or analyze findings, they should be considered over and against such subjective issues as:
   a. Accessibility/availability.
   b. Acceptability (stigma, custom, mores, etc.).
   c. Freedom (capacity or ability to appropriate/access, both spiritually and politically).
   d. Desirability (level to which it provides locally perceived satisfiers such as happiness, peace, well-being).

Things which cannot be assumed:
1. All development will be the same.
2. Basic human needs and quality of life are defined by all societies in the same way.
3. Meeting the most urgent and obvious need will necessarily bring a minimum level of satisfaction.
4. The acceptance of a program by community leaders will reflect the community as a whole and its response to the program or project.
5. What appears to be a successful venture during the first year will continue to meet the same needs in the future. Once a community has become aware of satisfaction of a need, the response which provided the satisfaction may be obsolete once the community has discovered other potential responses.

Value choices
Indicators should measure results, not inputs. Data must be easy to collect and process.

Data represents what needs to be collected in all societies. The composite must not require more precision than components already being used. The economic percentages should be expressed in relative levels of poverty/well-being such as the following:

Absolute poverty: The income level is below that which can provide for a minimum diet of at least 2,100 calories per person. Essential nonfood requirements are not affordable.

Relative poverty: The family actually receives less than one-third of the per capita income of that economy.

Below poverty: The total of the relative and absolute.

Adequate and acceptable: The family is able to maintain physical, emotional, spiritual, and economic stability.

Above basic or minimal needs: The family is able to add to basic requirements and live beyond adequate local standards.

Types of data which might be useful in developing a quality of life index which can be considered locally specific, yet universally measurable.

1. Characteristics of housing:

Status	Square Feet (per family member)	Number per room	Percent with facilities
% Home owners			
% Rented/leased			
% Squatters			
% Street dwellers	0	n/a	0

2. Educational indicators:
   a. Average level per family unit (local/national).
   b. Percentage of literate/nonliterate (male) (local/national).
   c. Percentage of literate/nonliterate (female) (local/national).
   d. Percentage of appropriate age levels in local/national.

	Elementary school	Primary school	Secondary school
Female			
Male			

3. Medical/health care indicators:
   a. Availability of hospital/clinic (indicate within 3, 5, 10, or more miles).
   b. Number of trained health-care personnel (indicate within 3, 5, 10, or more miles).
   c. Infant mortality rate (local/national).
   d. Average level of caloric intake (local/national).
   e. Percentage with access to excreta disposal (local/national).
   f. Birth rate (local/national).
   g. Primary preventable causes of death (local/national).
   h. Access to potable water/average (within 3, 5, 10, or more miles).
   i. Percentage of infants immunized (DPT) (local/national).

4. Economic indicators (all of these to be measured within the local community and on the national level):
   a. Unemployment rate.
   b. Number of children per family.
   c. Per capita income.
   d. Number of homeless children per 1,000.
   e. Number of single-parent homes.
   f. Density of population.
   g. Access to local market (within 3, 5, 10, or more miles).
   h. Percentage in each economic level:

Top 10% _____	Lower 20% _____
Top 20% _____	Lower 10% _____
Middle 40% _____	

5. Spiritual indicators:
   a. Number of Christian churches/congregations (within 3, 5, 10, or more miles).
   b. Percentage generally defined as Christians in community/country.
   c. Percentage of community who are active participants in a local church.

d. Percentage of community who are active participants in a local evangelical church.

e. Access to Scripture in their language (translated and available).

f. Access to gospel literature in local language.*

g. Ratio of adult baptisms per year per member of local churches.

h. Freedom to congregate without fear of intimidation or harm.

i. Freedom to witness/share publicly.

6. Potential or practical uses of index.

a. To develop a general profile of a community which could give a relative picture of major areas of concern through factor analyses.

b. To provide an instrument to point to specific areas requiring detailed investigation for purposes of strategy and/or project planning.

c. To validate/repudiate suppositions regarding intentions for programs of work.

*Access in this case refers to the average cost of gospel literature for use in Sunday School and training as compared with local PCI. If the cost is one percent of the per capita income (PCI) or above, it should be considered inaccessible.

Notes

[1]Kaunda, *A Humanist*, 68.

[2]Laurns Van der Post, *The Dark Eye*, 54.

[3]K. S. Sitaram and Roy T. Cogdell, *Foundations of Intercultural Communication*, Columbus, Ohio: Charles E. Merrill, 1976, 191.

[4]Ibid.

CHAPTER 3

CROSS-CULTURAL MINISTRIES . . . COMMUNICATING CONCEPTS THROUGH WORDS AND ACTIONS

Cross-Cultural Communications in the Context of Transformational Ministries

While this book is not intended to provide an exhaustive study of cross-cultural communications, there may be no more important subject to consider for missionaries and others who minister cross-culturally. Some of the finest and most innovative projects have ultimately failed because of an inability to understand the cultural dynamics of the situation and circumstances where they were to be initiated. A development worker does not have to become an anthropologist or sociologist in order to work in another culture, but a basic understanding of some of the pitfalls related to inter-cultural communications may keep the incarnational agent from a tremendous amount of stress and failure.

The term culture, here, addresses "the sum total of the distinctive characteristics of a people's way of life including such issues as: ideas, customs, skills, arts, religion, moral codes of conduct, etc., which are inherent in a people or group and passed on or communicated to succeeding generations." When expatriate workers move into another culture to work with and carry out human need ministries they must first go through the process of enculturation if they are to understand, minister, and communicate effectively. That process must include the acquiring of a clear understanding of the heritage of the larger community with which one will work.

One of the first dangers is the fact that the person ministering cross-culturally may presume to be communicating one thing in the process of doing good, while all the time the message being sent is just the opposite. Let me illustrate.

Some time ago, a group of well-meaning and dedicated laymen went down to an island in the Caribbean following a major hurricane. There had been tremendous devastation and loss of housing. It was their intention, out of a Christian motivation, to rush into the scene to rebuild some of the housing. It took a great deal of organization and Western know-how to get things ready for the trip to the island. After arrival and a brief orientation, they went into the area of the worst destruction to survey the damage and to start the rebuilding process. They made several serious mistakes in the process, however. First, they determined the criteria regarding which houses were to be rebuilt or repaired without consultation with the local people. Second, they took control from the beginning in the planning and preparation for the buildings. They had a limited amount of time to be away from their work and had to move as quickly as possible to set up the logistics and move materials and manpower into place. When the building actually started, they totally disregarded the way houses were normally built in the area, and decided that a structure built along good engineering design would resist future storms better than the pattern followed previously by the local people. Unfortunately, this decision was not communicated through the normal decision-making patterns or acceptable channels of communication.

The end result of their efforts was both positive and negative. They did build many houses and were able to get even more done than they planned by effective organization and minimal delays.

They won the admiration of some leaders for the speed and efficiency by which they worked. They may have missed out on the one major opportunity which impelled them to go, however—the opportunity to share the love of Christ. Because of an insensitivity to the people, their culture, their feelings, their sense of self-worth and personal dignity, they may have left more of a negative witness than a positive one. This is sometimes even worse when the cross-cultural messenger knows a little bit of the language, presuming therefore, to also understand the culture. They may have forgotten that in any cross-cultural ministry, one must first become an incarnational agent before one can serve effectively as a transformational worker.

Communications Model

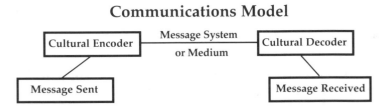

In the communications model above, the communicator uses a variety of message systems to transmit a message to the person(s) intended to receive that message. Every message sent, however, is first of all encoded in symbols representing the whole of the cultural setting and circumstances of the one sending the message. It is then decoded by the receiver, prior to understanding, into corresponding symbols representative of the second culture. In each case, the symbol will have a meaning unique to both the culture of the sender and the receiver. This may also be modified by tone, body language, appropriateness of a particular level of vocabulary used in the language to denote respect or honor, and sequence both in terms of the body of the information conveyed and the person or persons to whom it is addressed. The importance of this process was brought home to me early in my ministry in Africa. Early one morning I went to visit a pastor on some important business. When he came to the door, I immediately began to bring up the matters I wanted to discuss with him. I recall vividly as he took a slight step backward, bowed his head politely, and said calmly, "Good morning, Brother Cheyne, and how are you today?" The rebuke, expressed so eloquently in his greeting and concern for me as a person, was in stark contrast to my abrupt discussion of business. I have remembered it ever since. By failing to observe one of the fundamental courtesies of the culture, I had failed in one of the essential aspects of being an incarnational agent—respect for persons.

Edward Hall identifies a number of the message systems by which people communicate in what he calls the "silent language of culture."[1]

Language: Since language is essentially a special set of systems whereby meaning is transmitted, no two words carry exactly the same meaning in other languages, simply because the symbols are different. In Southern Africa, if one refers to a colleague as "one of the boys," the message received may suggest that he is no longer respected and that you considered him to be like a child. When one translates the word *God* into the parallel word used locally to refer to deity, it probably will not transmit the image of the Judeo-Christian understanding of God, but rather that of a remote being too far removed to be addressed by man. The particular culture will determine the symbol being received and the meaning which it gives. Language only has the capability of transmitting a perceptual model, but the actual meaning will need further clarification if one wishes to be sure that the listener understands. Tone in language may convey even more than the actual words spoken. When one first enters a foreign environment, one may hear two people discussing something with a high sense of emotion and come away thinking that they are in a bitter debate, when the tone used may actually express commonality and consensus.

In the Amharic language of Ethiopia there is a concept referred to as "wax and gold." In essence it refers to speaking with words that have a double meaning. The wax is the covering and the apparent meaning. The gold is the core and the real meaning. The spoken language works in a circular way from the outer covering to the inner meaning. Hence, two enemies may meet on the road. In greeting one another they may use the plural of respect, but actually be insulting one another. A rather simplistic illustration of this can be seen if one could imagines that the men are driving donkeys down the road, and the first greets the second by saying, "How are you all?" The plural of respect is used properly, but it can also infer that the man is one of the donkeys being driven. Hence, the apparent respect covers the intended insult.

When someone from the Western world speaks in a very direct manner, the Ethiopian may be asking himself, "What is the real meaning of what he is saying?" He would not necessarily anticipate that the real meaning would be found in the cover statements. Hence, the offer to provide certain types of help may be construed as having an ulterior meaning. One must patiently work through other message systems both to build trust and to convey the real meaning.

Temporality: (Attitude toward time, routine, and schedule.) One's respect for personhood is nowhere demonstrated more than in one's attitude and understanding of the relationship of time. In an African setting, the paramount chief may call for a meeting of all the subchiefs at a certain time and place. No one would consider starting the meeting, however, without giving ample time for all to arrive. The time waiting would be one of casual fellowship and renewing of relationships and the tardy person would not necessarily be considered negligent by failing to show up at the assigned time. An agriculturist may have in mind the development of a long-term breeding program to upgrade the local livestock. If the program should take as much as two or three years before any tangible results can be seen, the local farmers may not buy into the concept at all. The longer target schedule may be conveying the message that he really didn't plan to do much and was using the time frame to gain an advantage. It is often necessary to provide some type of short-term, high visibility-type project as a part of the long-term planning.

Territoriality: (Space, property.) Territoriality is the technical term used by the ethologist to describe the taking possession, use, and defense of a territory on the part of any living organism. This has to do with the sense of ownership or belonging in one's own community or territory. It has to do with position and appropriate respect for that position. In language it may have to do with the proper use of symbols toward those in authority or having a particular family position. In Korea, there are several levels of greeting depending upon whether one is speaking to a superior (in social custom), a child, a peer, or a total stranger. In each case, unless one is aware of the proper usage of vocabulary in relationships it would be easy to be perceived as putting someone down or looking down upon them. In Ethiopia, as in other countries, certain words and even letters of the alphabet are reserved for royalty.

Often this is reflected in following diplomatic procedures as one seeks to get approval for matters related to project proposals. One offended official can stand in the way of an excellent effort. This is true even in the marketplace. Beggars have beats, prostitutes work their own side of the street, salesmen and distributors have their territory. Junior officials safeguard their area of responsibility. Women often have defined roles and places. Children move through clearly-defined age sets, often by initiation ceremonies to mark the rite of passage. Each of these are systems of communication regarding the culture.

Exploitation: (The method of control, the use and sharing of resources.) The relationship between materials and language is especially important in developmental work. The value placed on things may differ widely between the alien and the local people. Hence, one can enter a ghetto where there are no facilities, no sanitation, extremely shabby housing, muddy streets, few schools, and limited income. Yet, one might see television antennas perched from practically every house. One might also see a relatively expensive vehicle parked outside the house. These may have value far beyond the perception of the newcomer, even causing him to make spot judgments on the apparent insensitivity it indicates toward the children or wife who have inadequate food or clothing.

Prior to making judgment, it is often better to attempt to understand the dynamics which make this so common around the world.

Association: (Family, kin, community.) Most societies have a clearly-defined, but not always apparent, pattern of social relationships. Like the animal world, chickens have their pecking order, horses have their "kicking" order, and all societies have their ethnic, clan, caste, social or racial orders or acceptance.

When in Zimbabwe (what was then Southern Rhodesia) in 1955, I was criticized by a very fine Christian friend (who was white) for allowing an African teacher (who happened to have a BA degree) to sit in my living room with me as a tutor while I studied the language. Back in those days one simply did not do those things. My persistence in the practice communicated loudly and clearly both to Africans and whites something of the position and place of our ministry in that country. Where one lives, how one identifies, the degree to which one associates on a social level, the relative acceptance and warmth of others as peers will communicate much more loudly than Sunday's sermon.

Subsistence: (Work, division of labor.) In terms of a primary message system, subsistence refers to everything from individual food habits to the economy of the country. The type of employment one may have communicates the particular place in society one has in many cultures. To be a worker with leather in Ethiopia is openly to identify with a low class. To have a job which requires one to wear a suit to work, regardless of how low one may be in the organization, places one automatically among a different social standing. It is important to recognize when attempting to initiate vocational training projects that one may be indicating by the choice of the work to be taught that the trainees are perceived in a particular way by the initiators of the project. In another way, the fact that a group of volunteers gets out among the people and participates in the manual labor of a project may help the people of the community to understand their acceptance as equal before God.

Intersexuality: (Differing modes of speech, dress, conduct.) No relationships send stronger signals than do those involving relationships between the sexes. Most countries have specific understandings as to the manner in which a man and a woman should conduct themselves in public. Hence, when a married American man and a single American woman are seen touching or embracing or spending time alone in a building, it is often interpreted locally as an indication of a more intimate relationship between the two. Dress conveys similar intense communication. In Malawi, a woman is not allowed to wear a dress with a hemline above the knee. In other countries a woman would not be allowed to wear any type of trousers. The importance of understanding intersexual taboos and restrictions cannot be overstated in terms of one's capacity to communicate a clear message of the gospel.

Learning: (Observation, modeling, instruction.) Language developed as people learned to communicate through shared behavior. Once people have learned to do something one way it is extremely difficult for them to learn to do it another way. The astute transformational worker will first discover the historic and socially acceptable way of doing things prior to the introduction of new methods. In many cases, certain jobs have historically been assigned to one or the other sex simply by tradition. It may take years and very special circumstances before change can come about. In a West African agriculture program it was observed that women always did the plowing with a short-handle hoe. The work was both tedious and ineffective. Before a change could be made, however, the initial phases of the project required conformity with the traditional standards. It was years later, after the introduction of animal traction, that the men were willing to accept the idea that handling an ox or mule was a *man's job* when the social change began to take place. Communicating this concept came through the example of the agriculturist who demonstrated the effectiveness of utilizing the animal over the hand method. Essentially, the thing that communicated most was the fact that more land could be cultivated and more money could be gained through the improved method.

Play: (Humor, games.) Some years ago one of the workers in our home thanked me for being able to laugh with me. At first I did not understand what he was talking about until he explained something of the customs of the country regarding levels of familiar relationships. In his country, one did not laugh with one's mother-in-law, or with a chief, or with others in certain social relationships. It was all a matter of just how familiar one was allowed to be with others in different relationships. My laughing with him was a method of communicating a familiar acceptance about which I had been totally unaware. During the years, in moving from country to country helping to plan or to open the door for developmental projects, I have discovered that humor is one of the easiest ways to open a relationship. Even with high officials, often the relaxed amusement of sharing humor brings an acceptance and breaks down otherwise difficult barriers.

Defense: (Health procedures, social conflicts, beliefs.) Defense refers to those primary message systems whereby mankind protects itself against outside intrusion. The relatively uneducated rural tribesman may reject modern medicine in favor of an herbalist with whom he is familiar and trusts. That same herbalist may represent the spiritual association ascribed to the healer and a perception of God. In much of the developing world, the masses of people do not compartmentalize religious activities from all the other activities which make up their lives. The rite or the ceremony attached to moving through age sets will often be secret to guard against any outside influence. The whole content of religion, its organization, and the manner in which it is integrated with the rest of life varies from culture to culture, but a lack of understanding of those relationships may communicate a lack of acceptance of the people themselves. This is particularly true of the Islamic world as well as other cultures in which religion infiltrates all of life.

Concepts for Cross-Cultural Communication

The transformational worker never works in isolation. He or she is always involved with and working through people. Incarnational agents, who recognize the importance of the individuals with whom they work, will be sensitive to every aspect of the cultural situation and communication systems in which they work. The incarnational agent must be known as one who has come to be a servant to the poor rather than one who has the poor for servants.

Things must be done through people. However sound the ideas or well-reasoned the decisions, they become effective only as they are transmitted to others and achieve the desired action, or reaction. Communication, therefore, is our most vital tool. Communication takes place not only through words but through attitudes and actions, for communication encompasses all human behavior that results in an exchange of meaning. Here are some concepts of communication that may help you to be more effective as an incarnational agent.

1. Be clear about what you want to say and how you want to say it before you say it. The more systematically we analyze the problem or idea to be communicated, the clearer it becomes. This is the first step toward effective communication. Many communications fail because of inadequate planning. Good planning must consider the goals and attitudes of those who will receive the communication and those who will be affected by it. Ask yourself whether or not the ones receiving the idea or concept can communicate it back to you correctly. If not, they probably haven't understood it.

2. Be clear about why you want to say something. What is the essential purpose of the message? Before you communicate, ask yourself what you really want to accomplish with your message—obtain information, initiate action, change another person's attitude? Identify your most important goal and then adapt your language, tone, and total approach to serve that specific objective. The sharper the focus of your message, the greater its chances of success.

3. Consider the time, space, circumstances, and situation before you attempt to communicate. Meaning and intent are conveyed by

more than words alone. Many other factors influence the overall impact of a communication and you must be sensitive to the setting in which you communicate. Be constantly aware of the total setting in which you communicate. Like all living things, communication must be capable of adapting to its environment.

4. Get help when necessary in order to be sure that what you need to communicate can be both understood and received in the way you intend it. Frequently it is desirable or necessary to seek the participation of others in planning a communication or developing the facts on which to base it. Such consultation often helps to lend additional insight and objectivity to your message. Moreover, those who have helped to plan your communication will give it their active support.

5. Be aware of the impact of subtle overtones and gestures which may convey an entirely different message than intended. When task-oriented individuals serve as missionaries in a person-oriented culture, they often fail to grasp the importance of interaction in the daily work routine and become extremely judgmental of their national co-workers. Your tone of voice, your expression, your apparent receptiveness to the responses of others, have tremendous impact on those you wish to reach. What does your eye contact or failure to make eye contact say in this particular culture? Did your physical gesture convey the same meaning in the foreign culture as it does in your home culture? Beware!

6. Always be conscious of your audience, whether large or small. Your communication should be addressed with them in mind and indicate your appreciation and/or respect for them as persons. Consideration of the other person's interest and needs, the habit of trying to look at things from their perspective, will frequently point up opportunities to convey something of immediate benefit or long-range value to people. People are most responsive to those whose message takes their own interest into account. Ask whether it is more important to do it your own way or to work together with the people around you, building

mutual understanding and cooperating to make decisions and solve problems in a manner acceptable and beneficial to the whole community. The incarnational agent is sent to people to serve them, to minister to them, to communicate God's love for them. Building relationships is central to ministry, and this can be done only through devoting one's time and life to personal interaction.

7. Your best communication may be in how well you listen! Don't be in a hurry for them to stop speaking so you can say something really important. When some people start talking they often cease to listen, in that larger sense of being attuned to the other person's unspoken reactions and attitudes. We are all guilty at times of inattentiveness when others are attempting to communicate to us. Listening is one of the most important, most difficult, and most neglected communication skills.

8. Request feedback by having them express in their way what they heard you say. Your best efforts at communication may be wasted if you do not follow up to see how well you have put your message across. Ask questions, encourage the receivers to express their reactions, follow up contacts, make subsequent review of performances. Make certain that every important communication has a feedback so that complete understanding and appropriate action results.

9. Illustrate what you say by what you do following the communication. In the final analysis, the most persuasive kind of communication is not what you say but what you do. When one's actions or attitudes contradict one's words, we tend to discount the words. You make a mistake when you assume that people have understood you when they have heard what you have said.

10. Be broad in your scope as well as narrow in your focus. While communications may be aimed primarily at meeting the demands of an immediate situation, they must be planned with the past in mind if they are to maintain consistency in the receiver's view. Most important of all, they must be consistent with long-range interest and goals.

How Communication Networks Multiply to Create Problems

Communications can become complicated in terms of the potential multiplication of interfaces involved as the number of people involved increases. In this respect, the larger the number of people the more likely it is that there will be a variety of perceptions both of the communications from the planner and the intercommunications between the units themselves. This becomes even more critical when there is also a difference of culture, language, dialect, or ethnic groupings. From the vantage point of the increasing world population this can be seen in another way. From 1930 to 1976 the number of people on earth doubled from 2 billion to over 4 billion, and the number of possible connections quadrupled. Based on current growth rates, the population could be expected to double again to 8 billion by 2020, bringing another quadrupling of possible connections. This amplifies the concern for attempting to force Western models on other societies. The transformational planner must be extremely careful to understand these dynamics throughout the planning process.

Notes
[1]Edward Hall, *The Silent Language*, 62-81.

CHAPTER 4

THE MINISTERING CHURCH . . . PROBLEMS AND POSSIBILITIES

The Bottom Line!

Is the church authentic? Does it really care about people? Can the church continue to function among the peoples of the Southern Hemisphere in the same way it has done during earlier great missionary movements? How will those areas classified as limited access countries respond to the continuing approach of Christian missions? As the forces of Islam become more aggressive and conservative, will the message of Christianity speak to the masses who form so much of the hungry and hurting world? Many in our world today are asking these questions of the church. Incarnational agents need to be certain when they answer that they have ample evidence to support their stance.

While this past century will certainly be seen as a time of extraordinary missionary outreach, the judgment concerning the future of missions, as we move into the next century, is still uncertain. One of the questions that is being asked and will be asked over and over again is that of the authenticity of the church. Nationalism, ethnicism, and political ideologies all rise up to ask the same question—"Is the church genuine?" In the context of real-life concerns, human suffering, isolation, hunger, displacement, loss of franchise, and basic freedoms, they may also be asking, "Where is the church?" In many countries of the Southern Hemisphere, as well as other developing nations, missionaries are no longer allowed to remain unless they can demonstrate ways in which they are involved in an aspect of some of these very practical human concerns. How tragic if the single most powerful catalyst for spurring the church to become more deeply involved with hurting humanity had to come from pressures by non-Christian governments.

One of the dangers confronting both the local church in these nations, as well as those who send missionaries to work with them, is that their concern for people might appear as a masquerade, merely as a means to an end, rather than authentic caring. People have a right to question at that point. Even John raised the question when he asked, "But if anyone has this world's goods, resources for sustaining life, and sees his brother and fellow believer in need, yet closes his heart of compassion against him, how can the love of God live and remain in him?" (1 John 3:17 AMP).

Preparing for the Future
If evangelicals propose to move into these next decades with the purpose of extending the gospel into all the world, they must, at least, be cognizant of the condition of the world's peoples, and consistent in ministry with the model of that message, our Lord Jesus Christ. To be unaware of the human situation binding the lost in conditions of life so deplorable as to be beyond human comprehension is to preclude the possibility of either an authentic witness, or a biblically-based strategy for winning a lost world to Christ. At the center of this concern is the local church, both those who have been the sending bodies and those who historically have been the recipients of missionary concern.

Some Facts to Be Faced as Churches Move Beyond A.D. 2000
A full 50 percent of the world's hungriest people live in countries

where they have not heard the gospel. Historically, these countries have been beyond the reach of customary approaches in evangelism. At the same time, these same countries have been subject to the worst kinds of economic, political, and religious deprivation. In most of these areas, the church is quite often perceived in the context of the formal state church hierarchy or, on the other extreme, some sort of sect. The universal fact of dire need has been one avenue where Christians have been given an opportunity to exert a spiritual influence by demonstrating the fact that they care, and that the gospel message is the motivation for their sharing.

From the vantage point of the continuing population explosion, the local church has never had a greater challenge. Some of the greatest growth, which will produce a population projected to be around 6.5 billion by A.D. 2000, will be in major city ghettos. These ghettos have the smallest percentage of churches within the developing nations. Some slum areas of Latin America, containing as many as 1 million people, do not have a single evangelical church. Most of those referred to as street children are located in these terrible islands of poverty, sexual perversion, and drugs. Statistics show anywhere from 145 million to over 200 million children around the world, between the ages of 6 and 20, make their homes in the streets. They know nothing of Christ or salvation and for the main part have negative feelings about religion.

Another issue confronting local churches in their total ministry relates to the plight of the desperately hungry. When the land can no longer sustain the growing population, massive migrations take place from rural to urban centers. People go there looking for jobs, food, and a way to sustain life. Instead, they end up in even more dire conditions than before and with no way back. Various agencies report from 700 million to 1 billion people suffering from chronic malnutrition. This rate will grow as we move into the next century. Of course, this is not a problem the local churches or international missions agencies can deal with in isolation. This fact, however, does not release them from responsibility.

The Scope of Ministry

Hunger is a dynamic, not a static issue, and must be faced. Hunger can occur anywhere that people are vulnerable to war, drought, pestilence, or poverty. While certain projections can be made concerning the most likely areas of need, local sensitivity and local initiatives will be required as part of a worldwide monitoring.

The problems involve government policies, economic priorities, religious persuasions, international trade, political pressures, environmental impact, social, spiritual, and ethnic relationships and, not the least, the human factor of personal freedom of choice and human dignity.

The local church is the key as it acts as the catalyst through ministry outreach. It is here that sensitivity to opportunities, desperate need, and social action must be demonstrated. More and more the local church must learn how to take advantage of the tremendous opportunity and impact it can have toward modeling the message of Christ's love. Only then will the larger community and the government begin to respond.

The local church is also a storehouse of experienced and committed personnel. Missionaries and professional development workers can accomplish a great deal, but it will require the involvement of local people at every level of expertise. They must fully identify with the community in which the human situation is most severe before the fundamental problems can be solved. In the same way that cities and institutions have related to sister cities or institutions overseas, farmers, builders, plumbers, and the whole range of those with special training and talent must reach across ethnic and tribal boundaries to identify with those who are physically and spiritually deprived. The local church is the first line of focus.

If churches are to deal effectively with the strategic human needs facing the world, they must begin to raise the issues, ask the important questions, and give serious consideration to their local and international planning concerning these areas of human deprivation and need in the context of their total ministries. Some of these issues are obvious and are already being dealt with to a certain degree. As we act in transformational ministries, we must guard against defining human need in light of a mere emotional response to the latest crisis shown on TV, in which it becomes the primary driver action. The plight of people and their human condition must become an integrated part of the church's spiritual and evangelistic ministry.

Some Areas of Essential Need and Primary Opportunity for Ministry

1. The extending scope and debilitating effect of massive world hunger and poverty will continue to impact many of the people groups which represent the largest numbers of the unreached in the world. Evangelicals are already developing strategic plans in cooperation with one another on an unprecedented scale to share the gospel with such groups. It has also been demonstrated in a series of world crises that these same people respond to the gospel most effectively when those who go to share the gospel do it in the context of caring and loving ministries centered at the point of their most immediate physical concerns.

2. Few churches have developed programs specifically designed to train their membership for ministry. Yet, when Christians become aware of their spiritual gifts and employ those gifts in sensitive ministries to the less fortunate, the Lord seems to bless the total evangelistic outreach of the church in ways never before experienced. One missionary in Uganda, who is an outstanding evangelist and loves to preach, indicated that following a program of food distribution in one of the areas of that country most ravaged by the internal conflict, he was able to share the gospel with about 40,000 people who had never heard about the Lord. They first saw him as a caring person and wanted to know why he cared so much.

3. Ministry evangelism opens doors which would otherwise be sealed to other forms of evangelization. Christian doctors from Korea are involved in developing a medical ministry in one of the most rigidly closed Islamic countries. Kurdish refugees are

responding to the gospel even as they flee from attempts at genocide by Iraqi leadership. Churches which were sparked by programs of Christian compassion are growing up in countries of the former Soviet Union. Any sincere analysis of human need in restricted countries will usually reveal windows of opportunity which would otherwise be closed to historic methods of *pure* evangelism. Nearly 75 percent of those most severely in need are among the unreached people groups around the world.

4. It is estimated that by the year A.D. 2000 over 50 percent of the world's population will be under the age of 20. Out of this group there could be as many as 200 million who live on the streets and who beg, rob, take drugs, become involved in prostitution, and are almost totally alienated from the church. Few, if any, churches have considered them a target group for ministry. Instead they have become the target for death squads, those who buy and sell body parts, slave traders, perverse and evil people who exploit children through pornography and sex tours, and others who ply them with drugs and alcohol. If local churches, missions agencies, and Christians as a whole do not respond to their need, the numbers will become exponential and the negative impact on society will be beyond imagination.

No government or relief agency, or missions board, or international body has a greater potential to minister to this need than does the body of evangelical churches working in unison. If and when they do, they also have the potential to unleash one of the mightiest forces for good in the world. Whole nations could be changed and evangelized if these young people were freed from their physical enslavement, and then spiritually set free to follow the Lord.

5. There are many kinds of poverty. We are all aware of the ever-growing economic crisis within the developing world. Part of that crisis has come because the poorer nations of the world have not been able to pay back the enormous loans made following their independence. Now cash crops have replaced food crops. People who lived in the rural areas have had to leave their

homelands and move to the cities in search of jobs to feed their families. At first it was a trickle, then it became a flood of people, creating situations where the urban growth rate exceeds the capacity of cities to absorb them. Ghettos have grown. The percentage of jobless grows astronomically every year. Soon most of the ten largest cities of the world will be in developing countries and will have all the associated evils of ghettos crowded with illiterate, unemployable, and homeless emigrants. The resulting poverty is more than financial. It is a social poverty which develops a cultural poverty. It also creates a psychological poverty of the mind and soul. Most of all, it engenders a spiritual poverty. The church has never had a greater challenge, and nowhere is the Scripture more specific than it is in the command to "do it unto the least of these."

6. One area where a little could do so much is in the area of community-based health. In much of the world almost 50 percent of the children die before the age of five. They really don't have to die. They do not starve to death, although malnutrition is the primary reason that so many cannot survive. Filthy water and a basic lack of information about sanitation are the largest killers. Governments are still spending huge amounts to build first-class hospitals from funds made available by the World Health Organization or other aid programs. A great deal of emphasis is given to training doctors to meet the urgent health needs of these same countries.

At the same time, it is estimated that 75 percent of the killer diseases could be prevented with less than 15 percent of the funds spent for training doctors and building hospitals through a concentrated program of community-based health care. The network of rural churches could become the most effective venue for training programs. With minimum education, many of the leaders within the local churches could become trainers and teachers who help those less informed by providing simple lessons in basic health care. Such a ministry might also remove many of the barriers of superstition and fear which alienate the most needy from seeking help.

7. The lack of financial resources which keep most local churches from becoming involved in major ministry efforts can be overcome through a concentrated utilization of other resources which are inherent in the local churches. It has been suggested, for instance, that in a crisis situation such as an earthquake or flood, one of the greatest needs is for someone to counsel with those who have lost their homes or loved ones. Churches have become temporary havens for those without housing. Members have aided in identifying relatives or lost children who have been separated in the crisis. In the civil unrest of the former Yugoslavia, individuals opened their homes to refugees, thus providing not only a temporary sanctuary, but also a model for Christian witness. In Romania, the evangelical churches became the channel through which major relief groups could distribute supplies without fear of corruption and loss. In the wake of hurricanes in the Caribbean, churches have been the primary channel of response in immediate aid and subsequent rehabilitation. Much of what has taken place in these situations has not been the result of spending large amounts of funds, but rather because of the involvement of lay men and women who have responded with their lives.

Remember 1 John 3:17-18: "If a rich person sees his brother in need, yet closes his heart against his brother, how can he claim that he loves God? My children, our love should not be just words and talk; it must be true love, which shows itself in action" (NIV).

Other Issues to Be Considered

Evangelism: In 24 countries, Christians represent less than 1 percent of the population, and in almost 200 other countries less than 10 percent are considered Christian. While the growth of Christianity has been phenomenal over the past century, the actual percentage of Christians in the world has decreased from 34.4 percent in 1900 to 32.8 percent in 1980. Much of that decrease is the result of population growth in countries that have been considered "highly inaccessible" to Christian missions.

It is estimated that there are over 1.28 billion people on this globe that have been beyond the reach of uninhibited missionary approaches in evangelism. Over 60 percent of all Christians live in countries where civil liberties are curbed. Sixteen percent must endure severe governmental interference and harassment of religion, and another 5 percent dare not confess their faith for fear of endangering their lives.

Some of the world's hungriest people are the least evangelized. A full 50 percent of the world's hungry people live in just five countries, where Christians make up only a fraction of the total population. Some 13 percent of all Christians in developing nations live in absolute poverty. About half of this number are in Latin America, a third in Africa, and the rest in South and Southeast Asia. By the standards of the world, they are paupers and live in a condition of life so characterized by malnutrition, illiteracy, and disease as to be beneath any reasonable definition of human decency.

Population:* For every two persons on the earth in 1975 there will be three in A.D. 2000. The main increase will be among the poor. Four-fifths of the population will live in less developed countries. Population growth will be 40 percent higher in A.D. 2000 than in 1975, but some 92 percent of it will occur in the least developed countries. Between 1990 and A.D. 2025, the population of South Asia is expected to double, that of Latin America to grow two-and-one-half times, and Africa's may increase by three-and-one-half times. Obviously, the most rapid growth will take place in the urban areas. Of equal significance is the fact that while the population structures of the industrialized nations become more column-shaped (characteristic of a mature and slowly growing population) with a relatively even age distribution, the structure of the developing countries will become even more pyramid-shaped (characteristic of rapid growth). By A.D. 2000 the number of megalopolises (connected groupings of major urban population areas) is expected to total 61 in the Southern Hemisphere and only 21 in the Northern Hemisphere.

The largest percentage of the population will be under 20 years of age, and hundreds of thousands will be abandoned children, especially in the massive urban complexes. It is conservatively estimated that there are some 40 million children at the present time who fend for themselves on the streets of Latin America.

In Rio de Janeiro and São Paulo alone, there are 4.5 million abandoned or semiabandoned children. They shine shoes, sell chewing gum, shoplift, pick pockets, prostitute themselves, sometimes kill,

Percentage of Population of the World in Different Age Groups

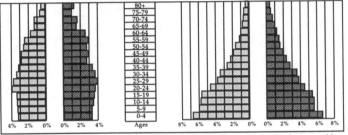

Characteristic age sets
of developed world

Characteristic age sets of developing world

Estimates and Rough Projections of Selected Urban Agglomerations in Developing Countries*

	1960	1970	1975	2000
		(millions of persons)		
Calcutta	5.5	6.9	8.1	19.0
Mexico City	4.9	8.6	10.9	31.6
Bombay	4.1	5.8	7.1	19.1
Cairo	3.7	5.7	6.9	16.4
Djakarta	2.7	4.3	5.6	16.9
Seoul	2.4	5.4	7.3	18.7
Delhi	2.3	3.5	4.5	13.2
Manila	2.2	3.5	4.4	12.7
Tehran	1.9	3.4	4.4	13.8
Karachi	1.8	3.3	4.5	15.9
Bogota	1.7	2.6	3.4	9.5
Lagos	0.8	1.4	2.1	9.4

*Population Today, March 1993

or do whatever is necessary to survive. Some go home at night, many more sleep out, with newspaper for a bedsheet, and all their worldly possessions for a pillow.

Hunger:* There are between 13 and 18 million deaths from hunger and hunger-related diseases every year. Some 15 million of these are children. At the same time, some 250,000 children become blind every year from lack of vitamin A. About 40 percent of the world's hungry are children; the remaining percentage are mostly women. Malnutrition is the underlying or associated cause in one-third of all deaths of the worldwide under-five population. Today some 30 of the world's poorest nations, representing almost 900 million people, do not meet the minimum caloric needs of their population. The majority of these live and work in rural areas. There is a large and growing number, however, in the sprawling urban slums, ghettos, and shantytowns, especially in Latin America, where 60 percent of the children under the age of five die as a result of malnutrition.

Poverty:* By A.D. 2000, the gap between the richest and the poorest will have increased. The difference in per capita income between the developed and less developed nations will widen from about $4,000 in 1975 to some $7,000. Within countries these disparities may even be larger. For every one dollar increase in the gross national product per capita in the less developed countries, a $20 increase is projected for the industrialized countries.

Economics:* In the foreseeable future, prices will continue to rise, and purchasing power will go down. The real price of food commodities may rise as much as 100 percent. Energy costs could rise as much as 150 percent, while the relative purchasing power of less developed countries will actually decrease. Because of the natural decline in many vital commodities such as water, land, wood products, fish, and other items affected by both environmental conditions and human demands, the pressure on inflation will continue and intensify. The inability of the poorer nations to cope with national debts, and the proportion of their productivity needed for currency exchange will create pressures that will affect the very foundations of the world economy, as well as the continuing political and economic instability of the less developed nations.

Resources:* The amount of arable land available per person will decrease from about four-tenths of a hectare in 1975 to only about one-quarter hectare in A.D. 2000. Fully one-half of the world's total petroleum resources has already been consumed. By the turn of the century over one-half of the remaining petroleum resources will be consumed. In the same period world per capita water supplies will decline by 35 percent. Available wood stock will decline by 47 percent. By A.D. 2000, 40 percent of the forests still remaining in the less developed countries will have been razed, thus the environment will have lost important life-supporting capabilities. The concentration of carbon dioxide in the atmosphere will be nearly one-third higher than preindustrial levels. Several inches of topsoil around the world will have been eroded from vitally needed croplands, especially in the less developed countries. Desertification may take a significant portion of the world's rangeland and cropland.

Health Care:* Even with the great advances made in health care during the twentieth century, the global health situation at the end of this century is far from optimistic. The contrast between scientific and technical advances and the impact of poverty and malnutrition is increasingly stark. Inaccessibility and high cost of health services, poor living conditions, malnutrition, lack of sanitation and water, the continuing population explosion, and lack of education all contribute to the negative prognosis for health in developing countries. In many of these same countries, 85 percent of the national health budget is devoted to hospital services which serve less than 10 percent of the population. Only 15 percent of the budget is left to provide basic primary health care for 90 percent of the people. For the cost of training one doctor for a hospital, some 30 community health workers could be trained to make available essential care at the village level. It is estimated that some 80 to 85 percent of diseases now prevalent in developing countries could be prevented by an adequate program of primary health care.

One major missions health care program follows the same pattern seen in the secular world. Presently 80 percent of its physicians and 38 percent of its nurses have a primary job assignment related to an institution. Only 12 percent of physicians and 23 percent of nurses are primarily involved in any form of community health. Today 79 percent of all its requests for physicians are for highly skilled specialists, and 77 percent of the requests for nurses are for institutional service. Out of the 44 health-care personnel requested in one year, there was only one request for a public health nurse, and one for a nutritionist. Too few doctors are assigned to community-based health programs.

By the turn of the century disease patterns will be changing worldwide. In addition to infectious diseases, nutritional deficiencies, and preventable diseases now predominant in developing countries, there will be significant increases in cancers, chronic illnesses, industrial and/or automobile accidents, and diseases of a stressful lifestyle (diseases associated with development). New diseases resistant to treatment, such as AIDS, are likely to rise beyond imagination. It has already been estimated that Africa will have 10 million children orphaned because of AIDS by the year A.D. 2000.

Vulnerability to Natural Disaster and Human Disruption:* The ethnic and tribal tensions that lead to war will have increased in almost every sector and, at the same time, weaker countries will be more vulnerable to the disruptive effects of war. For instance, the potential conflict over fresh water alone is underscored by the fact that out of 200 of the world's major river basins, 148 are shared by two countries and 52 are shared by three-to-ten countries. Food needs are likely to create more situations where food is used as a weapon to gain political conformity and military alliances.

Defining the Role for Churches
Relating to Human Need Ministries

The purpose of winning the lost should never be forgotten. Dynamic evangelism is really authenticated when it is concerned with the relationship between the biblical mandate to proclaim the gospel, and the biblical commandment to care about the life and integrity of those to whom it would share that good news. In this context, evangelism becomes incarnate within the evangels and ministry oriented within the organized bodies of believers.

Some criteria which must be considered relating to the principle of incarnational evangelism which results in ministering churches: It must manifest the Christ model in ministry, the mission of our Lord in reconciliation.

1. In drawing people to Christ, they must also be brought to Christlikeness.
2. The target priorities must be consistent with the priorities in the ministry of Christ.
3. Evangelism must include witnessing to all areas of God's truth in the life and body of society. Though evangelism is fundamentally spiritual, it is inevitably involved in the whole of life.

It must be clearly definable contextually. It cannot be separated from the demonstration of the whole web of human relationships in one's life. It is not disembodied truth. Proclamation loses its integrity when it is broadcast wholesale without dealing with persons individually in their real-life situations. Truth which is not clothed in life lacks authenticity (see 1 John 3:17).

Vital evangelism depends upon a strong community orientation—the church in community. The reconciled life is that which comes from being joined to Christ and growing up in proper relationship with God and others. Only when the church is genuinely a reconciled and reconciling community does it have the capacity to reconcile.

It takes transformed people to transform society. Evangelism is compromised when it fails to communicate its truth to those who, because of their circumstance or condition, do not have the capacity or opportunity to comprehend the message. *Koinonia* is not only the mark of fellowship within the body, but also the key to effective evangelism strategy in community. Evangelism is most effective when it provides for a balanced encounter for participation in the whole environment of the ministering church—worship, witness, and ministry.

The effective ministering church becomes the enabling center to equip for ministry-related evangelism. In this respect, effective evangelism depends upon the harmonious functioning of all leadership gifts (apostle, prophet, evangelist, pastor, teacher) in which the whole body participates.

If the church is to grow up to experience Christ's fullness, evangelism must be seen as a beginning rather than an end, otherwise it leaves no room for nurture and growth. Christ's lordship must affect the whole of life, and this can only happen as the body facilitates that growth.

Organization must become flexible, person-oriented, and culturally appropriate enough to allow for divergency in ministry and scope in function. Form should follow function. Witnessing and service should be an integrated, yet spontaneous, outgrowth of structure. Structures should never be allowed to stifle the life of the body by encouraging believers to become spectators rather than participants.

The approach must be a holistic one. It must focus concern on not only the humanitarian aspects of hunger, disease, and other human needs, but also on the deeper dimensions of spiritual poverty that are often at the root of human need. The unnatural and unscriptural division between wholeness of body and wholeness of spirit has no place in a ministry that would present the whole gospel to the whole person. If the approach is to be authentic, however, it means the church must not only minister to the whole person, but also that it must wholly minister to people in need. In other words, one not only has to see the whole need of people, but has to recognize that everything that is done must involve the incarnational agent in the whole life of all he or she would evangelize.

The goal in response must be transformational, not just developmental. As discussed earlier in the introduction, the best developmental plans often fail because of human greed, power politics, graft, or just plain lethargy. Real transformation calls for a change from a purely physical and material level of living to one of both spiritual and physical wholeness. To be valid, a transformational approach must be people-centered, rather than being program- or project-centered, and must recognize the importance of deliverance from every form of bondage that would inhibit or preclude the reconciliation of the whole of life.

The rationale for response must be biblically based. The Great Commandment is no less binding than the Great Commission as a mandate from our Lord. There is a biblical consistency demanding concern for the poor, the sick, the hungry, and the hurting in the "unto the least of these" kind of theology. John asks, "Whoever has this world's goods, and sees his brother has need, and then closes his heart to him, how can he say that the love of God dwells in him?" The question, "Am I my brother's keeper?" in the Old Testament is echoed in the New Testament which asks, "Who is my neighbor?" In essence both passages seem to say that to whatever extent one fails to become his or her brother's keeper, one participates in becoming his or her brother's killer.

Defining the Role of Incarnational Agents

The place and the role of the missionary and/or development worker has been dictated somewhat today by the sequence of events as much as by deliberate choices. However, the response of these in adapting to the new circumstances may largely determine the extent of their effectiveness for the future. The day of the expatriate as boss or supervisor is rapidly passing into history. In some cases, it may be just as difficult for a national to distinguish between a supervisor on the one hand and an advisor on the other, unless those who choose those roles relate with a servant attitude. Those who would work in the developing world must be identified in the framework of the social structure itself, e.g., as "a friend of the court." As a friend, one can have a role in the indigenous church, whatever that job assignment may be. In this respect, the role may be expressed in the following ways:

An earthen vessel—The incarnational agent must first of all be an instrument in the hand of God, which at once brings others to see the glory of God (and not the person or resources the agent may bring), while at the same time providing the channel through which God can speak to people about all their needs—both physical and spiritual. The agent is not just an apologist, one who propagates faith and practice, but a translator and interpreter of the whole truth of the gospel. The vessel is, at best, frail and unworthy of what it possesses.

A servant—To be a servant, in the sense that Jesus taught His disciples—the first-last principle, the foot-washing posture, the sheep-feeding precept, the ministering rather than being ministered unto purpose—is fundamental in the role of the incarnational agent. As a servant, the degree of involvement and the place of leadership must be determined, not by the sending agency, nor by one's own insistence, but rather by those being served.

A soul winner—The incarnational agent cannot expect to perform some professional function to the exclusion of that fundamental purpose of sharing Jesus Christ. This must be done in the context of a genuine love for people in which they are viewed in terms of their potential for living out the Christian life in relationship to their fellow man as participants in the presence of Christ.

An enabler—If incarnational agents have a weakness, it may be at the point of their desire to do good for others rather than enabling others to do good. If one is not very careful, this may promote a type of ethnocentric pride which leads one to believe that their way of doing things is of necessity better than that of a less developed nation.

A catalyst—By the very nature of the message and ministry demanded by the gospel, the incarnational agent is an agent of change. However, two things must be remembered. First, it is the Holy Spirit who will really effect the change in people's lives, even in the context of material help that meets the more urgent physical needs of the hour. Secondly, one cannot leave the infant in Christ without spiritual nurturing anymore than one can leave the physically deprived without empowerment to change the physical circumstances which keep him or her from an acceptable quality of life.

A resource agent—The incarnational agent must also be a source of new ideas and information. The agent is the voice of experience, but an experience based on one's own cultural background, and therefore always subject to modification. The task is to become a source of cultural alternatives for people to select if they want and need them. Those resources must never be limited to things. In some respects, the weakest part of any development program may be the external financial resources it becomes dependent upon. The incarnational agent must discover how to enable the people to develop their own greatest potential—both spiritually and physically.

A fraternal worker—Incarnational agents must always recognize their place as guests of the government, the indigenous people and, in most cases, the local churches where they serve. The fraternal worker is not there to rule but to influence. The extent of that influence is subject to the manner in which they conduct themselves and the perception thus perceived by the local people. It will also be reflected by their understanding of the local culture and language.

A church planter—Following the New Testament ideal, an incarnational agent will have an innate desire to see churches being born. Just as it is natural for a married woman to desire children, it

An Old Chinese Poem

Go to the people
Live with them
Learn from them
Love them
Start with what they know
Build on what they have.

But of the best leaders
When their work is accomplished
Their work is done
The people all remark

"We have done it ourselves!"

is natural for a born-again Christian to desire to see others born into the kingdom of God. This should in no way be in conflict with the goals for transformation in the physical realm. It does not presume that the agent will in every case, or indeed in many cases, be directly involved in the actual organizing of local groups. The function may only be to inspire those who appear to be uniquely able to share the Word of God to their own people to move out to share their personal experience with Christ. It may be to prepare the *soil* for others to come and develop and to nurture.

The Local Church Ministering

Before a church can truly become a ministering church, it must discover how to become an incarnational agent. Orlando Costas identifies four significant areas of church growth: numerical growth, organic growth, conceptual growth, and incarnational growth. He further defines incarnational growth as "the degree of involvement of a community of faith in the life and problems of her social environment." It is in this area that the ministering church must understand the mandate of Christ to "love our neighbors as ourselves." We would add another thought to this by suggesting that incarnational growth is the evidence of the manifestation of Christ within the body of believers being demonstrated in every aspect of the life and work of their community. It is more than just being a caring people. It demands a sensitivity to the world of poverty, exploitation, hunger, and despair, in which the members are prompted by the Holy Spirit to become agents of hope by becoming active participants in the very nature of Christ Himself.

Peter says, "His divine power has given us everything we need for life and godliness through our knowledge of Him who called us by His own glory and goodness. Through these He has given us His very great and precious promises, so that through them you may participate in the divine nature" (2 Peter 1:3,4f NIV). This is what is required of the church—participation in the divine nature in the context of human hurt.

Prepare the church for participation. Participation in the nature of Christ means understanding how Christ related to people in despair. Pastors might prepare a series of lessons, and through storying and dialogue with discipleship groups, reveal the variety of ways in which Christ manifested His divine nature and thus the nature of the Father in real-life situations. The Gospels are filled with vivid examples of this type of ministry. The following two examples suggest how this might be done.

The Samaritan Woman (John 4:1-26): Tell the whole story as it is related in the Gospel. The leader might begin by asking, "What do you feel is the most significant concept Jesus communicated to the woman at the well?" Most will answer that He simply asked her for a drink of water. The real message which He was trying to communicate, however, was that she was a person of value! Most of us tend either to figure out ways in which we can help people, or ways in which we can witness to them about Christ. Christ started out, however, by suggesting that she could be useful in helping Him. She was a person of worth! You notice that Christ did not ask her what she needed or what she wanted. He focused immediately on her real problem.

Ask the group to discuss what they feel were the woman's biggest problems and how they would deal with them. It is apparent that she had a number of problems.

She had an ethnical problem—she was from an outcast group of people. She had a social problem—she went to the well alone in the middle of the day without any company. Most of the women would normally get their water in the cool of the morning without inviting her. She had a moral problem—she lived in a progressive state of adultery. She had a religious problem—her people worshiped in the mountain rather than at the temple in Jerusalem. She had a spiritual problem—she was lost in sin. Her most immediate problem, and the one Jesus dealt with, was the fact that she was thirsty. She simply did not know how to satisfy her thirst so she went to men hoping that they would bring her the joy and peace she was looking for. No matter how many men she tried, she was never satisfied. This is why Jesus gave her living water which caused her to forget her water pot.

The man at the pool of Bethesda (John 5:1-14): Tell this story as it is related in the Gospel. The leader might ask the following questions: What were the Jews doing at the time Jesus stopped to help the man? Why didn't they stop instead of just going on to their worship service? Why hadn't the man been helped before? Name some of his problems. Which problem did Jesus deal with first? Second? Last? How did He relate His physical ministry to a spiritual one?

You will notice that one of the man's greatest problems was the fact that nobody cared. He had been crippled for 38 years, and not once had anyone ever stopped by to help him prior to the coming of Jesus.

Some of the greatest problems in any community start right there. People can live with hunger, poverty, disaster, and sickness, but if no one cares they may not be able to go on. It is also interesting to note that God's people who were going to worship and sacrifice never became sensitive enough to notice the level of suffering right at the door which led to the temple. It would appear from the story that those who did take time to stop and help others actually got in his way. Perhaps this truth could be developed further by asking the group how we as Christians tend to get in the way of those who are needy and don't know Christ.

It is interesting to note that, having first dealt with his social problem, (he had no one who cared), Jesus dealt with his physical problem, but He also involved the man himself in the healing process. He told the man to become a participant by telling him to "take up his bed and walk." It was only afterward that Jesus came to the man a second time and dealt with his spiritual problem. Now there is no magic order in these events, except to say that Christ was sensitive at the points where He could best communicate the love of the Father.

Select other stories from the Gospels which point out how Jesus ministered to individuals regarding their physical and spiritual needs. What did He deal with first? Why? How did He lead them to an awareness of Who He was? What did He ask them to do in

DEVELOPING A CHURCH MINISTRY ASSESSMENT

The following profile is designed to assist the local church in appraising its present program of activities in contrast with its perception of need and the relative level of involvement to address those needs. By comparing the level of involvement and the areas of known human need, the potential ministry opportunities can be prioritized.

Present Programs of Involvement	Perception of Importance					Present Involvement				
	1	2	3	4	5	1	2	3	4	5
Church planting										
Lay evangelism										
Partnership evangelism										
Leadership training										
Stewardship training										
Bible school extension										
Theological Education Extension (T.E.E.)										
Women's work										
Youth work										
Student work										
Men's work										
Elementary education										
High school										
Literacy										
Media:										
Radio (local)										
TV (local)										
Publications										
Tape cassettes										
Other										
Medical:										
Church clinic										
Public health assistance										
Dental assistance										
Nutritional training										
Day care										
Vocational training										
Job placement										
Urban/Rural development										
Counseling										
Drug rehabilitation										
Street children										

Areas of Known Human Need	Perception of Importance					Present Involvement				
	1	2	3	4	5	1	2	3	4	5
Chronic hunger										
Malnutrition										
Infant foods										
Water:										
Purification										
Wells										
Irrigation										
Disposal										
Primary health care:										
Under five										
Supplemental feeding										
Nutritional training										
Nutritional rehabilitation										
Vaccination/Immunization										
Children:										
Abandoned children										
Orphans										
Basic educational assistance										
Street children										
Secondary health care										
Unemployment:										
Job placement										
Documents										
Vocational training										
Food-for-work										
Drug rehabilitation										
Prostitution										
Alcoholism										
Halfway house										
Temporary housing										
Transients										
Others (list)										

KEY

Perception of Importance
1. No importance
2. Little importance
3. Moderate importance
4. High level of importance
5. Urgent

Present Involvement
1. Nothing planned
2. Little involvement
3. Moderately involved
4. Actively involved
5. High-priority involvement

the process of receiving help? How did He involve the disciples in participation with Him? In what ways did He encourage them to get firsthand experience? In the early church, what evidence is there that the disciples continued to carry out ministries of healing, feeding, etc?

Prepare for resource and ministry assessment. (See Chapter 6: The Project Planning Process.) If the church is really to get involved in the needs and problems of its community, it must be an example in areas of social action as well as direct humanitarian aid. It may be obvious that hundreds of people are out of work and need job skills in order to find work. It may also be true that there is inadequate nutrition, medical help, literacy, or educational facilities. In the context of determining the variety of needs within the immediate community, leaders need to assess the nature of the problems creating the needs. Joint action on the part of the entire Christian community may be called for in many cases to alert representatives of various government ministries to the problems.

Resource Assessment

Human resources: Your most important resource will always be people. This is particularly true within the local church. If the church is to become involved in a holistic approach toward ministry, it must look primarily to the gifts and skills within the body of believers. Prior to developing any kind of a questionnaire or assessment instrument to determine the particular skills and interests the congregation may have, a study should be made to lead the members to understand the nature of spiritual gifts and to discover their own spiritual gifts.** As the members begin to understand the meaning of spiritual gifts, they should be helped to understand how those gifts may be used in ministering to those around them. Participants should then be encouraged to focus on one, two, or three people within their immediate surroundings for whom they can exercise their spiritual gifts in a specific form of ministry. Expressing those gifts on a one-on-one basis within their immediate neighborhood will help them to see the potential of the wider application for a cooperative church effort.

Some of the least trained people may have the greatest gifts in communicating to those in need. Everyone should have an opportunity to participate regardless of education or special training.

José was a short-order cook. Having heard that some members in his local church were going from Southern California to Mexico to assist local people following a hurricane, he volunteered to go and cook for the group. When he arrived, however, the local church people had already set up the facilities for feeding the volunteers and it looked like José wasn't needed. He started picking up debris, sweeping up, and doing anything he could to help. A local person stopped to ask him who he was and why he had come. In his broken way, not even thinking that he was giving a testimony, he told the man that Christ had come into his heart and he simply wanted to help others because of all Christ had done for him. The man got so interested he asked José to tell him more about Jesus. It wasn't long before the man trusted the Lord. He then asked José if he would come to tell the same story to his family and neighbors. José did so and before he left to return home, this short-order cook with nothing to do had won more than a dozen people to the Lord. Never underestimate the power of Christ in an empty earthen vessel.

The following skills and gifts inventory may be helpful.

Personnel: Skills and Gifts Inventory

Name	
Address	
Home phone (if applicable)	
Business phone	

2 Describe what kind of work you do.

Where employed?

3 What languages do you speak?

4 What languages do you read and write?

5 What personal facilities do you have which could be employed in helping people?

❑ Car ❑ Truck ❑ Boat ❑ Spare room

❑ Typewriter ❑ Computer ❑ Portable bed

❑ Furniture (specify)

❑ Others

6 Check the appropriate items (x) if you are willing to help in this area. If well trained in the area mark with a star (*).

❑ Soul winning	❑ Plumber	❑ Music (specify)
❑ Children's work	❑ Tailor	❑ Office (specify)
❑ Builder	❑ Counseling	❑ Computer
❑ Carpenter	❑ Teaching (specify)	❑ Gardens
❑ First aid	❑ Electrician	❑ Youth work
❑ Care of children	❑ Farming	❑ Nurse (RN/LPN)
❑ Mechanic	❑ Poster art	❑ Photographer
❑ Sewing	❑ Driving a car/truck	❑ Radio/TV repair
❑ Cooking	❑ Typist	❑ Doctor
❑ Sports (specify)	❑ Animals	❑ Well digging

❑ Other (specify)

7	Would you be willing to participate in a project with this church?
	❑ Yes ❑ No
8	What days of the week will you be available?
9	What time of the day(s) will you be available?
10	Would you be willing to be trained to help in a church project?
	If yes, what is your preference?

Community resources: Determine what kind of municipal, government, school, agency, or other leaders might be available to provide specialized services to your church in the context of various ministry programs. This could include social workers, medical personnel, youth workers, counselors, psychologists, various artisans, local merchants, etc.

Physical resources: Check carefully to determine how the various rooms and facilities of the church building might be used during the day or other times when normal services are not being held. Check throughout the community to see whether or not there are other physical resources, such as sports facilities, schoolrooms, libraries, auditoriums, amphitheaters, workrooms, unused warehouses, etc.

Technical resources: Check with missionaries, other churches, government ministries, Red Cross, the United Nations Children's Fund (UNICEF), relief agencies, radio or TV stations, businesses, local merchants, artisans, and others in reference to materials, literature, or other resources they might make available.

Financial resources: Before going outside the church family, lead the body of church members to determine what they are willing and able to invest in such ministries. In many cases they may be able to participate in personal service rather than give cash. Some may be able to donate time. Too much outside funding, from whatever source, may stifle initiative and create dependency. If the project has a community application and deals with a community problem, it would be better to seek total community participation rather than go to outside sources. It is also possible that local merchants, factories, or national or multinational corporations would be interested in donating materials such as food, clothing, equipment in addition to any cash donations. However, beware! Anytime the church goes to the community or to other outside sources for this type of aid, it may compromise the essential purpose for its involvement, the sharing of a witness for Christ.

Feasibility and targeting: After the church has determined the problems and/or the needs it will target, a thorough study needs to be made concerning the feasibility of any proposed project. (See chapter 5.) The church must carefully count the cost in terms of the finance, time, and personnel it is able to commit to the project(s). Projects should be big enough to challenge the church into real ministry, but small and practical enough to be carried out within a given period of time. Focusing on a particular target group may be helpful. As the church gets experience in developing one type of ministry, it may expand to other aspects of ministry involvement.

Planning: Any plans should involve the whole church in some phase of participation. The more the church members know and understand the planning, the more likely they are to be committed to it. The whole ministry program should belong to the whole church rather than to an individual or small group within the church even though all may not be directly involved in carrying out the ministry.

Monitoring and evaluation: (See chapters 6 and 7.) In most cases, it would be more helpful for the church to ask either a local missionary or some other impartial observer to provide assistance in evaluating the programs of ministry. Periodic checks should be made by the leadership within the church to determine whether the programs are proceeding as planned.

Many different approaches have been attempted to deal with the overwhelming aspects of economically deprived urban people. More and more it becomes apparent that unless churches work together in ministry they will not be able to make a significant impact on human deprivation. Even working together, it will take the cooperation of others within the larger community beyond the slums to participate in providing jobs, training, and intermediate support for the systems to work.

The following urban church project in SOWETO, (Southwest Township) near Johannesburg, South Africa, serves as one model for cooperative efforts in urban slums.

A Cooperative Local Church Project Model—
SOWETO (Southwest Township, Johannesburg, South Africa)

Background. The area administrator for Eastern and Southern Africa requested a consultant from the Southern Baptist Foreign Mission Board to work together with the missionaries and national pastors in Soweto to research and develop a feasibility study of potential approaches in addressing the problems of human needs. At the time of the study, there were eight small cooperating Baptist churches in the township.

The overall purpose of the proposal was to involve the churches in a community-wide effort to reach the poorest of the poor. In the context of the program, each church hoped to extend its total ministry into the squatter portions of the township. They were concerned about meeting human needs while extending a spiritual witness to the communities involved.

Description of the area. The Soweto township is a major suburb of Johannesburg, South Africa. It is a sprawling slum of over 3.5 million people and in 1992 it was growing at a rate of 2,000 persons per day. The entire township area is approximately 15 kilometers from east to west and 12 kilometers from south to north. Because of the constant riots, tribal fights, and general disorder, all schools had been closed. World Vision, the Salvation Army, and a few other local agencies had some social programs targeted toward this same group of people. Because of the enormity of the problems, these were inadequate to meet the need. There appeared to be little coordinated effort on the part of the local or federal government to deal with the problems.

Within the township there were ten growing ghettos or squatter areas as well as thousands of squatters within the confines of regular housing. The unemployment rate was 50 percent within the township generally and 75 percent in the squatter areas. The vast majority of residents were under 25 years of age. The Baptist churches scattered throughout the township averaged about 150 to 200 in membership.

Following detailed research regarding the area, a human needs consultant met on the field with the missionary who was working within the township, the executive secretary of the convention, and pastors within the township. After briefing the group on the details of a week-long feasibility study regarding potential approaches to the problems, a meeting was held to determine the best possible approach to develop a holistic ministry through the churches.

Initial research involved the following:

1. A determination of the general demographics of the township from data already assembled by the local township government and/or other sources.
2. An understanding of the situation and circumstance under which the people lived. This involved mapping the township and identifying each of the squatter areas and other areas of temporary or unsuitable housing.
3. An investigation of the role of the government, relief agencies, and other denominations regarding the extent of any developmental or relief work being done.
4. An awareness of the economic environment in regard to the relative level of joblessness and other factors affecting the potential for producing income.
5. An investigation of the community health factors for an

understanding of need and potential for local church involvement in meeting some of the needs.

6. An understanding of the dynamics of social, political, and ethnic unrest in terms of what was obviously a hostile environment.
7. An evaluation of the level of existing church developmental ministries of all denominations and their relative impact on the communities in terms of outreach and evangelism.
8. The discovery of ways in which the local churches could extend their total ministries in evangelism and church growth.

(A map of the Soweto area and a tabulation of the various churches is included for illustration of the kind of research required for an adequate feasibility study on pages 89-91.)

Preliminary steps following research and data gathering:

1. A meeting was held with pastors, church representatives, and the leadership of the Baptist Convention of South Africa to discuss the data and to develop further planning.
2. The group decided to develop a body of materials and request competent leaders to train members of each of the local churches in methods of conducting a survey throughout the slum areas.
3. Following the survey, and in cooperation with the local missionary and convention leadership, training courses in ministry evangelism were to be taught in each of the churches.
4. Based on the information received, each church was asked to adopt a ghetto area in proximity to the church building. Church members were assigned to the area for the purpose of identifying and entering into a foster-care relationship with at least five families each from the adopted ghetto area. The purpose of this relationship was to minister to their spiritual, emotional, and physical needs in the context of the total ministry program to be adopted by the local church. It should be understood that one of the constraints in this effort was the fact that the township was under a virtual state of siege with a total disruption of the school system, normal commerce, and freedom to move about.

5. It was determined that it would be impossible to provide for a general food distribution program from the churches because of the lack of security. Alternate ideas included: a) providing food coupons which could be used at specific stores for a set type of food supplies; b) setting up soup kitchens or feeding stations within each area. Ultimately, these ideas proved to work the best as the local townspeople not only offered to provide the space for this, but provided additional protection for those to bring the food and serve. It also involved an increasing number of church members in ministry.

6. Attempts were to be made by the families ministering to set up small cell groups, starting with the families with whom they were assigned.

7. Following an additional survey of the surrounding area, a 45-acre site was chosen and purchased to provide for a training and conference center as part of a total outreach to the township. It should be noted that the township was growing rapidly in the direction of the new property. Because adequate buildings for a total vocational training program were already available on site, little had to be done in terms of improvements to set up the program.

8. A survey was done within the total Baptist community in Johannesburg of various businesses, shops, industries, and others to identify job opportunities and skill needs prior to setting up the vocational training center. Plans were made to offer training to men and women from the ghetto areas for specific job needs according to the specifications of the potential employers. They were asked to provide entry-level jobs for those trained for a minimum of six months trial, and following that to extend the job for those who qualified. (After two years, the plan has been so successful that employers are practically waiting in line to get the trainees.)

9. Because the site was adequate, the center was able to introduce agricultural subjects and actually raise much of their own food supply. Other produce was sold, as well as items manufactured by the trainees, to provide for operating expenses.

In the survey, it was important to determine the exact scope of the area considered to be a squatters village, because these were not marked out with specific boundaries. It was also important to determine the exact method for sampling the households within the squatter areas.

It was decided to use the general map of Soweto and divide each of the subdivisions in order to locate each ghetto/slum. It was then decided to identify some obvious landmark located near the center of the slum as a starting point from which to measure and/or identify which dwellings were to be surveyed.

Assignments could then be made based on specific directions from the center point.

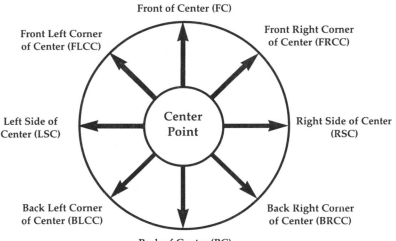

THE SOUTHWEST TOWNSHIP (SOWETO)
Johannesburg, South Africa

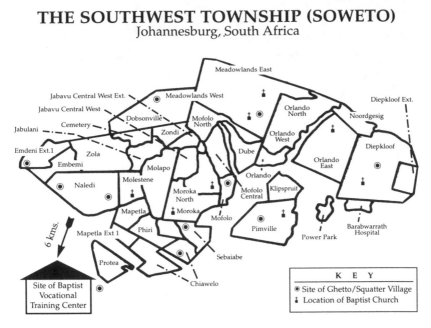

Soweto—Cross tabulations ranked by denomination

ID	Denomination	Member	Count	Mean	Largest	Smallest
1	TOTAL	148,385	211	703.25		
2	Roman Catholic	22,738	8	2,842.25	9,000	200
3	St. Paul's Anglican	9,415	1	9,415.00	9,415	9,415
4	Methodist Church	6,906	8	863.25	2,000	300
5	St. Peter Clever	5,000	1	5,000.00	5,000	5,000
6	Twelve Apostle	4,888	7	698.29	1,243	340
8	Seventh Day Adventist	4,618	7	659.71	2,720	120
9	Assemblies of God	4,169	9	463.22	951	225
10	St. Mary's	4,000	1	4,000.00	4,000	4,000
11	Church of Nazarene	3,917	12	326.42	784	92
12	N.G. Kerk	3,720	4	930.00	2,009	230
13	Church of the Province	3,122	3	1,040.67	2,500	311
14	Anglican Church	2,940	3	980.00	1,580	410
15	African Meth. Episcopal	2,624	5	524.80	819	209
16	Catholic Church	2,600	1	2,600.00	2,600	2,600
17	Apostolic Church	2,350	2	1,175.00	1,700	650
18	Evangelical Lutheran	2,160	4	540.00	700	340
19	Lutheran Church	2,097	4	524.25	797	300
20	St. John Apostolic Faith Mission	1,900	1	1,900.00	1,900	1,900
21	Presby. Church of S.A.	1,450	4	362.50	500	250
22	Jehovah's Witness	1,421	2	710.50	1,021	400

23	United Congregational	1,306	4	326.50	363	230
24	St. John's Anglican	1,200	1	1,200.00	1,200	1,200
25	Salvation Army	1,185	5	237.00	354	80
26	Paris Evangelical Mission	1,183	2	591.50	750	433
27	Old Apostolic Church	1,153	2	576.50	653	500
28	Church of England	1,140	2	570.00	800	340
29	Ethiopian Church	1,031	2	515.50	600	431
30	New Church Mission	1,030	1	1,030.00	1,030	1,030
31	St. Hilda's Anglican	1,014	1	1,014.00	1,014	1,014
32	Dutch Reformed	1,000	1	1,000.00	1,000	1,000
33	Good Shepherd	1,000	1	1,000.00	1,000	1,000
34	St. Eli Apostolic Mission	1,000	1	1,000.00	1,000	1,000
35	Intnl. Assemblies of God	977	3	325.67	430	247
36	African Congregation	976	1	976.00	976	976
37	Apostolic Faith Mission	959	4	239.75	300	209
38	Gereformeerde Kerk	958	3	319.33	619	89
39	Bantu Methodist	930	2	465.00	630	300
40	United Christian	912	1	912.00	912	912
41	Bantu Presbyterian	905	2	452.50	500	405
42	Central Sending Kommissie	900	1	900.00	900	900
43	St. Martin Catholic	900	1	900.00	900	900
44	Apostolic Church of S.A.	896	1	896.00	896	896
45	Evangelical Mission	860	1	860.00	860	860
46	Bethel Apostolic Church in Christ	780	1	780.00	780	780
47	Presbyterian	761	2	380.50	411	350
48	S.A. Baptist Mission	711	1	711.00	711	711
49	The Full Apostolic Holy Zion Mission of S.A.	704	2	352.00	352	352
50	Berlin Lutheran Church	700	1	700.00	700	700
51	United Methodist Church	700	1	700.00	700	700
52	A. Bantu Mission	690	1	690.00	690	690
53	Full Gospel Church of God	662	2	331.00	600	62
54	Nederduitse Gereformeerde	659	1	659.00	659	659
55	Nederduitse Gereformeerde Kerk van Transvaal	637	1	637.00	637	637
56	Lutheran Free Church	632	2	316.00	316	316
57	Lutheran	620	1	620.00	620	620
58	United National Baptist	608	1	608.00	608	608
59	A.M.E.	600	1	600.00	600	600
60	S.A. Baptist Church	600	1	600.00	600	600
61	Lutheran Berlin	587	1	587.00	587	587
62	Twelve Apostles Church	560	1	560.00	560	560
63	St. John Berchman	537	1	537.00	537	537
64	African Methodist	536	2	268.00	320	216
65	Christian New Salem	534	1	534.00	534	534
66	Presbyterian Church of Africa	509	1	509.00	509	509
67	Moravian	506	2	253.00	256	250
68	Apostolic Zion Assembly	500	1	500.00	500	500

69	Church of Holy Ghost	500	1	500.00	500	500
70	Zion Christian Church	500	1	500.00	500	500
71	African Evangelical Church	473	1	473.00	473	473
72	Christian Brethren	473	1	473.00	473	473
73	Paris Mission	461	1	461.00	461	461
74	Congregational of S.A.	457	1	457.00	457	457
75	African Gospel Church	450	1	450.00	450	450
76	Nederduitsch Herformeerde Kerk	450	1	450.00	450	450
77	United Congregation Church	430	1	430.00	430	430
78	Independent Presbyterian	417	1	417.00	417	417
79	Apostolic Church in Zion	413	1	413.00	413	413
80	African Evangelical	400	1	400.00	400	400
81	Bantu Congregation of American Board	380	1	380.00	380	380
82	Independent Presbyterian	365	1	365.00	365	365
83	The Holy Apostolic Church of Zion	364	1	364.00	364	364
84	Mahon Mission	361	1	361.00	361	361
85	S.A. General Mission	323	1	323.00	323	323
86	American Board Mission	310	2	155.00	180	130
87	Full Gospel Church	300	1	300.00	300	300
88	Naledi Assemblies of God	300	1	300.00	300	300
89	Nederduitse Gereformeerde Kerk	300	1	300.00	300	300
90	Church of Sweden	297	1	297.00	297	297
91	Holy Spirit Association for the Unification of World Christianity	280	1	280.00	280	280
92	Church of Nazareth	271	2	135.50	250	21
93	Methodist Church of North Africa	271	1	271.00	271	271
94	Methodist Church of North America	271	1	271.00	271	271
95	Bantu Church of Christ	260	1	260.00	260	260
96	African Congregational	250	1	250.00	250	250
97	Baptist Missionary	250	1	250.00	250	250
98	Christian Church of Zion	239	1	239.00	239	239
99	Order of Ethiopia	215	1	215.00	215	215
100	Scandinavian Independent Baptist Mission	215	1	215.00	215	215
101	African Gospel	201	1	201.00	201	201
102	Baptist Church	201	1	201.00	201	201
103	Church of Nazarette	200	1	200.00	200	200
104	Nederduitse Gereformeerde Kerk van S.A.	200	1	200.00	200	200
105	New Apostolic	195	1	195.00	195	195
106	Swedish	172	1	172.00	172	172
107	Zion Apostolic Church	170	1	170.00	170	170
108	Baptist Church	160	1	160.00	160	160

109	S.A. Baptist Missionary	152	1	152.00	152	152
110	Holy Spirit Christian Catholic Church in Zion	124	1	124.00	124	124
111	Swiss Mission	112	1	112.00	112	112
112	Native Gospel Mission	101	1	101.00	101	101
113	S.A. Baptist Mission Soviet	90	1	90.00	90	90
114	Full Gospel	81	1	81.00	81	81
115	Evangel Alliance Mission	77	1	77.00	77	77
116	United Apostolic Church	70	1	70.00	70	70
117	United National Lutheran	50	1	50.00	50	50

Notes

*Statistics in this section are found in *The Global 2000 Report to the President*, compiled by the Council on Environmental Quality and the Department of State, Volume 1.

**Note the list of books in the Bibliography on the subject of the Holy Spirit and spiritual gifts.

CHAPTER 5

LOCAL FACTS AND FEASIBILITY . . . SURVEYING AND APPRAISING THE POSSIBILITIES

Essential Research and Fact-Finding for Project Planning
This chapter is a general guide which may be used for developing research for transformational/developmental projects. Adaptations and changes may have to be made in consideration of local circumstances and cultural differences.

Background
There should be a general description of the target area for the proposed project, including a complete picture of the community situation. Project managers need to clearly understand the economic, social, cultural, linguistic, ethnic, and religious aspects. Investigation should be made into the nature and types of problems which create need.

Sources of Information
1. The community members, i.e., the target group.

2. Existing government and voluntary relief and development agencies working in the area.
3. Professionals in the areas of low income development.
4. Representatives of various churches, denominations, or agencies and social workers.
5. Demographic studies and previous records relating to the area.
6. Municipal, community, or other national government offices.
7. Community Survey

General Objectives of the Project Researchers

1. To provide a valid sociological, demographic, and statistical base for planning the extension of the total ministries of the churches and/or agencies within the area.
2. To provide the instruments necessary for carrying out the most effective and efficient approach toward meeting the needs of the target group in a holistic manner.

Specific Objectives of the Project Researchers

1. Related to the question "What is the social, economic, and spiritual situation and the problems creating felt needs of the target group of this area, and what awareness is there of the attitudes toward existing activities of churches and/or developmental workers?"
   a. To analyze the general demographic, geographic, and historic nature of the community for a proper understanding of the target population.
   b. To ascertain the physical environment of the residents for an accurate insight into the perception of the people toward both their needs and those who would minister to them.
   c. To come to an understanding as to how these factors might relate to approaches proposed by the planners.
   d. To provide a relatively accurate basis upon which to assess the general health of the community.
   e. To gain an understanding of the community's own perception, attitudes, and potential response toward various approaches to meet their needs.

f. To gain an awareness of the spiritual dimensions, values, and practices of the community in order to understand how those spiritual factors may influence their lifestyles, aspirations, and interests in church-sponsored transformational projects.

2. Related to the question, "What governmental and voluntary relief and development activities are being carried out in the area, and what are their strategies and past results?"
   a. To reveal specific activities/programs being conducted by these organizations in order to avoid unnecessary duplication, misunderstandings, or mistakes related to current problems in the context of formulating strategies.
   b. To evaluate techniques and procedures toward providing training, jobs, or physical assistance to the target population.
   c. To discover the holes or weak places in programs which may minister to needs, but do not deal with the essential problems creating the needs.

3. Related to the question, "What are governmental policies and professional viewpoints regarding the development of such programs?"
   a. To understand the government's role in assisting these communities and to ascertain their expectations, restrictions, laws, or other limitations regarding programs which may be introduced.
   b. To collect pertinent information related to potential problem areas and/or resources which may be available as strategies are being developed.

Community Field Surveys

1. The measuring instrument:
   a. The type of instrument must be chosen considering the specific purpose of the study, the cultural composition of the area as well as available resources, and personnel. The question is, "Can it be used where the educational level is deficient?" Normally, in a slum or rural area an interview schedule method

is employed to elicit attitudinal and demographic data because of the high illiteracy rate. Researchers have developed several interview techniques for the assessment of attitudes, beliefs, and behavior patterns. Before these techniques can be successfully implemented, however, there is a need to modify and redesign the instrument to fit each specific setting. The preparatory stage should include the following if available:

- *Secondary research*—consulting existing information of previous sociological studies.
- *Review*—of previous research methods used and tested in other localities.
- *Consultation*—with church and missions leaders of the area to determine what categories of data are needed to establish priorities and possibilities for (transformational) development work.
- *Interview*—the schedule needs to be constructed with care proceeding through several revisions to be sure that it is in a language that the interviewers and the people can understand and with which they can identify. The intent of the questions must be accurately perceived by all the people involved.

b. The interview schedule should be tested in a nonsample area to determine the workability of the measuring device and to ascertain what changes are necessary before conducting the field survey. During pretesting, the following areas need to be reviewed:

- Words or concepts which are difficult and require simplification.
- Vague or inappropriate phrases and questions which may be culturally offensive.
- Questions for which respondents request further explanation.
- Questions which respondents had difficulty answering.
- Interview length—especially if it is too time consuming from the respondent's viewpoint.
- Nonverbal reaction—which questions caused embarrassment or resistance.

- Problems in administering the questions either by male or female workers.
- Correction of difficult or imprecise explanations or translations.

c. The final interview schedule (see following sample) contains four basic measuring forms, or questions, which act as verification checks on each other as well as exploring different levels and areas of the society.

Projective statements: Projective statements are useful tools for probing cultural value systems. The statement or test materials provide a stimulus designed to bring reaction—the first answer that comes to the respondent's mind. This immediate reaction is usually a projection of a person's beliefs and values, and may be indicative of the person's personality traits or unconscious motivations.

Dichotomous questions: Yes/no questions. These are used to determine basic demographic socioeconomic data.

Open questions: The open question does not suggest any alternative answer which the respondents can choose. The technique is very useful in exploratory study where new thoughts and associations are sought.

Closed questions: This type of question gives the respondent a choice of answers to choose from and is especially helpful to ascertain the community's reaction to possible projects proposed.

Other types of questions or statements: These can be used such as true/false for giving values and/or priorities to list, etc.

d. The final questionnaire should contain the following areas of investigation:
The demographic and historic nature of the community:
1) Family unit: size, type, sex, age, marital status, births.
2) Migration: From where? Why? Length of stay, planned duration, ties to rural area, i.e., land, cattle, anticipated visits.

The physical environment:
1) Housing: type, condition, ownership, felt needs.
2) Clothing: quantity, conditions, felt needs.
3) Water: source, storage, felt needs.
4) Fuel: source, type, felt needs.
5) Food: source, diet, felt needs.
6) Refuse: disposal, toilet facilities, felt needs.
7) Bedding: furniture, blankets, felt needs.
8) Amenities: radios, TV, utensils, bicycles, other transportation, felt needs.

The psycho-socioeconomic environment:
1) Education/literacy: school completion, vocational training, literacy skills.
2) Employment: occupation, type of employment, permanency.
3) Social: entertainment, memberships, social networks, leisure time.
4) Money: usage, income, borrowing.
5) Aspirations/changes: education, employment, social, money

The general health:
1) Nutrition: adult/child consumption, approximate caloric intake per person (adult/child), preferences, infant feeding practices.
2) Sickness: kinds, treatment, causes, preventive measures, felt needs.

The community development programs:
1) Health and nutrition: awareness, participation, attitudes.
2) Family planning: awareness, participation, attitudes, preferences.
3) Education/training: awareness, participation, attitudes, preferences.
4) Social: awareness, participation, attitudes, preferences.

The spiritual situation:
1) Religion: What? How long? What level of involvement?
2) Knowledge and values: life, death, God, Christ, the Bible.
3) Christian practices: denomination (if any), attendance, Bible reading, activities, training.

2. Research permission: In many places this will not be required, but it is encouraged to be sure that there is full understanding and backing by leaders in government and/or other community organizations.

3. Interview intensity or sampling: Normally time, money, and personnel make it impossible to try to do a thorough research. Modern research statistics show that scientific samplings give an accurate picture of the whole.

   Unit sampling: Often governments have communities divided on a map into various blocks around a central area or water source. Utilizing such a map, the interviews can be divided among the blocks according to a fixed schedule. A designated number of houses in a designated direction from the central point is indicated for each interviewer. An example: 2FCP equals the fourth house toward the central point, and 6AFCP equals the sixth house away from the central point, etc., in each direction around the community center point from each set of interviewers. (See diagram on page 87.)

   Community sampling: In the absence of a map and any government organization in the community, a map should be made by the researchers or representatives in the community using main roads, pathways, power lines, and rivers or creeks as boundaries. Estimates should be made of population density and the areas divided accordingly and a number of interviews per section should be assigned. In one section a visit can be made to every sixth house until the number of interviews indicated is reached. In another section it could be every fourth house. Each section would have an Nth house predetermined to give a random but accurate picture of the community as a whole.

Other methods can be used like selecting smaller areas scattered around the larger community, visiting every house in those small areas, or do every nth house on every street, etc. The main emphasis is to have a systematic plan for the sampling.

4. Interviewing procedure:*Interviewers:* Interviewers should fulfill the following criteria when possible:

- recommended by the church.
- completed secondary education.
- fluent in the language to be used, both speaking and writing.
- complete the interview training sessions.
- successfully complete role playing and practice interviews.

Interview training: Interview training should familiarize interviewers with the interview schedule and sampling instructions. During this time the interview schedule and its various components need to be explained in detail, making sure the interviewers understand the purpose and the meaning of each question. Practice sessions including role playing between the interviewers, and mock interviewees should be used as an important part of the training.

Field work: Local community leaders and/or community government leaders should be contacted beforehand to ensure resident cooperation. Also, information should be distributed to the community so that the whole community knows about the research. All interviewers need adequate orientation as to who they should talk to upon arriving at a household. Normally the first person who comes to the door is interviewed, providing they meet certain basic requirements such as the following:

- be a resident of the community for at least six months.
- be at least 16 years of age.

- be a household head or responsible adult.
- speaks the language of the interviewer.

Field work should be done, if possible, on different days of the week, including weekends, and at varying times of the day to ensure representation from diversified segments of the population. Orientation should be given as to how to handle those who might refuse an interview. The interviewer should work under daily supervision and debriefing by the research team.

5. Analysis: A reference book should be developed before the actual survey is done in order to categorize and analyze the information gathered. After the field work, the response to each question needs to be tabulated. If a computer is available, each response should be given an alphanumeric reference, so that the data can be entered for analysis, tabulation, and cross tabulation.

Methodologies and Procedures

1. Survey of existing development programs: A list should be made of governmental and voluntary organizations that have been, are, or will be engaged in activities and programs in the area. This survey should include the following:

- policies.
- purposes and goals (programs).
- strengths and weaknesses of strategies.
- employment and income generating results.
- significant problems or constraints faced.
- nature and commitment of funding (time frame).

2. Overview of government policy and professional viewpoints should be taken into consideration. A data collection sheet should be developed for conducting interviews with appropriate government officials to secure notes and documents

related to urban community development. Also, through library research and personal interviews, viewpoints from sociologists and anthropologists concerning urban migration, development, and strategies for urban ministries can be collected.

Qualifying Note: No survey should be taken as a be-all, end-all community profile or analysis. Rather, it must be seen as a first step in an ongoing process of information gathering and evaluation. The model illustrated in the appendix may be used and/or modified for local use.

The Feasibility Study
The likelihood of the failure or success of a project is in direct relationship to the quality and scope of the preparation.

Of all the work done in planning a project, there is nothing more important than the feasibility study.

One of the purposes of such a study is to raise and answer questions which must be dealt with before finalizing the design and/or initiating a project. There will always be surprises after the project is implemented, but the more accurate the research and planning in response to the questions raised, the greater the possibility for success.

Designing a major transformational/developmental project requires a systematic approach, undergirded with a thorough study of the social setting and circumstances most likely to affect the outcome of the proposal. If any plan is to succeed, those factors must be identified and reckoned with. Sometimes, the more simple the social/cultural setting may seem, the greater the requirement for in-depth and more sensitive understanding. The planners must be able to determine what will be the potential impact of their project and what continuing relationship it will have on the target community. In order to do this, it is important that the planners, together with the participants, have as much information as possible concerning the feasibility of the proposal.

Sometimes feasibility studies will require special consultants or experts outside the project area itself. However, the study should be done jointly with the participants within the project area. Many of the questions can be answered with little technical research, but they should be dealt with as objectively as possible. Project participants should be clearly informed of the findings. Some projects will require very little expert study and can virtually be done on site. However, larger and more complicated projects will require a more thorough study.

Elements of the Feasibility Study

Appropriateness. The appropriateness of a project plan will most often be determined by the capacity, the ability, and the willingness of the people to fully participate in every phase of the planning, development, implementation, and maintenance of the project. In what ways has this been brought into the planning?

In addition, the potential social or cultural impact must be assessed. Many well planned projects have later been discarded and/or abandoned once the project organizers have completed their work and left the scene. Part of the reason for this has to do with the relative inappropriateness of the project idea in the first place.

Cultural Appropriateness. The cultural appropriateness may be as important or even more important than the particular level of technical appropriateness. Project planners must ask, "Is the project concept suitable in the local circumstances? Does it fit into the traditional and cultural ways of working? What are the roles of the men and women who participate—is it at once acceptable and uplifting to all involved? How will the project impact the historic, social, and cultural roles of the people in the community?"

Technical Appropriateness. In dealing with the appropriateness of technologies, it is not sufficient to introduce something that appears to be relatively simple or even inexpensive to operate.

A more important question may ask, "Is the level of technology to be used maintainable and sustainable by those whose cultural role would normally call for them to employ it?" Many simple technologies, such as passive solar ovens, have never been widely accepted or continued because of superstition, or failure by those who are to use them to understand the principle behind the concept. Often there are other socio-cultural reasons which may be difficult for the outsider to recognize. Many times simple technologies, which may seem appropriate at the existing educational level of a local group, may become delimiting or demeaning if they are not coupled with continued upgrading and adequate training in the application of higher technologies, as they become more socially acceptable and the participants are properly motivated and become capable of employing them.

In one instance, a missionary tried to introduce the use of a tractor for a village where the level of technology was that of using a short-handled hoe to chop the ground. The women who did the plowing knew little of any mechanical equipment or even proper cultivation, irrigation, or fertilization. The community had a very low per capita income as well. It is true that at first the use of a tractor did tend to raise the level of productivity simply by enlarging the scope of land under cultivation. Unfortunately, the plan did not take into consideration the potential operational costs, maintenance requirements, and replacement costs of the equipment, to say nothing of properly training the local people to handle such equipment, or the role of the women in that society and the wide motivational level required of the leaders to support the concepts involved. The project failed within a very brief period of time.

A gradual movement from the hoe to animal traction, to mechanical equipment accompanied by continued training involving the same objects succeeded in another very similar situation.

Obviously, there are many other technical considerations relating to environmental and agricultural principles that could be mentioned. Many elaborate programs have been presented on the naive assumption that the introduction of higher technology alone would solve a community's food production problems. Some have discovered too late the reason for their failure was the fact that the projects were both technically and culturally inappropriate.

Understanding of Root Problems. How is the proposed response to the apparent need related to the actual cause of the problems faced?

Planners are sometimes blinded by the obvious nature of the need. Polluted water supplies, a high level of parasite infections, diarrhea, etc., signal serious problems. However, it is virtually impossible to measure the impact a project may have toward solutions unless one first ascertains the total circumstances or conditions causing the problem prior to the implementation of the project. The problem may be an educational one, rather than a technical one. The problem could involve superstition, cultural prohibitions, fatalistic attitudes, or even specific religious values.

In one case, a clean water project was proposed with the objective of lowering the incidence of diarrhea among younger children in a community. However, the project planners failed in several ways. They had never determined exactly what the incidence of diarrhea was among specific groups such as those under the age of five. In addition, no study had been made as to the level of understanding the community had in regard to the relationship between impure water and diarrhea. No thought had been given to potential problems that might be created through the introduction of a clean water supply for the township.

An unanticipated problem arose when one of the leaders became upset because many of the families were using the pure water for their gardens as well as for drinking. To enforce his point, for three days per week, he decided to cut off the valve from the newly built water tower which contained the pure water supply. On those days, the women went back to the river for water. In this particular case, the incidence of diarrhea may have actually increased. They were not only mixing the pure with the impure water, but little or no consideration was given to sanitation, waste disposal, and other mitigating factors which had increased because of the additional water.

The planners had not taken into consideration a whole scope of probable causes, nor had they introduced an educational program to teach both the mothers and the leaders all the various factors that could cause diarrhea.

Environmental Considerations. What is the most likely or probable impact the project could have upon the environment as a direct or indirect result of doing this project? Obviously, one of the most serious concerns in project planning should be the study of the potential environmental impact.

A typical example involves the practice of drilling wells without consideration of the total impact both on the environment and the potential for subsequent pollution of the well. In most Third World rural situations, the dependency upon livestock is the basis of their economic well being. In areas of marginal water supply, the drilling of a well may cause the surrounding area to be stripped of grass and other vital vegetation by becoming the only viable source of water for the livestock. Animals most likely would also create a major source of potential pollution to the well. It is commonly known that improperly sealed wells, or wells which are used for both human and animal consumption will most likely become polluted. Yet, such wells are regularly being drilled or dug without corollary sources of supply for animals, proper safeguards against pollution, or teaching programs to inform the local population about such problems.

In other instances, the continued drilling of wells has caused the water tables in dry areas to be lowered to such an extent that existing wells run dry. Seldom is any thought given to the possibility of creating catchment areas or dams which might provide both for animals and some absorption to replace underground supply. Even when this is done it must be combined with educational efforts, literacy training, and other kinds of support related to the sociocultural aspects of rural development. Water ponds may also cause increases in health problems such as schistosomiasis (bilharzia) when they are not protected.

An irrigation project, designed to raise farmers' food supply through increased productivity, might actually threaten established relationships, the customary ways of doing things, and/or have severe environmental consequences. It may introduce new water-borne disease factors. It may have other unintended consequences which, in some cases, could be more detrimental than the positive impact of the project itself. In such a context, it would be much more beneficial to raise important questions, pointing to the kinds of concerns which one should have been aware of in the project planning stage.

Consideration must be given to the potential problems of pollution to existing pure water supplies. In addition, questions about the normal decision-making patterns and the participation of the local people in either the project design or the viability of carrying it on once the outside leadership and funding had been withdrawn, must be addressed prior to developing the project design.

Cost-to-Benefit Ratio. What is the relationship between the capital costs, the operational costs, and the actual benefit to the recipients?

One of the greatest problems related to approach in a top-heavy administrative structure in developmental funding has to do with the total cost of the project in relationship to the actual benefits it may provide to the participants. In some cases, the institutional structures, the equipment needed, and the operational costs can exceed the benefits obtainable for the participants. Again, let me illustrate. In one social ministry project, a proposal called for the establishment and operation of a free day care center in connection with a vocational training and job placement program for mothers. However, in analyzing the proposal, it was discovered that the capital costs, administrative costs, plus the costs of caring for the children per mother trained once the center was built, would have actually been more than the potential earning power of the mothers once they were employed. In that case it would have been far less expensive to have given the mothers the money and let them stay home to take care of their own children.

This approach would have also created dependency rather than allowing for self-sustainable and locally supportable processes. Many elaborate schemes fail to take into consideration the per capita cost or the potential earning capacity of those involved in terms of the sustainability of the efforts and the actual benefits provided.

Skill Effectiveness. Are there adequate and identified job opportunities for those who are being provided vocational training? Many vocational training programs are created with the assumption that, once trained, the participants will be able to enter the job market and fend for themselves. The concept may look good. It may employ appropriate technology. It may reach the right target audience, but at the same time fail to enable those involved to raise their skill levels to a point where they are actually better off than when they began.

In one case, a project plan called for training handicapped beggars from an extremely poor ghetto area. The concept was to train them in the very simplest of technology without the use of any modern equipment. It was felt they would not have access to such equipment once they completed the program, therefore, the technology was considered to be inappropriate. Most of the people involved had been beggars for an extended period of time. Little or no study had been done regarding the potential job market for laborers with the proposed level of training which would be offered them. Neither had the planners considered the market potential for the products they would be trained to produce.

As the students completed the course, no assistance was given to help them discover job opportunities, and virtually no follow-up was done to determine whether or not they actually entered the job market. It was most probable, considering their very poor level of craftsmanship, that most of the students would still have gained considerably more money by going back to begging than they could have from attempting to make and sell the simple furniture they were trained to make.

Resource Analysis. What is the total scope of all resources needed to assure the project will be successful? What assurance do you have that these will be available on time, in sufficient quantity or quality? What about continuity of resources, especially in terms of leadership?

Resource analysis is mentioned here only to point out the fact that many project planners tend to make broad assumptions about the availability of the required resources. They also tend to forget the vulnerability of depending upon existing commitments, whether financial or personnel. Managers, teachers, and other required leaders who sometimes offer their services at the planning stages of the projects, may be moved or otherwise be unable to carry out their commitments. Others may be interested for a short time, only to slack off once they understand the requirements for long-term continuing assistance. Missionaries who provide leadership may go on furlough, be transferred to other jobs, or even lose interest, while their replacements either have no interest in the project or prefer doing the whole thing another way.

Once the initial start-up financing is secured, planners tend to assume that everything else will fall into place. At times, one of the more vulnerable areas arises when the planners depend upon a commitment by the government in a joint venture. Often the project is initiated with outside funding only to discover that government resources are either delayed or no longer available.

It is important to ask such questions as: "What contingency planning has been done? What if the leadership drops out? What if the volunteer workers do not continue?" Underestimating the various resources necessary to carry out a project is one of the most common problems related to an inadequate feasibility study. Often the most optimistic scenario becomes the basis for figuring both budget and potential human resources needed to administer and/or to provide teachers for a program.

In vocational training projects, as indicated above, it is often assumed that the student will be able to produce a certain number of products in a given period and that these will sell for an average of a certain amount. Rarely does it work out this way. If something can go wrong, it usually does go wrong! It is not just a matter of figuring in contingencies, but rather of making more realistic projections, based on objective studies of the actual potential under the given circumstances. This leads naturally to the next consideration.

Market Potential. Many projects call for the production of commodities which are to be sold, thus proposing to provide for the sustainability of the project after the initial capital investment. On paper this usually sounds good. However, it is very easy to plan such projects without taking into consideration important mitigating factors. In the urban setting, many vocational projects are planned for people living in ghettos or slums. In most cases, they have little or no academic training. Often they are illiterate, and have not previously handled the equipment they are to be trained to operate. It is generally assumed, however, that after a brief course, they will be able to produce quality products, that there is a market for such products, that the cost-to-benefit ratio will be such as to provide adequate income, and that they will have the motivation, technical ability, and market knowledge to continue without further supervision. It is also assumed they will spend whatever added income that may be gained in improving the status of their families, rather than spending it for liquor or other unsatisfactory items.

In similar rural projects, such as farm-to-market gardens, most of the planning is centered in the production phase of the crops, with little or no thought being given to the potential market or the capacity of the farmer to deliver and sell the produce for a profit. In a very elaborate project in Central America, the plan for success was built upon the assumption that a national farmer, who knew the soil and did a reasonably good job of raising crops, could administer a farm training program. He was to teach the students what they needed to know about farm-to-market gardening, enable them to clear forest land on their own following the two-year training, and then keep the whole project viable by selling the produce the boys were being taught to grow. Needless to say, it was far more than he could do, and well beyond his training and ability. After a heavy financial investment the project failed.

Questions That Need to Be Raised
Initially it was stated that one of the most important purposes of a

feasibility study is to raise and answer questions which must be dealt with before finalizing the design and/or initiating the project. The following are some additional questions that should be raised:

- Can the project be done, or is it actually impractical to presume as much as has been planned?
- Why are you doing the project?
- How was the problem and need determined? Who determined it?
- Have you explored all the possible strategies and chosen the most viable one in terms of the basic objectives of the primary group(s) carrying out the project?
- Are you and the constituent community capable of carrying it out?
- Whose project is it (yours/theirs/both)?
- Have you looked at the risks involved? Who is taking the risks, and who will be responsible for them?
- What problems (technical/cultural/environmental/governmental/other) will you have to deal with in order for it to be successful?
- Is it technically and culturally appropriate?
- Are the human, technical, and financial resources adequate and readily available?
- What resources are absolutely essential for success, and what will happen if any element is inadequate or missing?
- What are the primary and secondary constraints?
- What are the problems, issues, or circumstances that could most likely keep it from being successful?
- What are the "safety nets" if the plan does not go as anticipated? Do you have a long-term commitment to the community?
- Are there government restrictions? In what way are you allowing for these?
- If the project involves the production of a commodity or includes vocational training, what is the market/job potential?
- What are the plans for quality control?

- How can you be assured that those trained will be able to improve their relative economic, social, or spiritual position as a result of the quality and quantity of training offered?
- How does this relate directly to designated resources?
- What are its relative chances for meeting the primary objectives within the scheduled time frame?
- Is the project likely to bring a solution to the problem causing the need? If not, why not? How do you then justify it?
- What problems (environmental, social, etc.) might be raised if the project is successful? If it is not?
- Can the project be maintained and continue to function when outside resources are withdrawn? Will there be sustainable results?
- What do you really expect to have happened when the project is completed? How will you know? What are the objective and impact indicators of success?

The Constraints to Be Considered

Constraints have to do with those forces, both natural and unnatural, that may confine, limit, hold back, or even compel alternate approaches upon proposals. The sensitive planner will want to be fully aware of these factors in developing the feasibility study. They may take many forms and/or involve multiple influences.

Political/Governmental: Do not presume that you already have legal authority to proceed with the initiation of a proposal, the organization of a cooperative or other types of institutional elements until you have checked the existing laws including taxation, importation of commodities, dollar exchange (where appropriate), or any other factors such as regulations concerning building codes, labor laws, minimum wage standards, etc.

Even food-for-work projects have come under government scrutiny because they have often been interpreted as ways in which alien agencies have avoided paying minimum wages. In one major project in Africa, workers were actually "paid" with used clothing that had been sent over for free distribution. The concept of food-for-work should never be intended to provide a wage for workers. The whole idea is to enable volunteer participation on the part of the recipient community, while providing adequate food for the volunteers when they are not involved in normal employment.

In some cases, a particular government worker may impose constraints because of personal problems beyond your control. Be sensitive in the case of government extension workers who may be put in a bad light because of your project proposal. If at all possible, they should be included in the project planning and, where practical, be able to receive much of the credit for its initiation and success.

Spiritual: It is important to understand clearly what perception the community has of outside planners in terms of local religious values. Do they present a threat to them? In what way? How may this be overcome in the context of meeting their needs? Who are the key individuals most likely to block progress? Why? How can they be approached? Planners must avoid, at all costs, the concept or impression that members of the local church will be the only recipients of assistance. The time is hopefully long past since the days of creating rice Christians, by insisting that any aid or enablement is reserved exclusively for those who are either members of the church or who are willing to join.

Social: Do you fully understand the dynamics of the social structures operating in the circumstance of the proposed project setting? What is the role of women? What are the primary antisocial activities which are most likely to interfere or cause difficulties in the successful completion of this project? What social realities do you need to be aware of in addition to the ones you may be dealing with?

Logistical/Physical: Time/space—Can the local community visualize the time span between the commitment to the project and the potential amount of time it will take to change their circumstances? Have you allowed for some short-term highly visible and tangible results prior to the actual completion of the whole project?

This kind of question is particularly important in two kinds of situations. First, in a rural, developing country community, it may be difficult or impossible for farmers to imagine the potential benefits from a five-year cattle breeding program intended to upgrade their livestock. They will most likely be looking for something to happen in the immediate, tangible future. Second, you could find yourself in a situation where other groups have made promises of great and wonderful proposals only to have them come to nothing after having raised high expectations. Local leaders may have become skeptical of some long-range planning which is not expected to show results for several years.

Personnel: Educational/leadership—Are those involved from the local community capable of continuing the project without outside assistance? What plans have you made for training local people to assume full responsibility? What orientation have you given to any foreign volunteers who may be involved, that they refrain from imposing their own Western ideologies and methodologies?

Can you be assured that teachers and others on whom you may be counting to support the program will be consistently available? What kind of backup system have you allowed for?

Sustainable results: Many tend to measure the number of dollars spent, medicines shipped, buildings built, or hours utilized in training as an accurate way of estimating the effectiveness of development projects. These factors can be indicators of progress and can be tabulated and measured. However, they do not give an adequate indication of "output." When planners focus on specific physical indicators, they may lose sight of real development. Sustainable results will always examine the impact the project has had upon the lives of the target community.

Notes
[1]Adapted from workshop material prepared by Beth Spring for Evangelical Press Association annual convention, May 7-9, 1984.

CHAPTER 6

THE PROJECT
PLANNING PROCESS . . .
IDEAS FOR ACTION

First Thoughts

People are more important than projects. They should be involved at the beginning of planning, continue to participate in the process of planning and, ultimately, be empowered to carry out the planning. It is always easier to provide relief to people in need than it is to enable them to solve the problems which create the need. Good project planning shifts from helping people primarily in terms of giving them something, to enabling people by empowering them to *do* something.

Transformational (developmental) projects must be understood as being different than relief projects. Relief tends to be a stopgap measure filling a short-term need for human survival. There are times when this is absolutely necessary, and one should not shy away from meeting needs this way. However, transformation has as its goal the enabling of people to become self-sufficient, and is characterized by local participation in every phase of the planning process. One must, of course, work within the existing systems and social structures to help individuals discover their own potential for solving the problems which create the needs. Having said this, it must be understood that material progress without spiritual transformation is difficult to achieve and impossible to maintain. In this context, good planners recognize that it takes transformed people to transform society. However, transformational processes demand incarnational agents!

Projects should be developed in the context of holistic concern. In other words, effective development should be concerned with spiritual, emotional, and physical needs. Rather than focusing upon improving or changing those things associated with certain amenities of life, a holistic approach begins with a biblical understanding of the importance of people. This is especially important when a poverty mentality has replaced a sense of worth and dignity within those for whom a program or project may be targeted.

Transformational ministries meet people in the context of their local circumstances. Those circumstances may be physical, political, social, economic, educational, or even a combination of circumstances, but will always involve the spiritual circumstances of life. Each circumstance must be understood by the planner, and may become either a bridge or a barrier to ministry. The difference will be determined by the insight of the planner in relating to those in need. The task is to set them wholly free from all that keeps them from becoming what they can be as newborn creatures in Christ.

True freedom may be understood as the power and privilege to give expression to the greatest potential within a person—this is true transformation. Men and women, boys and girls, are created in the image of God. A person's greatest potential is always in the spiritual realm. However, men and women may never discover this great truth while they are still in the bondage of physical circumstances which blind their eyes to God's word.

The person is more important than the activity. From the vantage point of the sense of purpose, the goal in any given project must be to help people discover their true worth in the eyes of God as the object of His love. They do this when they also discover a sense of self-reliance and spiritual dignity rather than just becoming objects of charity.

All persons have talents waiting to be discovered and used, but real growth can only come from within each person. There are resources and skills within each community that are underutilized and waiting to be harnessed. A large part of transformational ministries is to move individuals from a position of latent talent by enabling them to give expression to gifts which grow out of a spiritual relationship with the Lord.

People grow in responsibility as they are helped to accept responsibilities. People will never be ready to take over the job until they, along with their leaders, pass through the process of discovering what they are really capable of doing. Too much help leads to dependency. People should be helped only insofar as it enables them to become more self-reliant.

Learning becomes most relevant when it is built into a life experience. Ideally, each recipient of the project must be able to identify with some phase of the project that is specifically targeted toward a conscious need of which they are aware. The energy put into community action will be proportionate to the involvement of the community in the planning.

The most effective venue for training for the community's gain takes place within the community environment. This is especially true in rural development. The student may learn that he or she can accomplish great things within the ideal environment of an agricultural center, only to be disappointed when the facilities which made it possible at the center are not part of the real life situation back at the farm or village. As communities are comprehensive social systems, they are best served by development methods which are locally applicable, rather than methodologies which work in isolation from one another.

Community leaders know their problems and the solutions that may work better than others know them. Remember, the leaders are survivors. Much of what they know and do has been built on centuries of tradition and cultural experiences. Work in the context of those experiences before you attempt to modify them. The pace of development will be determined largely by the community. A change will be permanent only if that community is ready for that it.

The most effective agent to act as helper is a person who strongly identifies with the community, and who develops a relationship based on mutual trust and respect. This can only happen when the agent acts incarnationally as a servant.

Development involves people and cultures. Anthropology can help us greatly in understanding both of these as well as ourselves in new cultural settings. But, we can only move from development to transformation when culture is transformed not only physically, but spiritually.

One best communicates the love of Christ at the point where the message of reconciliation is consistent with the ministry of reconciliation (2 Cor. 5:18-19).

Ideas for Action

1. Any successful project will be dependent upon the degree to which local people have participated in every phase of the project from beginning to end. This includes their commitment of resources to the project—physically, materially, and economically.

2. People tend to identify with a project as being theirs when it deals with a problem they understand and meets a need which they feel is important.

3. Human need ministries must not be seen as a means to an end. They must be an integrated part of the essential purpose for a missions body being overseas. One must minister because Christ cares about people, and the servant-agent too must care if he or she is to be authentic. The basic motivation for ministering should be clear to the recipient group.

4. The recipient group should be able to sustain, maintain, and/or improve on any progress which results from a project.

5. Projects should result in an improvement of the position of the recipient groups within a given period of time.

6. The recipient group must be made aware of and trained to assume the responsibilities, obligations, and economic implications as well as the risks in any given project.

7. The initiators of the project are also accountable to the recipients. Monitoring and evaluation must include both impact assessment and goal attainment.

8. Cultural values are important. One cannot overlook the way people have always done things and expect to win their respect or response. A spiritual emphasis must first manifest a love and respect for persons.

9. People communicate what they are, not just what they say. One may go about doing good, but nullify the result by manifesting attitudes or lifestyles which are condescending or just plain un-Christian.

10. Project plans should be totally integrated to meet spiritual, physical, and other needs rather than emphasizing certain areas to the exclusion of others.

11. When planning a project, take into consideration the general planning of government, other relief agencies, local efforts with the area and/or other denominations. Projects should be coordinated. Don't reinvent the wheel!

Managing Transformational Projects

Management consists of carrying out tasks to produce the desired results. The goal of development is human well-being, both in the local communities and their individual members. The goal of transformation moves beyond physical well-being into the whole of the human dimension by acknowledging that "man does not live by bread alone." Management is a means of ensuring that the goals of development are reached. Good management gives one the tools to ensure that a transformational/development program is effective. If the objectives of programs are not the right ones then management will not be able to make them good.

Management helps one see where the objectives and implementation of a transformational/development project can be improved. Good management is always needed. But worthwhile objectives are also necessary.

- Projects must be realistic in their overall goals and time frame.
- Projects must allow for the fact that development can cause disagreement.
- Projects must allow for the involvement of those who will benefit.
- Projects must be inclusive in the use of local resources and experience, etc.

Effective management is the way to make a transformational project succeed. This success does require that the objectives of any transformational program are well-defined and understood. Management is the tool to do the job, but first you must make sure the job is properly defined. Transformation is not something one does for people. There are times when immediate relief is needed and one must act. But transformation goes beyond this, looking not only to successful projects but also to transformed communities. Success on this level requires relationships of mutual benefit and trust between the people and the incarnational agent.[1]

Rules of Thumb for Transformational Projects[2]

1. Become comfortable with looking at the world in terms of meaningful groups and with the need to organize to produce change.
2. Recognize that values are not taught, but caught from social systems to which they are essential.
3. Serve local processes and needs, rather than slavishly importing foreign models.
4. Be alert to the social systems in which the groups of interest are nested, and be prepared to react positively to conflict.
5. Create new formal forms of organizations as necessary to maintain momentum in transformation.
6. Make the church comfortable with exercising organized influence for positive change.
7. Recognize and welcome the urban institutions as allies.

"If it takes 100 actions to accomplish 100 results, carefully selecting 20 actions can often accomplish 80 percent of the desired results." This is called the "20-80 principle." It means that care must be taken to establish and carry out the priority concerns.

The Planner

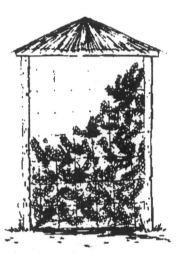

The Anti–Planner

Transformational Project—Preplanning

Before serious work can be initiated on any project, the project planners need to demonstrate that they have a thorough awareness of the contextual situation in which the project may take place.

The first presumption the planners will have made is—there is a need. One also presumes:

- The philosophy and motivation behind the desire to meet the need is consistent with biblical principles.
- There is a real concern for the people represented in the target area.
- Responding to the need is part of the essential purpose for the personnel, mission, or agency for being in the area.
- Any response is reflected as part of the total strategy of the organizing group.

Quite often attempts are made to deal with needs prior to any assessment of the problems creating the need. In most cases, merely attempting to meet the need will create a situation of dependency upon the project organizers and the organization supporting them. Needs will not be dealt with adequately until the problems creating the needs have been taken into consideration. In some cases, if not most, missions agencies are not equipped to deal with the whole area of problems creating needs. They may, however, become extremely influential in bringing focus to the problems as to encourage some redirection on the part of other agencies, municipalities, or government offices. Missions should never consider themselves and their work in isolation from the whole context of the environment in which they choose to work. There will always be a tension between attempts to meet human needs and the evangelistic impulse of missions groups, unless they understand the interrelationship between human needs and evangelism as related to their essential purposes for being in a country.

> *If you are not helping to solve the problems creating the needs, you may be creating a new need.*

Strategic Planning—The Bottom Line in Problem-Solving

While this book is not intended as a manual in strategic planning, it is essential that an organization have a clear understanding of its strategy and essential purposes prior to initiating project planning. The following outline details the essential steps in the process of project planning in the context of strategic planning.

Strategic Planning may be seen as: The art or science of devising or employing careful planning based on comprehensive and targeted research to undergird the application of specific programs of work (tactics) in harmony with the mission (essential purpose for being) and primary objectives and goals of an organization.

Operational Planning, on the other hand, may be seen as being geared to the present operational functions and how they can be improved or carried out. (How can improvement be made on what is already being done?) This is where most organizations spend their time planning. Strategic planning is geared to the changing environment, our changing world, and what one must change to be able to function there.

Strategic Planning Requires:
1. A careful analysis of the target situation, including all homogeneous groups and their particular priorities.
2. A study of any mitigating factors likely to affect the successful outcome of the planning.
3. An understanding of the environmental circumstances.
4. A knowledge of any limitations or constraints impacting the planning.
5. A review of any competitive factors, groups, or attractions which may divert the target audience from consideration of the planning.
6. A study of any other factors likely to cause the plans to be modified, such as those with opposing priorities.

Strategic Planning Insists That the Organization Know and Understand:
1. The central purpose and objectives of the organization—the mission.

     a. What kind of work is primary?

     b. What kind of services will it offer?

     c. How will it conduct its affairs?

     d. What is the relationship between message and ministry?

2. The total situation and circumstances in which it operates.
3. The trends and critical issues it faces in accomplishing its purpose.
4. The adequacy of the organizational structures to carry out the strategies—form follows function.
5. The most effective and efficient use of resources—both personnel and physical.
6. The potential impact of the competition, (that which stands in opposition to its purposes).
7. The limitationswhich will be imposed by all sectors.
8. The actions needed to carry out the objectives.
9. The scope and content of the various programs to which it will commit itself.
10. The indicators which will be used to measure both accomplishment of objectives, goals, and subsequent impact.
11. The possibilities of unexpected circumstances (developing specific scenarios).
12. Local attitudes, customs, taboos, traditional ways of doing things.
13. Who and/or what are the primary forces or agencies which could keep the primary mission from being accomplished?
14. Communication factors, both cross-culturally and interculturally.
15. The perception of the target people relating to their problems, needs, or concerns.
16. The marketplace possibilities and trends.
17. Government regulations, attitudes, or restrictions.
18. The major religious factors most likely to impact the planning processes.
19. The political circumstances. What is the government's plan or concern about the target group?
20. The physical circumstances which impact logistics.

Strategic Analysis—The Basic Information and Data Required Prior to Project Planning

Resource analysis: The planner must first answer the following three questions:
- What are the areas of resources you will consider?
- What are the strengths and weaknesses of local resources?
- What is the criteria for utilizing resources?

Generally, resources may be categorized under four headings:
- Human resources
- Cultural resources
- Physical resources
- Spiritual resources

1. *Human resources.* Again, the most important resources will always be people, especially those who are representative of the target group. In this respect, it is vital that you make a thorough study of every aspect of community life. In order to do this you should consult with appropriate government/municipal officers for any data they make available. In addition, you may want to use the Community Survey material suggested in the Appendix, page 233.

Government offices may offer vital resources. On a trip to West Africa a missions consultant was helping to get permission for staff to enter the country as a recognized organization. The local missionary had been able to set up appointments with most of the ministries of the federal government. As they visited each of them, they asked the same series of questions, primarily focusing on the "five-year" plans of each ministry. They were concerned to find out what type of vision local leaders had for their country and what were the top priorities in their long-range planning. Even though the consultant recognized there was little or nothing that could be done about the broader needs of the nation, they were trying to find an area where they could offer the kind of service which was within their capacity to respond. After several days and many ministries later, they discovered that the country had no dentists. That was their opening. The offer to send a small group of volunteer dentists into the country for the purpose of doing a complete dental survey in every primary and secondary school was quickly accepted. This was followed up by appointing a full-time dentist as a missionary along with continuing teams to meet the most urgent needs. Needless to say, the mission was not only fully accepted by the government, but also had an inroad into every one of the schools where the survey had been done. The basic resource in this case was not a heavy investment of capital, but volunteers, people who cared enough to give their time and witness. Within a very short time churches were planted and a holistic ministry was initiated. The missionaries not only continued the dental work, but launched out into other areas of transformational ministries including well digging, agriculture, and nutritional training.

In order to make the most effective analysis of human resources, one must ask the questions, "Who has a vested interest in the condition of the people in the target area? Who is most likely to cooperate with you in supporting and providing additional resources to accomplish the work?" For instance, in many developing countries young people are required to give at least two years of service to the country in return for a subsidized university education. Many of these young people will be assigned to rural areas as clinic workers, agriculture extension workers, or some other specialty. Often they are given little with which to work and little budget with which to operate. Some planners have failed to recognize the contribution they would make if they were brought fully into the earliest phases of planning. Not only do they learn from the experience, but their position with their leaders is enhanced when projects are successful. They are often the best communicators with the local population, and may be the bridge necessary to gain acceptance.

In Brazil, the problem of street children grows every year. There are estimates of nearly 17 million[3] in 1993 with the potential of over 20 million by the year A.D. 2000. A conference was held in early 1993 to discuss what evangelicals might do to become deeply involved in ministering to the young people and helping to solve the problems which create the dilemma. It was clearly recognized that they would not be able to solve this tragedy by themselves. Instead, they began to ask, "If all the resources were brought together in a coordinated way, where would evangelicals fit in?" The first part of the strategy called for identifying groups who might have an interest in seeing the problem solved.

Many of these groups may also indicate a real concern for the children. These included the following:

- *The municipal governments*—Street children have long been a black mark against the larger cities of Brazil who most likely would be happy to find a solution.
- *The federal government*—In 1992 a special commission was set up to deal with the problem after international pressures were brought to bear.
- *The local shopkeepers*—They have been accused of hiring the so-called "death squads" to take large numbers of children out of the city and to kill them.
- *Special ministries*—Every level of government is charged with social service responsibilities. One can imagine that the ministry of tourism would be very happy to see the gangs of children taken off of the beaches where the loss of tourism costs the government millions of dollars every year.
- *National and multinational companies*—The public relations offices of companies would benefit from seeing the problem solved.

Now the question remained, "How could they bring interested, and, hopefully, evangelical representatives together from each of the groups to think together about combining and coordinating resources to deal with the problem?" The plan called for some radical thinking on all their parts. Each group identified would have to participate in a significant way. The group focused on the types of things the churches could do, such as: offering to have every church in Brazil assume responsibility to provide foster care for 5 children for each 100 members. Someone suggested that the government might provide a small subsidy to provide for some of the care of the children. Municipalities and the federal government might be persuaded to provide assistance in developing academic and vocational training as appropriate. The companies and shop-keepers could be asked to provide entry-level jobs for those trained. The ministry of social affairs could be asked to provide additional materials and services to the families involved. Multinational corporations could be approached about providing trust funds for those capable of advanced training.

The group felt other avenues would open up as the process began. It would take tremendous cooperation and trust on the part of all groups involved, but it could be done! It would require the greatest resource of all, people who cared and were willing to commit themselves to the task.

2. *Cultural resources.* Probably the most overlooked and the most needed resources of all in any kind of transformational or develop-mental projects are the cultural resources. The planner will spend no more important time than in discovering everything that can be known about the local culture. Some significant aspects of cultural resources are:

a. *Kinship*: especially the extended family structures of much of the developing world. An understanding of the interrelation-ships between the nuclear family and the wider circle of the extended family, clan, totem, tribe, or caste may be the differ-ence between the success or failure of the project.

b. *Social structures:* The careful observer will attempt to discover how decisions are made within each of the various levels of social structures. Let me illustrate. I was once with an Indian tribe in Central America. The subject at hand was a request that we come to help them have adequate water by drilling a bore hole and providing a pump. The small community was called together. The men sat in one group and the women in another group. The apparent leader started the discussion, explaining the need and making an appeal for us to provide the well. We began the dialogue with an exchange of questions and group responses. Each question caused the two groups, men and women, to go into a time of intense discussion with one another. For that time, it was almost as if they had forgotten I was there. After their discussion ended, a spokesperson from each of the groups responded. The women always spoke first, but addressed themselves to the men. Following this, the more obvious leader of the men, not the one who had started the discussion, gave his response. There was a short period in which several others spoke to give support to the position of the group. This process took most of the day from early morning until late evening. By the end of that time they had defined a clear rationale for the well, the method by which they would maintain it, the scope of people for whom the water would be made available, the cost per bucket for training and hiring a local person to be in charge of the well, and everything else they needed in terms of their way of doing things. Most of all, in the end, it was their project—not ours.

c. *Political organization:* Missions have had a tendency to isolate themselves from any kind of government involvement for fear of entanglement in local politics. The reasons for this are clear. Yet, chances are in most cases, the government, the United Nations, other denominations, or other international agencies will have already developed materials, brochures, posters, class programs, and a whole host of other valuable helps in areas of greatest need. These may be used effectively to supplement any materials needed. At the same time, utilizing them may help to gain the needed support and credibility to carry out the task. Enlist the best, filter out the worst, and work harmoniously with all. In Zimbabwe, a missions group set out on a major program of rural development in a remote part of the country. A significant part of the plan called for the drilling of bore holes to reach artesian water 700 to 800 feet below the surface. Visiting the government mapping office, the mission received all the maps needed, and additional information on the location of every government well, the substructure and rock formations where water might be found, and a copy of the government plan and procedures for developing the water needs for the area. This not only saved time and money, but lessened the possibility of serious mistakes.

d. *Ideology:* Ideological resources are dynamic resources including such things as homogeneous relationships, beliefs, values, names, symbolism, forms of worship, patterns of behavior, music, educational patterns, ethnic identity, the immediate political situation, group consciousness, ancient rivalries, and/or prejudices. This is an illustration of how homogeneous relationships might impact planning: Imagine you want to enter into a major ghetto area of a large urban city. The area has well over one million people living in it. There are few facilities. Housing is substandard and typical of slums around the world. There is a high percentage of illiteracy and almost no schools. The jobless rate is over 50 percent. There are thousands of street children, drug addicts, prostitutes, and a host of other problems. How and where will you begin? The tendency is to initiate a small center which may provide some vocational training, recreation, a reading room, nutritional classes, and other such ministries. The center normally will cater to a relatively small segment of the population, but actually do little to alleviate or solve the major problems of the ghetto. It might be possible to do a more effective job by concentrating on one or more of the homogeneous groups within the township. See page 130.

For the sake of illustration, look at the homogeneous group called taxi drivers. Prior to any other thing, make a thorough study of the situation and circumstances regarding the drivers. What are the major problems they face? Do they own their own cabs? If not, what is the arrangement with the actual owners? How many drivers are illiterate? What are the local laws concerning ownership? What is the typical family situation? What do they perceive as being their primary needs? Problems? What is the average longevity of employment and why?

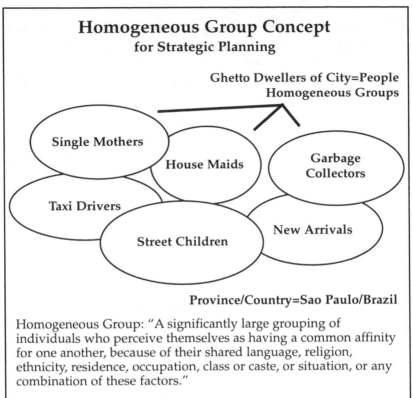

Homogeneous Group Concept
for Strategic Planning

Ghetto Dwellers of City=People Homogeneous Groups

Single Mothers

House Maids

Garbage Collectors

Taxi Drivers

Street Children

New Arrivals

Province/Country=Sao Paulo/Brazil

Homogeneous Group: "A significantly large grouping of individuals who perceive themselves as having a common affinity for one another, because of their shared language, religion, ethnicity, residence, occupation, class or caste, or situation, or any combination of these factors."

Concept from John Robb, Focus!, "The Power of People Group Thinking," 8.

Attempt to create a complete profile on this group. Now, having determined the situation as far as you can ascertain, build an imaginary scenario. Presume you have found that 80 percent of the drivers are functionally illiterate. Because of the low wages, they work 10 to 12 hours every day, seven days per week. Much of their spare time is spent drinking. Generally, self-image and morale is extremely low. Their home life is severely affected and many of their children are part of the street gangs. The average family consists of six children.

Some of the drivers will have families back home working on a farm. They have no union organization, and there is a large turnover because of the relatively small amount they earn after paying for the operating costs and a percentage to the owners.

At this point there is a tangible group with which to plan. Something is known of the situation they face, but it has not yet been determined what specific problems should be dealt with or what approach may be taken to alleviate their dire needs. However, you may be the only person to have considered the possibility of focusing on this particular group. The potential is enormous. Just imagine what might happen in time if 10,000 born-again cab drivers set out into the city giving their personal witness to riders, projecting a Christian lifestyle and, just perhaps, combining to form some type of a cooperative from which they could better control their environment and earn an honest wage.

3. *Physical resources.* The easiest resource to rely upon is money! It is also the one most likely to cause failure. Most major country-to-country aid programs are designed with the budget as the primary item on the agenda. Relief agencies and denominational workers tend to follow in their footsteps. At the same time, there is probably nothing more misused than the financial aspects of resource development. By relying too heavily upon financial resources planners tend to create far too much dependency and move away from local initiatives. Money is often used to support an artificially heavy superstructure of administration rather than being used to encourage more indigenous innovations. It is also used, unfortunately, to control rather than to allow for local initiatives and culturally effective programs of work.

The recipients are often able to provide many more physical resources than sometimes supposed. In rural projects, many of the natural resources such as gravel, clay, wood, bricks, and even buildings can be provided by the people themselves without relying on outside help. In urban centers, the resources are as wide as one's imagination. Government officials, private businessmen, and others are often willing to provide a variety of resources for well-designed projects targeted to meet the needs of population segments for which they are responsible.

Problem Solving—Discovering the Cause Behind the Symptoms

One of the first steps in project planning is the process of discovering the nature of the real problems which need to be dealt with. Most often, planners become aware of a need and immediately set out to respond to that need. In many cases, this response is built solely upon the perspective of the individual(s) who feel the urgency to deal with the apparent need. Their perception may very well be quite different than the perception of the target people themselves. The cultural setting, taboos, ancient ways of doing things, and social structures as well as many other dynamics may mitigate against both the alien perception of the need and the presumption as to the way it should be dealt with. An exercise on the art of problem solving is included on page 145. The exercise anticipates the kind of group interaction that can be experienced on the field.

Perception of Need

Any planner anticipating the possibility of initiation of a transformational project will first of all become aware that a specific need exists. The more skilled the planners, the more they will want to make a thorough study of the target area prior to making any long-term commitment to meeting the need. Obviously, in emergency situations, response will be made to the urgent needs to save lives or otherwise resolve the critical nature of the situation. But the local people are still the best group to make the decision. Many have seen the sincere first-world visitor arrive in a Third World situation and be so overwhelmed with the need that they rush back home to start a campaign either to raise funds or donations to meet the need. I can recall receiving a crate of used shoes targeted for an African village shortly after the visit of good meaning church members. There were slippers, high-heeled shoes, worn-out shoes, summer shoes, winter shoes, all kinds of shoes for which the customs agents wanted to charge a tremendous amount of duty. Actually, some of the people could have used the shoes and did. However, it neither solved a serious problem nor met an urgent need. It was simply the perception of someone facing culture shock, combined with an inappropriate attempt to do good.

Missionaries and other development-type workers are not immune to similar mistakes in perception. Identifying real needs is the first step in discovering what may be the problems creating the needs. How do we then ascertain what those needs are and the problems which create them?

1. *The perception of the community:* Caution! The planner must first realize that any investigation of the perception of the people regarding their needs may be seriously colored by the people's perception of the planner. Many times, people will express their needs in a way that reflects what they perceive the one doing the investigation wants to hear. If they perceive the planner as one who is interested in providing a school or hospital or whatever, chances are this is what they will often express as being the need. On the other hand, needs may be expressed in terms of the latest frustrations they are experiencing. They may not fully understand the root of the problems creating their needs. An experienced planner will attempt to ascertain the people's perception of need by asking questions about the daily problems they face, or what kind of frustrations and troubles they are having to put up with. Asking "Why" questions, or "What would you do if you could?" questions may come closer to providing the answers you are looking for.

In one rural situation, the people expressed their concerns in terms of "heartache," "backache," and "headache." The problems creating the heartache had to do with the fact that they would save up their seeds for planting during the early rains. When the early rains came the seeds would begin to sprout, but often the larger rains were either too late or too small and the young plants would wither and die. Having no alternate water supply the people were wholly subject to the whims of nature. In another case, the people expressed their concern about the fact that their children were subject to diarrhea and vomiting. They had no clinic or doctor to attend them. They also had no understanding about the relationship between impure water and diarrhea, not just because of a lack of knowledge or resources, but also because of their cultural background and the historic beliefs about the involvement of the tribal herbalist and the spirit world.

2. *The perception of the government:* The perception of the government may be colored by many different dynamics. Local politicians, tribal leaders, influential businessmen, current financial concerns, proximity to elections, etc., all may have an influence on the way particular government officials respond to the matter of human needs or problems. The government may look at the problem from the vantage point of hard currency problems on the international scene, to local politics on the local scene. They will, in most cases, have a five-year plan that covers some of the concerns for the area, but be blind or indifferent to them. In some cases, certain officials may be more than happy to see someone fill a need about which they are aware, if for no other reason than the political advantage it would bring them. Others are genuinely concerned for the people and will welcome honest efforts to assist.

3. *The perception of the planner:* For the planner to obtain a realistic perception of problems and needs, he or she will first of all need to have a clear and complete picture of the situation and circumstances of the target community. This should involve not only a study of the present demographics and physical circumstance under which the people exist, but also a serious study of the social structures, the cultural background, and the political and religious context in which the people live.

4. *Synthesis:* Synthesis takes place when the perceptions of all the various groups who may either have an interest or involvement in the target area are combined to discover the areas of commonality and priority concern. This still may not deal with the underlying problems creating the needs, but will guide the planner in using the correct methods of discovering the problems.

Now let's look at some preproject perspectives again:

1. **Community's Perception of Need:** (Be sure to distinguish "needs" from "wants.")

COMMUNITY Depending on the local situation and circumstances, it will help the planner to bring together small groups within the community in order to discuss the potential for working with them in the development of a response to their needs. In rural situations, be sure to identify any hereditary leaders such as tribal chiefs, respected elderly people, etc. The formal and official leaders may not always be the real leaders. Your purpose for calling the meetings should be clearly stated at this point, indicating that no commitments are being made, but that you need their input prior to moving any further in potential project planning. At this point, you should take the part of a very interested listener, raising significant and sometimes leading questions, but not expressing your own opinion.

Some interviewing ideas:
1. Before you interview, know all you can about those to whom you will speak.
2. Maintain the highest respect for each individual, no matter what!
3. Gain the group's trust and put them at ease.
   a. Identify yourself and state your purpose clearly.
   b. Arrange to meet at the most convenient location and time for the group.
   c. Be on time even if the custom is for others to be an hour late, but don't get upset about those who do come in late.
   d. Share any pertinent nonleading information you may have about the community.
   e. Maintain respect for any who do not wish to be identified in sharing their opinion.
   f. Come as a friend, but don't be artificial.
4. Establish a natural, friendly, informal rapport.
   a. Maintain eye contact with each person to whom you speak.
   b. Remain unshakable and unshockable.
   c. Don't get involved in debate or taking sides with any issue. Stay neutral, but understanding.

5. Think like a servant or pastor.
   a. Be observant: What do they see, hear, feel, like, fear?
   b. Learn to screen (evaluate) as you listen. What do they think, believe? Separate the one who may like to hear himself speak from those with honest concerns.
   c. Emotion: Listen to tone and body language. What is behind what they say?
   d. Anticipate: What are their goals, intentions, and personal desires?
   e. Action: What have they accomplished? What could they accomplish?
6. Ask the right questions at the right times. Learn how to ask leading questions which will maintain the direction.
   a. Closed-ended questions elicit facts, figures, specifics. They include yes-or-no questions, basic identification, and selection.
   b. Open-ended questions put the subject in control of the conversation.
7. Prepare questions based on your research.
   a. Focus upon specifics and stick to them.
   b. Ask one question at a time, and keep it simple.
   c. Anticipate pauses in the conversation and let them alone while they consider either the answers or other questions.
   d. Beware of hypothetical questions. You may promise more than you want to.
   e. Be sure not to raise any red-flag words or questions which have a judgmental tone, or involve the group in sensitive issues they do not wish to discuss.
   f. Always be specific, not ambiguous.
   g. Don't be afraid to ask for clarification. Ask, "I understand you to say . . . Is that correct?
   h. Be alert for bridges from someone's answer to other lines of questioning you want to pursue.
8. Don't hesitate to raise tough issues.
   a. Lead up to those with some softer preliminaries.
   b. Ask the tough question spontaneously as it occurs to you.

    c. Put the question in someone else's mouth if you can. "Did you mean . . . ?"

9. Keep the discussion moving.
10. Be observant.
   a. Be alert to sideline comments and discussions being held while you listen.
   b. Take special note of the appearance of the group, their dress, mannerisms, cultural peculiarities, their responses to one another, especially those in authority.
   c. Ask about anything special which you have observed and interpreted. Check to see if you are on target or not.
11. Close out with appropriate words of appreciation and your initial intentions without revealing any specific plans at this time.

LISTENING

"The important role of dialogue continues through the whole of a person's life.

We come to be who we are through conversation with others.

This is true on the level of information and it is also true on the deeper level of self-knowledge and values of life.

We listen to others in the family, the school, the community, our friends, and our adversaries, and our consciousness continues to be created by our response to the reality addressing us.

We are created through ongoing communications with others."

RESPONDING

"The word dialogue suggests that we are never simply the creation of the community to which we belong.

We listen and respond.

We become ourselves, distinct from others by responding. These responses are truly our own.

To the extent that we make them freely we are responsible for who we are and who we come to be as a person.

Our thinking, our religion, our entire mental world is thus created by a process in which the entire community is involved, and yet in which we ourselves consciously or unconsciously make the important decisions."

*Baum, Gregory, *Man Becoming*, New York, 41-41.

2. **Government's Perception of Need.** (A blending of official planning, personal opinions, and off-the-record remarks.)

First determine the appropriate channels of government personnel who will need to be involved in gaining permission to work in an area, or, if you are already working in the area and are anticipating initiating a wider response, those who will need to know what is going on. Having befriended local leaders, you will more readily gain access to others whose input will be necessary for a clear understanding of the kinds of ministries which may be open to you. In some cases, the government may look upon the situation in such a way as to be hesitant to have a missions agency or relief group become involved. There may be religious or other ethnic restrictions which should be clearly understood prior to making contact. Find out what has happened in the past which may inhibit or otherwise restrict a free dialogue with particular people.

a. Ask about government plans, hopes, and dreams for the community. Presume they already have grand plans in mind. Don't show any dismay or criticism of any apparent lack of preparation and planning on their part.

b. Find out which of those plans is underway and which, if any, await funding or other restrictions.

c. Ask about their perception of the greatest needs and the problems creating those needs. Do not express judgment or contrary opinions. You are looking for their viewpoint, not trying to debate the issue.

d. Emphasize the positive areas of your concern to help without committing yourself to any specific projects or programs. Let them know that you are still in the exploratory stage, but wanting to consider the areas of greatest concern to the people and the government.

e. Note, without comment, any significant differences from various staff or line officers in other offices. Especially listen to any field staff regarding their interpretation of needs as may be contrasted with top officials.

f. Do NOT promise more than you can deliver. Even suggesting that you will "look into it" will often be taken as a commitment. Be clear about what you are committing yourself and your organization to doing and what you are not promising. If possible, deliver more than expected rather than less. It will amaze some and win others.

g. Follow the interview suggestions on the previous page which may also apply to individuals as indicated for the group discussions.

h. After each discussion, list those areas which appear to be of the highest concern and priority. Be sensitive to areas that may have a more personal value to the official, but may not really represent a concern of the people.

3. **Planner's Perception of Need.** (Based on a keen observation and analysis of known facts and demographic data as well as personal insights of obvious need.)

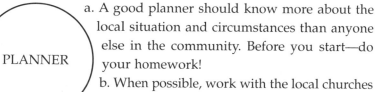

a. A good planner should know more about the local situation and circumstances than anyone else in the community. Before you start—do your homework!

PLANNER

b. When possible, work with the local churches in the community using the Community Survey information in the appendix on pages 233-243.

c. Deal with both facts and educated understanding.

d. Always attempt to differentiate between the needs of the community and the problems creating the needs. Determine if any one person is causing the problems. In what way?

e. Categorize needs according to specific areas:

1) spiritual needs   4) emotional or psychological needs
2) physical needs   5) educational needs
3) social needs

f. Determine the interrelationship of these identified needs.

g. Evaluate how you came to perceive the needs and problems. How valid was your observation or research?

4. **Synthesis:** (Real needs and problems as perceived by combinations of the groups.)

In order to bring about a valid synthesis of the perception of needs, one should rank the selection of each of the three groups in priority order as indicated by the group. Following this one can make a comparison of the levels of priority listed and develop strategic planning based on the results.

CP perceptions Indicates areas where both the community and planner agree in their perception of real needs and problems.

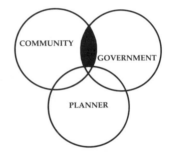

CG perceptions Indicates areas where both the community and government agree in their perception of real needs and problems.

GP perceptions Indicates areas where both the government and the planner agree in their perception or real needs and problems.

CGP perceptions Indicates areas where all three groups agree in their perception of real needs and problems.

5. **Needs Synthesis:** In each of the circles, list the first five priorities as indicated by the group listing the needs. Compare the various priorities and rank by the items which receive the overall highest level of agreement. This does not necessarily mean that one would be bound to choose the need which all three agreed upon, but rather gives a basis for developing strategic planning in accordance with verifiable concerns.

A. The Community
  1.
  2.
  3.
  4.
  5.

B. Government
  1.
  2.
  3.
  4.
  5.

C. Planner
  1.
  2.
  3.
  4.
  5.

D. Other Sources
It may be that the planner will want to consult other sources for information to help determine additional problems or areas of need. These sources could include the national churches, the missions body, other agencies involved in meeting needs, or committees concerned with the total strategic purposes of the organization.

In any case, every avenue should be investigated prior to determining what emphasis should be made. As indicated, the investigation of perception of needs and/or problems is only one aspect of the larger picture of the strategic planning cycle.

RANKING SCALE TO PROVIDE INDICATORS OF RELATIVE LEVEL OF COMMUNITY PARTICIPATION

Indicator	1. Very low	2. Low	3. Medium	4. Good	5. Excellent
Needs Assessment	Done from outside without internal consultation	Some minor consideration but dominated by planner	Local leader actively participated in assessment	Local committee worked as team to assist in assessment	Community as a whole has specific input in assessment
Leadership	One-sided, expatriate assumes basic responsibility	Some part-time involvement by local leader	Local committee works directly with national leader	Active local committee takes initiative	Local committee in control of all activities
Organization	Imposed as part of plan by outside agent	Allowed some small leeway in organization	Fully active organization but still controlled from outside	Local committee has significant say in organization and functions	Existing local committee designs and implements organization
Resource Mobilization	Insignificant or no contribution by local group	Some resources in-kind provided, but under control of planner	Community/ church make significant contribution but have no control	Local church or community provides funds and local committee controls	Majority of resources are local and fully controlled by local staff
Management	Directly under expatriate or outside person	Some minor management under supervision of expatriate	Local committee manages, but does not control leadership	Committee manages and supervises local leader	Local leader manages with supervision of committee

Diagram for Plotting Community Participation

		Need Assessment	Leadership	Organization	Resource Mobilization	Management
Excellent	5.					
Very Good	4.					
Medium	3.					
Low	2					
Very Low	1.					

Problem Solving—the Process

Up to this time we have been talking mostly about need perception. Unfortunately, the tendency is to see the needs through whatever way they may be perceived, and attempt to meet the needs in the best way possible. Too often the planner fails to determine the problem which is creating the need and/or discover the most effective and appropriate way to solve the problem or problems creating the needs. We tend to spend most of our time putting bandages on the sore rather than dealing with the infection.

Planning, in this respect, usually originates with one eye on the total financial or other resources available, another on the obvious personnel needed to carry it out and a focus on the most urgent need to be addressed in the context of those resources. It may or may not take into consideration the strategic purposes inherent in one's essential purpose for being present in the first place. Instead of allowing for innovative approaches in meeting needs, this type of thinking is more often extremely restrictive and inhibiting. It fails to take into consideration the wider range of resources already mentioned or to determine the long-range implications of the ongoing aspects of the apparent needs being addressed.

In order to look into the process of problem solving we have adapted a process developed by Charles E. Wales and Robert A. Stager of the Center for Guided Design at West Virginia University. The exercise on page 145 and following has been created to emulate a typical Third World rural situation which might be confronted by a missionary or development worker attempting to deal with a critical need. See the instructions for the conference leader on page 148.

As the group finishes the work, help them to understand the process which they have followed. In most cases, the resources available tend to become the drivers in determining the kinds of projects that will be planned to meet human needs. However, without careful evaluation of the situation and circumstances, the planner may never fully realize the single problem which is most likely to keep him or her from being successful in responding to the perceived need. In the case of the illustration presented, many planners are

**Let's concentrate on solving problems
not just meeting needs.**

likely to suggest the idea of building a bridge or a better road. Some will suggest digging a well (without understanding any of the potential cultural restraints which have kept wells from being drilled in the past). Few, if any, will think of the fact that their major problem may initially lie in the area of communications.

The focus of the group should always be pointed in the direction of the value of group consensus and the involvement of the local people both in the determination of the real problems which create the needs and the potential solutions to meeting the needs.

The Remote Mountain Village
An Introduction to the Process of Problem Solving

Introduction

You may have had the experience of arriving at a new assignment and feeling ill equipped to deal with the responsibilities assigned to you. Now, imagine the problem you might have if you had just been asked to start new work in a remote rural area. You wish to develop a program of evangelism and church planting. The tribal people in this rugged mountain area have always been resistant to the gospel, and previous efforts by other groups have ended in failure. Now, you have discovered that the people are in dire need, and unless someone comes in to help them with their problems, many will surely die. First, we want you to complete an individual exercise in which you will be asked to prioritize a list of resources. Then, you are asked to work as part of a group to explore the best way to deal with the situation which confronts you.

The Setting

You are assigned to a people group living high in a remote mountain area. While you have not learned the tribal language, you understand that several of the leaders in the tribe speak the national language, and there is at least one government worker residing near the area who is fluent in both the national and the tribal language. One of the tribesmen is said to speak a little English. You have been informed that the village is extremely poor. After three years of extreme drought, the rivers in the area, which usually dry up even after a good rainy season, are completely dry. There is no other local water supply. The situation has now become critical. There is evidence (reddish hair and bloated tummies) that a large percentage of the children may have severe malnutrition. There is a high mortality rate among infants and those under the age of five. There is also talk of severe diarrhea. Normally, the people live on a primary diet of cassava (manioc/yucca). There is little supplementary food, but the government has no specific plans to intervene.

For years the women of the village have had to walk nearly 15 kilometers along a narrow treacherous mountain pass in order to haul water from another area. Many times rock slides have destroyed the mountain path, making the trip even more hazardous. Because of the dire need for water and limited local food supply, the women continue to make the journey even though many have fallen, either to be seriously injured or even to die on the mountain slope. Fortunately, a Baptist hospital is located just across a gorge on another mountain and a few of the villagers have come to the hospital for help, thus establishing a relationship with the villagers. However, the village is at least nine hours away over a very rough road—and four-wheel drive vehicles would be required. It can be reached in a shorter time by a more direct route by foot or donkey. In your desire to enter the village, you recognize that you will first need to become involved in providing some level of assistance for the people concerning their physical problems, if you hope to share the gospel effectively. You, together with a local national pastor, a national public health nurse, and one missionary evangelist on the hospital station have agreed to work as a committee of four to work out plans to deal with the situation.

The committee agreed that they first should make a survey of the potential resources available to them. They have come up with the following list. First, without discussing it with anyone else, we want you to prioritize (rank) the resources. Choose only the top five most important to enable you to respond effectively. Put your answers in column A. Second, we want you to work in an assigned group to reconsider and rerank the five most important resources based upon a consensus of the group. Record these answers in column B.

RESOURCES AVAILABLE

	A	B
1. A special gift of $10,000 designated for human needs work in the country which could be requested from the mission.		
2. A sophisticated rotary (down-hole) water drilling rig on a trailer.		
3. A civil engineer (with special training in water resources) willing to come, if requested by the mission through the area office.		
4. A village leader who has been to the hospital and was healed of what many villagers thought was a fatal disease.		
5. A 35mm camera with a variety of lenses and film.		
6. A young national agricultural extension worker assigned to the area by the government.		
7. A four-wheel drive jeep with a heavy-duty hitch.		
8. Five hundred Bibles translated in the local tribal language.		
9. Five thousand packets of nutritional food for children.		
10. Reference/resource packet (Guidelines for use of hunger/relief funds, a planning manual, and an appropriate technology textbook.)		
11. A public health nurse who is a national.		
12. A government survey of the tribal area containing demographic and topographical data.		

Action to Be Taken by the Committee: (Limit each to one specific action)

1.

2.

3.

4.

5.

Instructions for the Conference Leaders
1. After the individuals have completed the assignment, ask them to give their answers and the reasons for their ranking. (Allow about 7 minutes). Place the answers in column A.
2. Following this have the group count off, creating individual groups of not more than six in each group. Have each of the groups choose a group reporter, then discuss the prioritizing again, and come up with a group consensus on the priority ratings. Place the answers in column B (allow about 10 minutes). Let each group report and give the rationale for their choices.
3. Find out how many changed their rankings because of the group discussion and emphasize the importance of group interaction in decision making.
4. Once all groups have reported, ask them to determine the three top priority actions they would take in beginning their response to the situation facing them. (Allow 7 minutes for this.)
5. When they report, compare the actions they list with the priority ranking of the group for a comparison of the priorities they have made and the actions they have taken. Is there a direct relationship between the two or have they forgotten the priorities they listed?
6. Next, indicate to the group that up to this time they have not actually determined the single most critical problem that is likely to keep them from dealing effectively with the situation described. Have the groups discuss this and determine a group response.

Leader's Interpretation of Material
The single most critical problem to be dealt with by the committee is to discover how to relate/communicate with the leaders/village group in such a way as to get them to become fully involved in identifying the causes of their problem(s) and participating in all phases of planning and/or subsequent efforts to deal with those problems.

The Resources: In order of priority and rationale based on the nature of the situation:

1. **The village leader who has been to the hospital for help.** Since the essential problem may be one of establishing communication and relationships, this contact may be vital in opening the door to other village leaders and the tribe as a whole. He will have to be convinced that the committee has the desire to work with and listen to the leadership and has the ability to respond effectively.

2. **The young government agricultural worker.** He may not only represent one of the best lines of communication to the people, he may also represent the best way to get the local government's cooperation in assisting the people.

3. **The government survey of the village** containing demographic and topographical data. Until you know the details of the population and area as well as the scope of the various needs, chances are you will deal only with the manifestation of the problem and not the problem itself.

4. **The public health nurse.** First of all, she may be able to communicate with the women better than any other person on the team. Second, she should be able to determine the exact nutritional state of the children and their need for fortified food, oral rehydration, and/or other emergency responses that may be required. She may also be better able to enlist the cooperation of the women toward any future response beyond the immediate emergency needs.

5. **A four-wheel drive jeep.** It is going to be important to be able to get to the villagers to deliver emergency supplies and/or to visit on a regular basis. Without the vehicle this would be extremely difficult, if not impractical.

6. **Five thousand packets of nutritional food for children.** This should be high on your list for two reasons. First, many children may die if they are not fed before you have a chance to deal with long-range problems. Second, the villagers will be looking for some immediate solutions to their problems, and

not just promises of what might be done in the future. This could well establish a strong relationship with the people.

7. **The civil engineer who is willing to come for three months.** This person may be able to do a preliminary feasibility study about potential water supplies and recommend the best possible solution toward involving the people in helping to obtain it.

8. **The reference/resource packet.** It is going to be important to understand the guidelines related to the financial resources which may be available. In addition, it will be important to be fully conversant with the other materials prior to designing a proposal, conducting a feasibility study, and determining the exact response desired.

9. **Five hundred Bibles in the local language.** The chances are literacy is very low, however, these could be used to teach literacy as well as to share with those who already know how to read. It will be basic to the long-range concern of evangelism and church planting.

10. **The special gift of $10,000.** However, before you rely on outside resources, first discover what local resources are available which may be used to enable the people to help themselves. You can't solve problems by throwing money at them. On the other hand, there are some things that may require an initial investment in order to deal with the major aspects of the program. If wells are to be dug or drilled, pumps, and/or other appropriate equipment will be needed to enable the rest of the program to proceed.

11. **The sophisticated drilling rig.** This may be valuable in the lowlands, but it may be impossible to get into the high mountain village. It may also be impractical as the best means of getting water based upon the ability of the local people to maintain and operate the rig pumps once they are installed.

12. **The 35mm camera.** It would be nice to have the pictures to raise funds or to show people what is being done to help, but it will not solve the problems of the people.

The Action Planning Model

Someone has said, "planning is . . . figuring out how to get from where we are to where we want to go, or . . . figuring out what we want to happen and how to make it happen.

Is planning, especially "strategic planning," biblical? What about research?

These are the spies Moses sent to explore the land. When Moses sent them out, he said to them, "Go north from here into the southern part of the land of Canaan and then on into the hill country. Find out what kind of country it is, how many people live there, and how strong they are. Find out whether the land is good or bad and whether the people live in open towns or in fortified cities. Find out whether the soil is fertile and whether the land is wooded. And be sure to bring back some of the fruit that grows there" (Num. 13:17b-20 NIV).

The Strategy of Moses:

1. He was committed to survey the land. He recognized that he needed to know everything he could about the target area and the people who lived there before he determined the direction and timing of their move. Obviously, he waited for the specific leadership of the Lord, but in that context he needed a "database" in order to proceed.
2. He started the survey in a specific direction with a specific purpose. They were to go to the hill country where they would discover the first constraints regarding their potential to push further into the land. This would also give them a logical vantage point from which to view the land.
3. He asked about the demographics: (a). What kind of country? (b). What kind of people? (c). How many people? (d). How strong are they?
4. He asked about the quality of the land for future farming. "Is the land fertile? Is it wooded?"
5. He asked about the strongholds. "Do they live in open towns or fortified cities?"

6. Finally, he asked the spies to bring back samples of the fruit. He wanted something tangible that he could measure.

An Action Planning Model

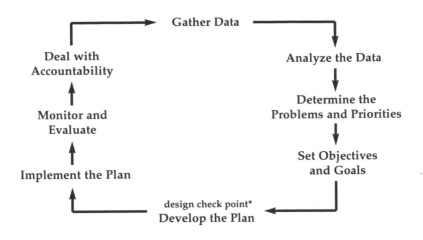

Gather Data
1. It can be demonstrated that the most successful transformational projects are based on the felt needs of the community. It will be important for the planner to follow the concepts laid out in reference to the process of discerning the perception of the community and others regarding needs and problems.
2. Those who have the problem must perceive it as their problem, believe it is in their interest to solve it, and be willing to commit themselves to becoming part of the process for solving it.
3. Often, the outsider and local formal leaders are blind to what are the true felt needs of the community or the actual problems causing the need.
4. It is one thing to identify problems. It is much more difficult to come up with acceptable solutions. Gathering data specific to the problems of a community and why they exist is the first step to innovative and community supported solutions.

5. On a micro or community level, this is simply a process of looking around to find out what are the unmet needs and, logically, what are the problems creating the needs.
6. In many developing countries there is an overwhelming number of needs. Since one cannot gather all the information about everything which creates a need, an immediate solution process usually takes place to determine priorities.

Analyze Data
1. Analyzing the data helps you to understand the problem areas and the interrelationship among causes. Once basic data is in, the process focuses on determining the relative importance of various problems and needs.
2. If you are working alone, this may be as simple as saying, "Given all that I know (data), this appears to be the major problem area, one which is identified and felt by the community."
3. In a developmental project you would sit with the community leaders to analyze and interpret the information gathered, and come to a common understanding of the problem areas and their relative priority to the community.
4. Reference is to problem areas since it is usually premature to say that the problem is already clearly defined. Within the problem area there may be many different problems.

Set the Objectives, Goals, and Write the Action Plans
1. Once the problem area is decided upon, the objectives and goals are written to describe the changes which one plans for the project to bring about.
2. For a project to be successful, planners and implementors must know where it is going.
3. The objectives are the destination of the project. They must be clearly stated and have a single focus in order to assure that the project itself is clearly focused.

> *An objective or priority concern is a concise statement of a long-term aim or desired end result, which is sought in the context of a project. Objectives should be consistent with the overriding purpose for the presence of the mission or national body in the country.*

Criteria for the formulation of objectives:
1. They should be broad in context and time span.
2. They should be realistic in terms of the planner's capacity to carry them out.
3. They should have a definable rationale to support them.
4. They should be listed in priority order of importance.

Sample – Not intended to represent a complete project design.

OBJECTIVES

List all project objectives (what you hope to accomplish ultimately).

1. To help people in the community of _____ improve nutrition and general health through developing water resources.

2. To enable residents of _____ become more self-supporting through irrigation and agricultural development.

3. To strengthen the Christian witness at _____ by coordinating evangelism with a response to physical needs.

Criteria for formulation and evaluation of goals:
1. They should be achievable within a specific time period.
2. All goals should be interrelated for the accomplishment of the objective for which they are stated.

3. They must have clearly-defined indicators to enable the project managers or evaluators to measure the results.

Goals are intermediate steps that lead to the attainment of an objective.

---

4. They should be flexible to respond to unforeseen developments and changes such as those indicated by project monitoring. (See Implementing and Monitoring, p. 159).
5. They should be listed in order of priority (i.e., short-range, high-visibility goals may provide momentum and build trust for the accomplishment of more difficult, broader goals and objectives).

Sample – *Not intended to represent a complete project design.*

GOALS

(Complete one goal sheet for each project objective)
Objective 1: To help people in the community of _____ improve nutrition and general health through water development.

1. Construct one sand-filtered river bottom well as a potable water source for the village of ____. *Completion date: April 1, 1995.*
2. Construct one 20,000 gallon, overhead water reservoir to store drinking water for 500 residents. *Completion date: June 15, 1995.*
3. Install well water pump and chlorination system in the well in the village of ____. *Completion date: June 30, 1995.*
4. Install water distribution lines to 200 homes in the village of ____. *Completion date: September 30, 1995.*
5. Train maintenance and operation crew from local village. *Completion date: November 11, 1995.*

Criteria for formulation and evaluation of action plans:
1. They must include specific statements as to who, what, when, how, and how much (an actor and the completion date are necessary for each action plan).

> *An action plan is a listing of specific short-term steps toward the attainment of a goal.*

2. Actions are arranged in a logical progression for attainment of a goal.
3. Actions should be clean and unambiguous.

Sample – *Not intended to represent a complete project design.*

Action Plan

Objective 1: To help people in the community of _____ improve nutrition and general health through water development.
Goal 3: Install well water pump and chlorination system in the village of _____ by (date).

(List each action, with its actor, date, and costs [if any] necessary to accomplish this goal.)

Action	Actor	Date	Costs
Obtain data needed to size pump and chlorinator.	E. Jones	5/1/95	(Eng. fee)
Calculate pump size and chlorinator capacity.	Eng. Samueri	5/7/95	(Eng. fee)
Order pump and chlorinator.	E. Jones	5/7/95	$4,000
Contract plumber for pump and chlorinator installation.	Jones/Joabe	6/1/95	
Install pump and chlorinator.	Plumber-Jack	6/22/95	$600
Test all equipment.	Plumber/Eng.	6/25/95	
Instruct local operator in maintenance operation.	Eng. Samueri	6/30/95	

Checkpoint: After the last action plan has been written, it is important to review the design with a critical eye.

• Have the spiritual steps been integrated into the design?

- Have actors been selected for a distributed workload and maximum involvement of national and expatriate personnel?
- If the action plans for each goal are successfully carried out, will the objective be attained?

Asking questions and making corrections as necessary will enhance the likelihood of producing a well-balanced project design.

Look at the samples of objectives, goals, and action plans on the preceding pages.

Try to write out some objectives for a project which you might want to propose. List three or four objectives and test them against the definition given for an objective: Do they describe a long-term aim or desired end result? Are they consistent with the overriding purpose for the presence of the mission, church, or national body in the country?

Do proposed goals under each objective provide logical intermediate steps which lead to the attainment of the objective? Does the criteria required for goals fit?

Do the proposed action plans describe clear, short-term steps toward the attainment of the goals? Do they list who, what, when, how, and how much? Do they meet the criteria?

Finally, have you gone back over the whole plan to check each aspect of the project idea and proposal?

Notes

[1]Childhope, "Attacking street children, attacking family economies," *Together*, December 1991, 6.

[2]Adapted from workshop material prepared by Beth Spring for Evangelical Press Association annual convention, May 7-9, 1984.

[3]Paul Heibert, "Anthropological Insights for Whole Ministries," *Christian Relief and Development*, Edgar J. Elliston, Word, 1989, 81.

[4]Rules of Thumb for Transformation, *Christian Relief and Development*, Lynn E. Samaan, 156-158.

TIME AND SEQUENCE CHART
Determining the "critical path" for planning

OBJECTIVE	GOAL	ACTION	ACTIVITY DESCRIPTION	TIME SPAN	Nov. 15, 1994	Nov. 30, 1994	Dec. 15, 1994	Dec. 30, 1994	Jan. 15, 1995	Jan. 30, 1995	Feb. 15, 1995	Feb. 30, 1995	March 15, 1995	March 30, 1995	May 1, 1995	June 15, 1995	June 30, 1995	July 30, 1995
2	2	1	Early discussions with community leaders about irrigation	2 wks.														
2	1	1	Hire engineer	1 mo.														
2	1	2	Initial discussions with engineer	2 wks.														
1	5	1	Discussions with government officials about water system	2 wks.														
1	1	1	Complete well design	1 mo.														
1	2	1	Complete storage tank design	1 mo.														
1	2	1	Let contract for well	1 mo.														
1	5	1	Written agreement with community assumption for water system	2 wks.														
2	2	2	Presentation of initial plans for irrigation to community leaders	2 wks.														
3	1	1	Plan for special prayer meeting	2 wks.														
2	1	4	Revision of irrigation plan	1 wk.														
2	2	3	Presentation of revised plan to engineer	1 day														

• = Critical points
- - - - Critical path to completion

SAMPLE
Not intended to represent a complete plan

PROGRESS CHART

Date/Action #s by month	Actor	Accomplished	Or Not	Comments/ Difficulties
November 94	Pastor/Director			
G1-A1	Project Director			
December 94				
Ob2-G1-A2	Project Director	January 5, 1995	Delayed	Delayed until January 15, 1995
		Checked on December 1994		
January 95				
Ob1-G5-A1	Project Director	OK		
Ob1-G1-A1	Engineer	OK		
G2-A1	Engineer	OK		Checked on January 2, 1995
February 95				
Ob1-G1-A2	Project Director			
G5-A2	Pastor			
G5-A1	Mission Lawyer			

CODE EXPLANATION
Objective Number
Goal Number
Action Number

SAMPLE
Not intended to represent a complete plan

Chapter 7

Implementing and Monitoring . . . Tracking the Indicators and Keeping on Track

Monitoring is generally considered to be an ongoing process in the context of a project, for the purpose of assessing whether the administration of resources is being applied in an efficient and effective manner in terms of the original intentions. Normally, both performance and process will be monitored.

Performance Monitoring

Assesses whether or not the resources are being used as intended according to the budget, in keeping with the time frame and in a cost-effective manner. The four basic steps which make up performance monitoring include:

Establishing indicators. These are strategic control milestones, stated in a quantifiable and measurable way, that lead toward the attainment of the specific goals stated in the project design. These indicators will be stated in terms of time, quantity, quality, and costs. They are recorded as a part of the action plans and goals.

Comparing intermediate results against indicators. Regularly gathering information at designated times about the process of the project will enable comparison with the predetermined indicators. Generally some variation is permitted.

This comparison process is facilitated if all actions of the project are listed on a progress chart, by month. (See p. 158.)

It will also be useful to plot all project actions on a time and sequence chart. (See p. 158.) Each action must show the earliest beginning date and anticipated completion date. Some actions will be dependent upon the completion of other actions. Some actions will be dependent upon weather conditions, the availability of personnel and/or equipment and supplies as well as other variables. Normally, the proposed date for completion would indicate the order of actions on the chart.

Taking corrective action. The action required to get back on target is dependent upon the type of deviation. It is important to gather the facts about the situation and weigh the alternatives before a decision is made. Various types of reports and methods are used to gather information in the monitoring process. These may include:

- On-site inspection.
- Informal oral reports.
- Formal scheduled reviews with various staff.
- Budget briefings and updates.
- Activity or progress reports (normally every six months).
- Financial audits as required.

Personnel assessment. It will be important for overall effectiveness to monitor the individual effectiveness of various staff, community volunteers, local leadership, and/or others directly involved in carrying out the project. Your understanding of cross-cultural communication will be vital at this point. Human reaction to control is generally negative. The ultimate success of any system is determined by the effectiveness in getting people to make the necessary modifications in their own performance. People are sensitive to monitoring because it generally focuses on the things they do poorly and, as a result, reflects on their self-image. The evaluative process must have positive affirmation as well as corrective recommendation. Some of the attributes of a good monitoring system for workers include:

- They must see the monitoring as both helpful and meaningful to the effective carrying out of their responsibilities.
- Praise must exceed criticism.
- They must be capable of carrying out the expected changes within the time given.
- They must be able to expect the necessary help to make the changes required.

Process Monitoring
Process monitoring is primarily concerned with the delivery system. At this point it is related to impact evaluation. It looks at how the project is being perceived by the target audience, how it actually functions in relationship to them, and whether the communication and organizational linkages are effective. It asks, "How have relationships between the recipients and surrounding community been affected during the process of the project thus far?" It will also consider the possibilities of modifications if the timing and cost factors are not in line. In terms of cost-effectiveness, it will compare the actual cost per person being assisted with alternate possibilities for accomplishing the same thing.

A project was targeted at providing clothes for a population group which had lost everything through a major catastrophe. They compared the cost of importing free clothing from overseas with the cost of providing a few centrally-located sewing machines and materials to allow groups to make their own clothing in a cooperative effort. It was not only far less expensive, but allowed them to participate in solving their own problem.

In another instance, one might need to compare the cost of shipping donated bulk food supplies overseas with the purchase from local markets or adjacent countries. Each area of monitoring and evaluation should be considered together as part of a whole. For instance, on the one hand, you may be evaluating a clean water project to supply a village where diarrhea has cost the lives of numerous children through the years. One might need to ask if the pumps, pipes, and reservoirs have all been installed on time and as planned? On the other hand, one must evaluate the relative understanding of the local women regarding the relationship between clean water, clean vessels, and sanitary procedures.

In one Central American project, the local denomination had requested funds to build 100 "outhouse" toilets for the rural population. It was decided that two toilets would be built at each church with the rationale that it would be a good place to demonstrate an effective waste disposal system. Another part of the objective for the project was to reduce the incidence of various diseases related to poor waste disposal practices. No one ever took time to teach the local people about this, however. In time, the buildings became so filthy, drawing flies and other organisms, that the disease factor actually went up rather than down as planned. Midterm monitoring could have caught this and corrected it prior to the completion of the project.

The Importance of Determining the Key Issues to Be Monitored
Many project directors become completely frustrated when the project does not appear to be going as planned or expected. Early monitoring of the initial phases of the delivery system sometimes can help avoid serious problems in the middle of the project. Planners tend to overestimate what they will be able to do and how quickly they can do it. In some cases the anticipated staff is either unavailable or seriously delayed. In one case an agricultural project had been planned by a missionary working with the nationals prior to the arrival of the agriculturist. Agreements had been made, materials had been purchased, and the concept had been approved all the way up the administrative ladder. When the expert came he disagreed with almost all the plans and made a unilateral decision to scrap the whole thing and start over. The program never recovered.

The impact of delivery systems on project outcomes:
A labor intensive project was initiated in Africa. The community, made of a number of small villages each having a subchief, agreed to send a specific number of laborers to work on the site for building an earthen dam. Some of the villages were very responsive and did their part. In other villages few showed up and put the whole schedule behind by several months. Because of the delay the rains came and wiped out the work that others had done.

The Mission finally had to resort to purchasing an expensive bulldozer to complete the task before the next rainy season. In the end, the dam was constructed, but it was no longer the community project which had been part of the original philosophy of total involvement.

In an urban slum area a small church decided to develop a combination clinic service and a vocational training program. They requested funds to expand the facilities by building extra classrooms and equipment. The project plan indicated that the training staff for the vocational program and clinic would be volunteers. It was assumed that these would be available and that many had made some commitment to work in the program. Then, two of those expected to work in the center were transferred. The doctor was unable to fulfill his obligation because of extra duties, and finally the equipment which was ordered from the United States arrived a year late. The new buildings sat idle for over a year and the program as planned was never actually put into operation.

Communication problems:
In an urban literacy project the planners had failed to discover that the target audience was made up of two different ethnic groups. While the project seemed to work in certain sections of the community, in other parts of the community it was almost a complete failure. Planners failed to recognize the ancient rivalries which separated the two groups. The literacy trainer was from yet another group which was accepted by neither of the other two.

In the context of a cholera epidemic, women from one region of their country refused to boil the water as had been encouraged by a widespread media blitz. They said, "Our husbands do not like to drink hot water." Somehow in explaining the urgent need to have pure water to combat the disease, they had failed to indicate that the water could be cooled and used later.

In a squatter relocation project in Brazil the implementing agency believed that the community had been informed by their leaders as to the nature and the costs of the project, and that most families were in agreement. A quick study showed that most families had not even been told and were actually hostile toward the project.

Vocational training and job placement programs (monitors will want to ask some of the following questions):

a. Do those who have the greatest need actually have access to the project? What is the criteria for the selection process?

b. Are the training programs realistic in terms of the actual market or job opportunities which trainees anticipate being available upon completion of the training?

c. Is the raw material readily available at a cost which those trained are able to afford? How well can their product compete against larger highly-equipped and well-organized shops producing similar items?

d. What consideration has been given to alternate avenues of retailing or wholesaling products from the center?

Nutritional training and health care programs:

a. In what ways do traditional cultural beliefs and practices affect the success of the total program? What changes do you see taking place at midterm?

b. How well understood is the program in the larger community? What efforts are being made to expand the information channels?

c. What groups, if any, do not have access to the program? Why? How can this be corrected?

d. How cost-effective is the program in comparison to municipal, government, or other health care programs available?

Agricultural development:

a. To what extent are the participants able to replicate the concepts taught on their own land without additional help?

b. To what degree have the families of the farmers accepted the introduction of new crops or varieties which may produce more protein, etc? In a West African project an experienced agricultural missionary experimented with the introduction of the mung bean, noted for its nutritional value. He worked for over three years attempting to get the local farmers to grow the beans, but failed to get it introduced. Thinking through the problem, his wife invited some of the women of the village to her home for a meal at which time she cooked some of the beans. The women loved them. She then taught them how to cook the beans so they could introduce them to their husbands. When the men of the village tasted the beans, cooked in the manner the women were taught, they asked if they could get some seeds to grow them for themselves.

c. How dependent will the farmers be on imported materials, equipment, and extra funding in order to be successful in the training received?

d. How appropriate is the technology being introduced or taught? Does it have cultural implications about which you have not been aware? Is it readily adaptable and acceptable by those who you intend to use it? Does it allow for change and growth?

e. To what extent have you examined or considered the environmental impact of the project? A missionary agriculturist in West Africa, where the soil was highly acidic and basically laterite in composition, wanted to introduce new methods and crops for a very backward community. The traditional method of farming was merely to broadcast the seed once the women had broken the surface with short-handled hoes. He first tested to see what crops would grow in the soil with a minimum of chemical fertilizers. Once he determined what could be done in a simple and inexpensive manner, he introduced the idea to a paramount chief. He suggested that the chief mark off about one acre of land. Then he divided the land into two equal sections. One section was to be farmed by the women as always. On the other side he worked with the same short-handled hoe, but developed rows according to the contours of the land. He helped them dig a well near the spot and showed them the technique of trickle irrigation. He demonstrated how to fertilize with cow manure and then cultivated the crop as it grew. He had told the chief he would help under three conditions.

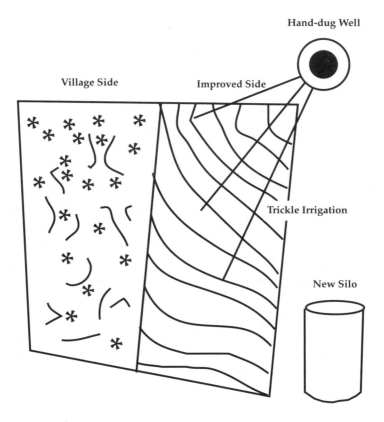

First, it wouldn't cost the chief anything the first time. Second, if he failed to produce as much as usual, he would make up the difference. Third, if he were successful, he expected the chief to use some of the proceeds to help another farmer the following year. All was agreed. At the end of the first year they had not only succeeded, but actually grew almost twice the amount as the other side of the land. They also constructed an inexpensive silo to store the crop. Within three years at least a dozen other farmers had used the approach. During his next tour of duty he introduced animal traction. In doing this, he taught only the men to plow with the animal. So, instead of the women breaking their backs using short-handled hoes, the men started plowing with animals.

Notes

[1]Adapted from workshop material prepared by Beth Spring for Evangelical Press Association annual convention, May 7-9, 1984.

168

FRAMEWORK FOR MONITORING AND EVALUATION
OF THE PROJECT IMPLEMENTATION PROCESS*

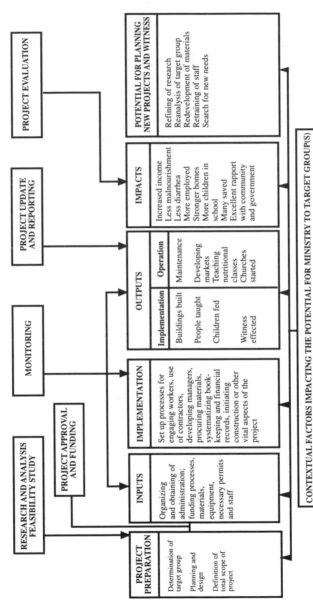

*Adapted from *Monitoring and Evaluating Urban Development Programs*, by Michael Bramberger and Eleanor Hewitt, 6.

CHAPTER 8

EVALUATION . . .
PROCESS AND IMPACT

If you don't know where you are going, it doesn't matter what road you take!

The What, Why, Who, and How of Evaluation

What is it all about?

Evaluation is the application of a system of research procedures in determining the relative validity and effectiveness of the initial concepts, designs, implementations, and results of various programs within a specified location and time, among a given group of people.

First of all, it is helpful to know what kind of criteria will be applied. The word *evaluate* means to measure. This is usually interpreted as meaning the measurement of performance against intentions. But, unless objectives and quantifiable indicators of success are carefully attached to a program before it is begun, then even quite simple measurements of achievement can rarely be made with confidence.

The second question which will need to be determined is: How are the results to be used? Will a written report be required and for whom? How will the report be used?

Why do it?

The intention of an evaluation is to measure relative achievement against primary needs/causes, concerns, and goals in terms of physical, material, and spiritual change. It may also introduce multiple self-initiating activities, and to influence thought and action during the investigation, implementation, and/or carrying out of a particular program or project. It is important for the evaluator to have the ability to gather information, analyze that information, and interpret the conclusions by documenting the observations in a clear and plausible manner.

Key Questions in the Evaluation Cycle

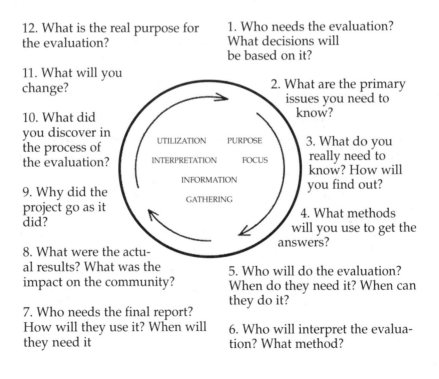

12. What is the real purpose for the evaluation?

11. What will you change?

10. What did you discover in the process of the evaluation?

9. Why did the project go as it did?

8. What were the actual results? What was the impact on the community?

7. Who needs the final report? How will they use it? When will they need it

UTILIZATION   PURPOSE

INTERPRETATION   FOCUS

INFORMATION

GATHERING

1. Who needs the evaluation? What decisions will be based on it?

2. What are the primary issues you need to know?

3. What do you really need to know? How will you find out?

4. What methods will you use to get the answers?

5. Who will do the evaluation? When do they need it? When can they do it?

6. Who will interpret the evaluation? What method?

The purpose of the investigation should be primarily aimed at ministering to the total needs of the target group while at the same time providing a constructive and positive basis for making any corrective adjustments.

In addition to actually measuring the relative success or failure to accomplish the established objective, it is well to bring into focus the question of the underlying assumptions supporting the activities under review. It is relatively easy to examine a program within its own terms: did it work; how well did it work, what will make it work next time, etc? This may only add legitimacy to a program which is founded on some extremely shaky assumptions and be colored by the expectations of the donors, or the need for information by the home office. It may not measure actual efficiency, effectiveness, impact, environmental consequences, or lasting value.

Who should evaluate?

Using an outside consultant
The advantages of using an outside consultant:
1. The evaluator may bring to the situation a fresh, trained, and critical mind. The objective observer may be able to identify and explore those aspects of the program which are likely to prove central to the achievements and to the problems encountered.
2. By being a good listener the consultant may provide a necessary forum for expressing personal understandings of the working situation. This may result in a more rounded review of a program than is possible by other methods.
3. The beneficiaries of a program may often feel more at ease in giving their comments to an outside evaluator than they would to the working staff.
4. Areas of conflict can usually be brought into the open without the bias of vested interests.
5. An outside trained consultant may find it easier to ask questions which are more appropriately tied to an adequate hypothesis based on the data.

The disadvantages of using an outside consultant:

1. Managers may feel that they are the ones being examined. It is extremely important that the consultant emphasize the purpose of the evaluation in terms of ministry to reinforce and/or assist in reaching purposeful outcomes.
2. The outsider may first have to be educated as to the nature and content of the program. This may become time consuming and burdensome for those who are called upon to supply the information, especially if they should come to feel that they themselves are under examination.
3. The time between requesting the outside examiner to come and the published report may create an unsatisfactory delay in the effective use of the results.
4. It may be very difficult for the outside examiner to collect sufficient and accurate information, particularly if this is clouded by issues that are either sensitive or politically dangerous.
5. It may not be possible to bridge the gap between discovery and learning, i.e., to find out what needs to be done and convey it in a positive and acceptable manner.

Self-evaluations

Self-evaluation will require a disciplined and systematic review of a program being carried out, but can only be valid if it takes into consideration, first, that everyone involved in the program has something to learn as well as to offer, and second, that managers will learn most from the people whom they are trying to assist and from the experiences of their own field-level workers who have seen for themselves the successes and the problems. Finally, it must be based on clear indicators at the outset of the project planning.

A self-evaluation should include those for whom the benefits of a program are intended—the members of the community served, as well as officials and volunteers invited to assist.

The advantages of self-evaluation:
1. It enables the people who have been most directly involved with a program to contribute what they know without having to filter their observations through the medium of an independent reporter. This may provide for a more creative dialogue and produce more exciting results than written analysis.
2. The program managers are more likely to learn the lessons coming out of the evaluation if they themselves invest the effort. The evaluator thus becomes the primary user of the information.
3. The evaluation can become a learning experience for all those who participate in the process. Thus, it can be part of the process of accomplishing the ultimate goals.
4. It can enhance a positive relationship between the enabling body and the community by indicating the strong concern for results that reflect the community's perception of need.
5. It may create more openness and honesty by being less defensive. It would assume, however, that there was a willingness to face obstacles as objectively as possible.

Some disadvantages of self-evaluation:
1. It is difficult, if not impossible, to be wholly objective.
2. There is a built-in tendency to become blind to weaknesses in an attempt to justify the continuation of a program.
3. Thorough evaluation takes time. It may be put off or done ineffectively because of time constraints. It also implies a willingness to make the necessary adjustments, or even discontinuance if the present project is failing to accomplish valid objectives.
4. It may expose the managers to criticism from participants which they are not prepared to deal with openly and honestly. If one is not prepared to look at the whole program objectively, it would be better not to invite or involve those whose opinions would be most incisive.

Key concepts of evaluation
A comprehensive evaluation: An analysis covering the conceptualization

and design of planning, monitoring, implementation, and the assessment of a program.

Conceptualization and design analysis: Studies (1) the extent and location of problems for which intervention is needed, (2) ways targets can be defined in clear terms, and (3) whether the proposed project is appropriate in terms of technical, social, or other areas of measurement.

Cost-effectiveness analysis: Studies of the relationship between project costs and outcomes, usually expressed as costs per unit of the outcome achieved.

Delivery system assessment: Organizational arrangements, including staff, procedures and activities, physical plants and materials needed to provide the necessary program services.

Need assessment: Design and development testing to determine if the project is dealing with underlying causes, real and felt needs, and/or whether it might tend to create artificial expectancy and future dependency.

Monitoring: Deals with the project's process. It takes place in the context of the project and is intended to provide information in tracking: timing, direction, goal achievement, cost, and organizational effectiveness. "Are we where we planned to be, doing what we planned to do?"

1. It should allow for intermediate corrective and flexible decision making.
2. It should provide periodic checks to assure that expectations are being met in terms of the responsibilities given to various managers of the project and that cost factors are in line.
3. It should act as an intermediate evaluator of personnel performance.

Impact assessment: Impact looks at some of the intangibles which could not always be predicted at the onset of the project. Like monitoring, it should be considered periodically during the process of the project, but should be focused on the factors and/or people most influenced and affected by the project.

1. It will focus upon the social, economic, political, and spiritual situation in the immediate target area. It will attempt to determine whether these areas of influence are in context with the specific measurable goals which were predetermined in the project design.
2. It will examine those experiences, changes, decisions, and responses which have had the most influence in fulfilling both the anticipated goals and any unexpected results.
3. It will involve a periodic value judgment of the qualities of social, spiritual, and relational values which have been most affected in the process of the project.

Types of information an evaluation may provide

The kinds of questions asked on an evaluation will be determined by the type, the scope, and the use to be made of the evaluation. The precise questions will vary according to the type of program on hand. Here are some central questions which should be considered.

Questions which should be asked in the conceptualization and design phase of a project:

1. What is the nature, the scope, and the cause of the problem requiring actions?
2. What interventions may be undertaken to deal with the problem significantly?
3. What is the appropriate target population for the intervention?
4. Has the target audience been involved in the need assessment, proposed approaches, decision making, or tentative planning?
5. Will the proposed plan reach the target population in terms of solving the underlying problem?
6. How much will it cost?
7. What are its costs relative to its effectiveness and its benefits?
8. Are the plans consistent with the philosophy and purpose of the sponsoring group?
9. Who else is attempting to meet this need? How? Is there any overlapping or contradiction in the approaches?

10. Define the primary concerns (objectives)—where do you want to be when the project is complete?
11. Specify realistic and definable goals.

Questions which may be asked in the context or completion of a project:
1. What were the program's primary objectives and goals?
2. To what extent have these been achieved?
3. With hindsight, how realistic were the objectives and goals when set against the wider context of limitations under which the program operated?
4. What is the relationship between the program's objectives and the fundamental causes of the problems addressed?
5. What alternate objectives/goals were considered, and why were they rejected in favor of the course eventually taken?
6. Who was expected to benefit from the program, who actually benefited, and who did not? To what extent did those with the most critical need benefit?
7. How did the timing of the project correspond with the timing of the needs? Were the benefits actually realized when they were most critically needed? If there was a delay, was the delay avoidable? What can be done to avoid a similar problem in the future?
8. How did the organization and the use of funds affect the program's objectives? How did the structure affect local decision making? How did this facilitate or adversely affect communications with the target group?
9. What pressures were exerted on the program and the personnel attempting to carry it out? Where were these pressures generated, internally or from external sources? What effect did they have?
10. What opportunities did the beneficiaries have to express their views or to influence the way in which the program was set up and managed?
11. Has the program facilitated growth which enables communities and organizations to learn from one another and/or to cooperate with one another?

12. What effect did the program have on local social processes, both formal and informal, by which things get done in the society? Did it enable recipients to become involved as participants?

13. What effect did the project have upon the community's ability to cope in the context of its own built-in ways of dealing with circumstances? Did it provide for ministry through the church, the extended family, the nuclear family, or within the social structure?

14. What effect did the program have on the physical environment? Is it possible to compare problems created with the problems alleviated?

15. What issues emerged during the setting up and carrying out of the project which might be generalized to other situations? For instance, what was the relationship between alleviating suffering and creating dependency? Should beneficiaries have been required to contribute more to their own welfare? Were national staff salaries in keeping with the total philosophy and purpose of the broader program? How could funding have been more wisely used?

16. What policy lessons have been learned from the program? If the program were to be repeated, what changes could be made up front to create a better framework within which to operate?

17. What evidence is there that the beneficiaries are moving on in self-initiated activities to solve these and other problems?

18. To what extent, if any, are the local people making decisions for themselves and accepting greater responsibility for management?

19. What evidence is there of a decreasing dependency on external personnel and financial resources?

20. To what extent, if any, is there an increased commitment of local resources (money, land, labor, management, etc.)?

21. If information on any, or all, of these and other possible questions is not immediately available, what steps can be taken to find out?

Three Key Words in Effective Evaluations

Participatory—Systematic—Simple

Participatory: Projects will be more effective if community members are actively involved in all phases. This stresses that participation is what development is all about—gaining skills for self-reliance.

Systematic: Every agency should employ all practical means to gather evidence, both quantitative and qualitative, about the impact of its programs. Evaluation should be integrated into the management cycle of programming, which includes budgeting and policy decision-making.

This may include several levels of evaluation. The basic level is usually the project itself. In the next level, projects are often clustered in country programs or in some cases by sections. The agency's overall impact in terms of its strategic goals represents another level. A system of evaluation must recognize that although each project ideally has its own evaluation process, the amount of information passed on from level to level should be restricted. The object is to create a steady flow of information essential for making decisions, without overloading the system.

Simple: The evaluator would do better to think of the trial lawyer gathering evidence for a jury or a good investigative reporter looking for corroborating clues to put together a story.

Uses of Evaluation

Decision-making: Program developers can use evaluation findings to obtain information in order to make better decisions. Results may help determine whether to continue a program, to add or drop a program component, or to institute a similar program in another context.

Assessment/Improvement of Performance: Information from evaluations may be used to identify weak points within a program.

Allocation of Resources: Neither all programs nor every aspect of a single program are equally effective in bringing about desired change. An analysis of a program may reveal that one part of its strategy is successful (as defined by the program's objectives) while another is not.

Personnel Development: Evaluation results may suggest the relative effectiveness of existing staff regarding training needs and/or other types of personalities which should be involved in a program.

Program Justification: This justifies program expenditures or indicates whether the program warrants the investment already made in the program.

Determination of Policy: Were the structures and mechanisms that have been developed appropriate for the task as defined by the organization's policies?

New Knowledge and Understanding: These can provide a rigorous test of lessons learned and suggest some generalizations that may be of use to other practitioners.

The Control Group

Whenever possible, a control group should be used for developing the most accurate assessment of the project. In order for the use of a control group to be effective, studies must be made both prior to the project and immediately following the completion of the project. If the project has as one of its goals the reduction of malnutrition within a given group of people, it will be absolutely essential that the level of malnutrition be accurately determined prior to the introduction of whatever aspects of the project that are targeted to deal with the reduction of malnutrition. The same group should be tested again within the given time frame set for the project's completion.

Evaluation Guidelines and Instruments

The following materials are designed to assist the planner in developing evaluation instruments for specific types of projects. In each case, the planner will want to use the suggested instruments as a guide for developing his/her own instruments—ones that are geared toward their project and situation. These are meant only as suggestions.

The following are included:

General Project Evaluation Guide which may be applied to a variety of rural developmental projects. In each case, specifics about the local project should be included in the final instrument which may be developed on the field. The guideline is included to assist the student in forming an instrument which may be applied to the specific project being developed.

Model Evaluation Instrument* developed from the above mentioned guideline. The instrument is divided into five sections. Each includes a series of questions which are then rated on five levels of responses including poor, inadequate, adequate, good, and excellent. The number of questions in each section determines the relative weight given to the section. The combination of the weight of the 20 questions and the ratings gives the total score for each section.

Section One: Initial Phase of the Project. There are 20 questions included in this section which are designed to weigh the issues in relationship to the other portions of the instrument. Section one deals with the overall strategic purposes of the project, the understanding of the problems and needs to be dealt with by the project and, finally, the underlying assumptions of the community and the planner regarding commitment to the objectives of the project.

Section Two: Planning. This is the heart of the evaluation instrument and includes 50 questions. In each section a redundancy has been built in regarding certain aspects of the whole project, which are particularly important in evaluating the particular aspect of the project reflected in the section. As an illustration, both section one and section two ask about the involvement of the people. This is meant to reflect both consistency regarding the answers given and the potential impact that involvement would have regarding the issues raised in the questions.

Section Three: Monitoring. This section includes 30 questions and emphasizes the importance of whether the project has stayed on track in reference to the original objectives, goals, and budgeting. It also provides a checkpoint in the area of the holistic aspects of spiritual emphasis within the project design and implementation.

Section Four: Accomplishment of Objective and Goals. The section has 35 questions and covers both process analysis and impact analysis.

Section Five: General Questions. This is the narrative portion of the instrument. It allows the individual filling it out to respond about other aspects of the project not covered in the other portion of the questionnaire. While it is more subjective, it may be the most important part of the evaluation instrument.

The instrument is designed for easy calculation on a computer. It is recommended that it be given by personal interview, with the evaluator putting down all answers except the narrative in section five.

Additional instruments are included in this book for evaluating special areas of work. These may be included as part of the general evaluation instrument for issues concerning the following types of projects:

- Vocational/technical training programs
- Community health programs
- Urban ministry programs

The following additional ideas may be incorporated in an evaluation instrument for vocational and technical training programs.

1. Establish and verify a rationale for the training program: (Sample questions you may need to ask.)
   - Does it deal with basic problems and issues realistically?
   - Will it make an impact on a significant number of people?
   - Is the per capita cost within reasonable limits?
   - How does it enhance the primary purpose of the mission/church/convention/agency?
   - Could the program become self-sustaining?
   - Is the rationale within the agency's policy guidelines for the use of designated funds?
   - Is it a valid response to a documented need?

2. Has a thorough community survey been done? This will encompass all segments of the target community and relevant government offices which will be affected by the activity, for the purpose of establishing baseline data.
3. Are specific goals and objectives clearly indicated and understood from the beginning?
4. Do the goals contain indicators which are:
   - *clear:* simply stated and understood by all?
   - *specific:* not too broad or general?
   - *observable:* can be seen by all?
   - *reasonable:* most people agree with the conclusion?
   - *measurable:* allows comparison between cases?
   - *attainable:* not beyond the capacity to be carried out?
5. Has a careful market study been conducted to determine:
   - What is the potential market for the proposed product/skill?
   - What level of skill/training is required to enter the market successfully?
   - What plans have been made for quality control?
   - Are local resources/materials available for producing the items to be made?
   - What commitment, if any, has been made by employers in the job market to employ those trained?
6. If skills training is for self-employment, what training has been planned for teaching marketing, management, quality control, financial record keeping, etc?
7. Has the selection process been based on the level of relative need, and does it reflect a cross section of the community without bias toward religious affiliation, social standing, ethnic background, or other such areas?
8. Has a resource analysis been done by the sponsoring organization?
9. Has realistic resource planning been incorporated? Ongoing financing is always a difficulty. Plans for decreasing outside funding need to be included from the beginning of the training program. Availability of required material, equipment, and supplies must be verified.

10. What assurance of qualified personnel has been planned?

11. Does the program provide training in marketable skills which can alleviate the indicated problems in measurable ways? Parallel programs in nutrition, handling of finances, and/or other courses are included to encourage proper use of added income that may result from training.

12. What plans have been incorporated for monitoring and evaluation to determine if the objectives and goals have been met?

Below are examples of the types of questions and information which will assist in measuring the results and impact of vocational/technical training programs. Relevant questions and information may vary slightly according to the uniqueness of each situation. The important point is for relevant information to be provided.

I. Measuring the training programs.

A. List the subjects planned in the proposal.

1._____

2._____

3._____

4._____

5._____

B. List the subjects that were actually taught.

1._____

2._____

3._____

4._____

C. Give the length of each course? _____Weeks _____ Months
    (a) inadequate   (b) approx. right   (c) too long   (d) other

D. Give the number of students/trainees enrolled? _____

E. What was the ratio of male/female? _____Males _____Females

F. Of those who began, what percent completed training? _____

G. What percent of the target group of trainees was actually
   reached?
    (a) 10% (b) 11%-33% (c) 34%-66% (d) 67%-90% (e) 91%-100%

II. Assessing problem areas. The major problem areas were: (Check
    those that apply)

❑ Training staff   ❑ Training space
❑ Program leadership   ❑ Finances
❑ Equipment and/or supplies   ❑ Finding employment for trainees

❑ Other (explain)_____

III. Evaluating the impact of the program:

A. What percent of enrollees have obtained employment?_____

B. Indicate what relative economic impact has been made on the
    trainees.   (a) very little (b) some improvement   (c) significant

C. Indicate how those trained have applied training/economic
    improvement to provide increased nutritional benefits for their
    families.   (a) none   (b) partially   (c) significantly

D. The program has dealt with root causes of hunger-related issues in the community: (a) not at all   (b) partially (c) significantly

E. The health status of the recipients has been affected:
(a) not at all   (b) partially (c) significantly

F. The impact made on the church/community/area by the program was: (a) none at all   (b) small   (c) moderate (d) great

G. Measurable spiritual results of the program were:
(a) professions of faith   (d) baptisms
(b) additional church members   (e) other (list) _____
(c) Bible classes

IV. Project overview:

A. What evidence is there of enhanced national awareness of ministry outreach and their ability to lead it?

B. What evidence is there of decreasing dependence on external assistance?

C. What interest is there in increasing the commitment of local resources to this type of program?

GENERAL PROJECT EVALUATION GUIDE

Name of evaluator	Relationship to project	
Location	Project number	Project name
Project director		Date of project initiation
Anticipated completion date		Date of project evaluation
Status of project:		

1. Objective: State the primary objective of the project:

(In responding to the following questions, be especially aware of measurable goals under the objective. Please evaluate other objectives in this project with the same instrument.)

2. This objective was achieved:
   ❏ not at all   ❏ partially   ❏ as expected   ❏ better than expected

3. When considered against the limitations experienced (financial, personnel, cultural, etc.) and the actual need, this objective was:
   ❏ unrealistic   ❏ on target and reasonably achievable
   ❏ somewhat off target   ❏ on target and easily achievable

4. The objective, as stated, is related to the fundamental causes of the problem it attempts to deal with:
   ❏ not at all   ❏ remotely   ❏ indirectly   ❏ specifically

5. Determine the organizational structure of the program. Is it directed by: ❏ an individual ❏ a local committee ❏ a board ❏ the mission
To whom is it accountable?

6. Background data and surveys used to justify the proposal were:
   ❏ inadequate   ❏ partially adequate   ❏ adequate

7. Early planning anticipated and allowed for later unexpected developments: ❏ inadequately ❏ partially ❏ adequately ❏ better than expected

8. In initial planning, what did you fail to take into consideration?

❏ If nothing significant, check here

9. What specific input did the people in the local community, or those most immediately involved, have in planning:
❏ none ❏ small but appropriate ❏ significant ❏ primary

10. What input did/do the local people have in monitoring and/or suggesting modifications during the project?
❏ none ❏ small but appropriate ❏ significant ❏ primary

11. To what extent was the project modified by midcourse correction:
❏ not changed ❏ modified little
❏ radically changed ❏ not applicable

12. To what extent have the time frames for meeting goals been modified?
❏ time significantly extended ❏ minor increase of time
❏ within time frame ❏ ahead of schedule

13. In terms of the original expectation for the project, what percentage of the potential target audience actually achieved/received what was expected from the objective (i.e., higher nutritional intake, adequate clean water supply, increased income, job placement, etc.)?
❏ less than 10% ❏ 11%-33% ❏ 34%-65% ❏ 66%-90% ❏ 91%-100%

14. What percentage of those who actually participated in the project achieved/received what was expected from the objective? (See examples for number 9.)
❏ less than 10% ❏ 11%-33% ❏ 34%-65% ❏ 66%-90% ❏ 91%-100%

15. Of the total number who have achieved/received, what was set out for them in this objective:

a. What has been the total cost per person thus far in terms of the total investment? US $_____ (Excluding expatriate salaries)

b. What has been the average cost per person in terms of the current operational budget? US $_____ (Excluding expatriate salaries)

c. How does this compare with the local area per capita income?
Per capita income in terms of US $_____

16. How did the use of funds affect the recipient community?
   ❑ Created unhealthy dependency
   ❑ Created minor short-term dependency
   ❑ Created basis for self-reliance
   ❑ Provided significant self-reliance factor
   ❑ Other

17. To what extent has this project operated within original financial expectations?
   ❑ continuing additional support needed
   ❑ onetime significant cost overrun
   ❑ onetime minor cost overrun
   ❑ accomplished within budget
   ❑ accomplished under budget

18. To what extent has the program been replicated or attempted by other communities?
   ❑ not at all ❑ very little ❑ significantly ❑ not applicable

19. To what extent have the recipients in the program been active participants in carrying out the program?
   ❑ not at all ❑ very little ❑ significantly ❑ fully

20. To what extent have the evangelistic goals of the project been successful?
   ❑ not at all ❑ very little ❑ significantly ❑ fully

21. In what ways has/have the local church(es) been involved in the project?
   ❑ not at all ❑ a minor role ❑ a major role ❑ wholly responsible

22. What evidence is there that the beneficiaries are moving on to think through and initiate things to solve these and other problems, or to improve their lives?
❑ none (no survey)   ❑ little   ❑ significant   ❑ very positive

23. To what extent, based on this project, are local people now making a commitment of resources or time to deal with similar or related issues?
❑ none   ❑ little   ❑ average   ❑ significant

24. To what extent does the project have potential for becoming self-supporting?   ❑ none   ❑ little   ❑ increasingly   ❑ completely

25. To what extent has an attitude of trust been enhanced/engendered as a result of this program?
❑ not at all   ❑ very little   ❑ significantly   ❑ not applicable

26. If you had it to do all over again, what changes would you make?

27. Describe any major problems, failures, unexpected successes/ rewards which took place either in the context of the project or as a direct result of the project.

28. Other comments: (Such as impact made on church/community/ area)

*(Note: The model evaluation instrument may be found in the appendix on pages 244-248.)

CHAPTER 9

PRIMARY HEALTH CARE . . . A NEW DAY, A NEW CHALLENGE

Introduction
Historically, missions have been the front runners in providing health care to countries in the developing world. In the earliest days of missions work, one of the approaches was that of establishing hospital care in some of the most remote and inaccessible parts of the developing countries. During the past several decades there has been an evolving change as the World Health Organization and Western nations have begun to attack some of the more serious problems which have been beyond the capacity of rural clinics and missions hospitals to handle.

Some Patterns of the Past
Poverty, which continues to be pervasive in many of the Third World countries, has contributed much to the rampant spread of major diseases that afflict the population. Such problems as gastroenteritis and pneumonia, when combined with persistent malnutrition and neonatal tetanus, have been the leading causes of

death in children. Malaria and other parasitic infestations have also had a widespread impact on basic health and take a heavy toll on both children and adults. In the context of this, population growth, especially in Africa, has not abated. Because of this, large numbers of those in the relatively healthy environment of the rural sectors have moved into crowded shanties within the urban centers, thus exacerbating an already serious problem. In much of the Third World it is estimated that one-fourth or more of the children do not live beyond the age of five. Many of those who do survive are permanently affected because of the severity of nutritional deprivation in the early months of their lives.

Poverty, particularly in the urban areas, along with the failure of many countries to come to grips with the problem, contributes more to ill health than almost any other factor. One of the reasons for this is the decreasing amount which many Third World countries are actually spending for health care. Generally, this is said to be decreasing by an annual rate of almost 2 percent. In many countries, the budgets for health care provide less than one dollar per person per year. Once again, this has been made more critical because of the emphasis upon training highly-qualified physicians rather than community-based health workers.

There are few illustrations of widespread efforts to improve on these conditions. In the largest part of the Third World, people still do not have adequate access to reasonable health care. Throughout Asia and Africa only 10 to 30 percent of the population are reached by health services. In some rare cases the number reaches 40 percent. In Ethiopia, the figure is said to be less than 5 percent. In much of Latin America, only 30 percent have access to modern health services. Unfortunately, there are too few indications of any widespread efforts to improve the quality and the scope of health services. Much of the funding which has been spent has gone into highly visible and modern hospitals in urban centers. The problem is that most of the population does not have access to the facilities which are being built or the specialists who work in them. It is obvious that the total amount of resources available is limited.

This is even more true with the various missions who continue to be involved in health care. Yet, it is possible to accomplish much more than is being done with far fewer resources than are now required to operate modern hospitals.

This is not to suggest that hospitals per se should be closed, but that missions and the local churches involved in developing countries will need to reconsider health care strategies, if they are to continue to be effective in alleviating human suffering.

Recent breakthroughs mean that health workers with a few months of training can help parents to halve the rates of child death and malnutrition in poor communities.

The Health Pyramid

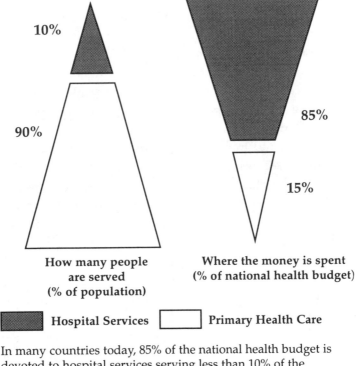

10%

90%

How many people
are served
(% of population)

85%

15%

Where the money is spent
(% of national health budget)

Hospital Services   Primary Health Care

In many countries today, 85% of the national health budget is devoted to hospital services serving less than 10% of the population, leaving only 15% of the budget to provide basic health care for 90% of the people.

Value for Money*

At the moment, two-thirds of the developing world's people have no modern health care. For the cost of producing one doctor (approximately $60,000 in the developing world), at least 30 community health workers could be trained in basic health protection. Latin America, for example, is planning to produce 200,000 more doctors by 1999. For the same cost it would be possible to train fewer doctors—say 150,000—plus one million primary health care workers to live in poor communities and make available basic care, and child protection, for the majority of the population.

Many of those countries which increased their health spending between 1972 and 1989 are among the poorest while some very rich countries slashed their health spending during that same period.

Generally, the pattern of health services is similar around the world. Normally this takes place in three specific areas. It usually includes major national and regional hospitals capable of handling reasonably complex cases with smaller district hospitals having one doctor. In many cases the smaller hospitals are operated primarily by nurses or doctor's assistants. Secondly, there is usually a network of small health centers or dispensaries, some of which will have a few beds. The third setting is the community itself where there is an increasing interest in community-based health care. These centers are normally under the leadership of health workers who specialize in health education and prevention. By relating to the local people and listening to their concerns, one can involve them in a participatory way in a total network of health education.

One of the major questions that now arises is the place of the local church and the historic missions bodies which have pioneered health care for the future. Without the massive funding required to keep up with the advance of modern medicine and the elaborate and expensive technology, what is the future place of health care services in the strategic planning of missions agencies and their local counterparts within the Third World?

The Challenge for the Future of Missions/Church-Based Health Care

1. *Sharpen the Focus.*

Churches and missions have a biblical and historical mandate to the poor, but in some respects they have been part of the problem by placing the highest priority on the most expensive and least effective manner of helping the masses. Too often they have been excluded from health care simply because of economics and ignorance. Yet, by far the largest number of those needing health care fall into this bracket. The challenge is both to the mission and the professional physician who has been highly trained to work in the context of a modern medical center where the technology is available to enable them to use their skills. How can they serve the poor and most needy while still carrying out the evangelistic mandate of sharing Christ? It would seem logical that when 85 percent of the people can be reached with 15 percent of the expense, and thus prevent the largest number of health care concerns, that major consideration needs to be given to this approach in strategic planning.

2. *Redefine the Criteria for Measuring "Quality of Life."*

In order to achieve what may be considered a minimum quality of life standard in the area of health care, certain services must be made available to the poorest of the poor within the urban areas and the most neglected in the rural areas. In order for people to grow in self-reliance, dignity, and full participation in their communities, some basic human needs must be met. Churches and missions have the greatest opportunity of ministering in these areas while at once reflecting the kind of caring concern that draws men and women to Christ.

In most cases protection against preventable diseases (through immunizations, providing access to essential nutrition and safe water, primary health education, and appropriate assistance to gain access to major health care when needed) can be accomplished with only a small portion of the resources needed for major hospital ministries. At the same time, these very ministries can be conducted by local churches, through the network of churches and in the context of holistic approaches in ministry.

3. *Determine the Foundational Principles for Missions-Centered Health Care Strategies.*
   a. Health care resources should be directed toward providing essential health education and health services to those most in need. Any limitation in resources should focus those resources on the priorities which will allow for the greatest level of prevention.
   b. Local churches and missions agencies should become the catalyst toward guiding various levels of government and municipal authorities toward equitable health care for the masses.
   c. Emphasis should be given to training community health care workers within the local churches to serve in the larger rural and urban communities.

4. *Study Your Community for Signs of Malnutrition*
   a. If less than 1,000 people live in a community, all of the children must be measured to get an accurate understanding of the level of malnutrition. If the community is over 1,000, generally about 25 percent of the children must be measured to get an accurate estimate. As the number goes up the percentage required for accurate estimation may go down to about 5 percent.
   b. It is better to measure all the children in 25 percent of the houses, than to take a sampling of 25 percent of the children in each house.

5. *Utilize Effective Ways to Measure Children Under Five Years of Age for Malnutrition.*
   a. Arm circumference: This can be done very simply with a simple measuring device. The upper arm of a child can reveal malnutrition. If the distance around the upper arm (circumference) is less than 13 centimeters, the child is malnourished. If the circumference of the upper arm is more than 13 centimeters, the

196

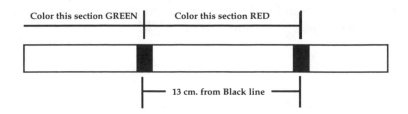

Color this section GREEN | Color this section RED |

├─ 13 cm. from Black line ─┤

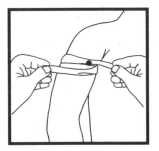

child is not malnourished. This test can easily be done. You may use an old piece of X-ray film with clear spaces. Cut out strips of film 20 centimeters long (or use a piece of cord or string). Make black marks to divide the strip as shown in the above illustration. It is important that the measurements be exact.

If the black line touches the red part of the strip, the child is MALNOURISHED. If the black line touches the green part of the strip, the child is WELL-NOURISHED.

b. The Bracelet: A bracelet is another way of measuring a child's arms for signs of malnourishment. The bracelet must be exactly 4 centimeters in diameter on the inside. This will equal exactly 13 centimeters in the circumference around the inside of the bracelet. It is possible to order bracelets already measured from TALC, 30 Guilford Street, London WCIN 1EH, England.

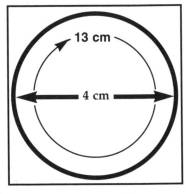

Take the bracelet and push it over the child's arm and wrist, but don't force it. If it goes above the elbow, it indicates that the child is MALNOURISHED. If the upper arm is too fat for the ring to go above the elbow it indicates that the child is WELL-NOURISHED.

c. Weight-for-age: If it is possible to know the exact age of a child, good measurement of the level of malnourishment can be determined by comparing the weight of the child with the normal weight expected for a child of that age.

d. Weight-for-length: A well-nourished child will come within certain standards for a comparison of weight to height. A malnourished child will be too tall for its weight. In this case, the age of the child is not as significant.

Note: The listings for weight-for-age and weight-for-length are on the next page.

6. *Develop a body of trained national workers as a first-line approach toward community health care.*

Probably the most efficient and effective method of local community-based health lies within the gifts of the people themselves. Expatriate leadership can provide both immediate assistance and long-term guidance. However, transformational workers must learn how to reproduce themselves if they expect to make a serious impact on primary health issues in the Third World.

a. Gather the resources necessary for the training and equipping of local health care workers. Many of these resources can be found within the ministry of health within each country. In other cases, books such as *Where There Is No Doctor* and *Helping Health Workers Learn* can form the basis of simple courses of instruction to equip locally qualified people to learn the fundamentals of health care. A training curriculum developed by Franklin Fowler, of the Foreign Mission Board of the Southern Baptist Convention, is included on pages 201-208 of this book.

b. Work with community leaders to determine the most appropriate way to select trainees for courses in community-based health.

c. Help the community to develop a system of support for the trainees once they have completed their training.

d. Provide a system of referral and backup for proper medical treatment in the closest medical center.

WEIGHT-FOR-AGE LIST		
Age of the child	If the child weighs less than this amount he/she is MALNOURISHED	Standard weight for this age
0 months	2.4 kg	3.2 kg
1	3.1	4.2
2	3.7	5.0
3	4.3	5.7
4	5.0	6.4
5	5.4	7.0
6	6.0	7.5
7	6.4	8.0
8	6.8	8.5
9	7.2	8.9
10	7.6	9.2
11	7.9	9.6
12	8.1	9.8
13	8.4	10.1
14	8.6	10.4
15	8.8	10.6
16	9.0	10.8
17	9.1	11.0
18	9.2	11.2
19	9.4	11.4
20	9.6	11.5
21	9.8	11.7
22	9.9	11.7
23	10.0	12.0
24	10.2	12.1
25	10.3	12.2
26	10.5	12.4
27	10.6	12.6
28	10.8	12.8
29	10.9	13.0
30	11.0	13.2
31	11.2	13.4
32	11.3	13.6
33	11.4	13.8
34	11.6	14.0
35	11.7	14.2
36	11.8	14.4
37	12.0	14.6
38	12.1	14.7
39	12.2	14.9
40	12.4	15.0
41	12.5	15.2
42	12.6	15.4
43	12.8	15.5
44	12.9	15.7
45	13.0	15.8
46	13.1	16.0
47	13.3	16.2
48	13.4	16.4

WEIGHT-FOR-LENGTH LIST		
Length of child	If the child weighs less than this amount he/she is MALNOURISHED	Standard weight for this length
55 cm	3.5 kg*	4.5 kg*
56	3.7	4.6
57	3.9	4.8
58	4.1	5.0
59	4.4	5.4
60	4.6	5.6
61	4.9	5.8
62	5.2	6.2
63	5.4	6.4
64	5.6	6.8
65	6.0	7.0
66	6.2	7.4
67	6.4	7.6
68	6.7	7.9
69	7.0	8.2
70	7.2	8.4
71	7.5	8.7
72	7.8	9.0
73	8.0	9.2
74	8.2	9.5
75	8.4	9.7
76	8.6	9.9
77	8.8	10.2
78	9.0	10.4
79	9.2	10.6
80	9.4	10.8
81	9.6	11.0
82	9.8	11.2
83	9.9	11.4
84	10.1	11.6
85	10.2	11.8
86	10.4	12.0
87	10.6	12.1
88	10.8	12.4
89	11.0	12.6
90	11.2	12.8
91	11.4	13.0
92	11.6	13.2
93	11.8	13.5
94	12.0	13.7
95	12.2	14.0
96	12.5	14.2
97	12.8	14.5
98	13.0	14.8
99	13.2	15.0
100	13.5	15.4

e. When possible, initiate an itinerant or mobile program for combining the preventive approach through those trained with qualified medical assistance on a periodic basis throughout the communities being dealt with.

Health Care Guidelines
In thinking about the establishment of community health and development programs, there are several steps for identifying the areas and types of activities which should normally precede the initiation of the work.

The following questions should be raised by the project planners.

Factors to Be Considered in Identifying the Target Area
1. How great is the need in this area?
2. Are there other services offered in the health and development field in the area which are specifically addressing the problems you have identified?
3. Will the proposed program be providing a duplication of services or will it be seen as a competing service?
4. Will you be cooperating with governmental or other existing programs? In what way?
5. Is the area governed as a single political unit? Are there more than two political units in the community? Is so, will you work with one or both?
6. Will work in this area require permission from the government, city council, or other groups?
7. Logistics—how much time is spent in travel to the area? Would it be better to offer a service in a community where the contact person(s) already live?
8. In what area would a community health and development project have the most impact on the evangelistic ministry?

Planning Community Health Activities
1. Identifying health and development needs:
   Talk with the community leaders: Establish opportunities to meet

leaders within the community, as well as people within their homes, to discover their perception of needs. Discussions with groups from the community will help identify group concerns as opposed to individual or general government- suggested concerns.

Prepare community survey and mapping: Problems encountered in the various communities will be similar. Dialog with personnel from various organizations will help you to know the major problems and needs which might be encountered.

Identify existing indicators of health in the country and local community: How different would these indicators be from those seen in the selected community? If not significantly different, these country indicators may be used as baseline data.

2. Choosing priority activities:

It is important to consider trying those activities which meet the most important health needs with the fewest resources.

Early in a program, it is good to identify activities which can be completed quickly, have a good possibility of succeeding, and which produce good public relations for the program. All of these aid in building trust.

Different groups will identify different priorities. Begin activities which are considered a high priority by the target audience, the provider, and the government.

Consider activities which meet needs of those at greatest risk, such as women and children. For this reason many community health programs center their activities around the needs of these two groups.

Identify activities which will meet needs of many, not just a few from the community. There may be existing activities which will help meet identified needs. Lack of knowledge about these, or means of access to them, may be the cause for the people not participating.

Identify resources which are available to help solve the problem.

Consider combining health activities with other development activities. Only when there is a change in the social and educational standing within a community can there be lasting changes in the health status of the community. The educational level of women is a key factor in the health status of children.

Solicit ideas from the community. Offer advice. Act as a catalyst to produce a change in the community. Getting the community involved in suggesting ways to meet their needs allows them to become part owner of any program which develops.

Get commitments from community members as to how they will help overcome the identified problems.

Deciding How to Carry Out Priority Activities

1. *Define the purpose of each activity (component of the program). Why should the activity take place?*
2. *State objectives and goals for each activity.* These should be measurable, realistic, and have clearly-defined indicators to know when they are reached.
3. *Decide how to reach each objective.*
   a. What training for people is necessary?
   b. What materials and supplies will be needed?
   c. What records will need to be kept for reporting and evaluation purposes?
   d. How will the success of this aspect of the project be evaluated?
4. *Develop plans for reaching each objective.*

A Training Curriculum for Community Health Care Workers
by Franklin T. Fowler, M.D.

Course Description: This is a practical study for student pastors, their wives, and other local church leaders. It is designed for them to gain a basic knowledge in the components of health and disease, the causes and prevention of the common diseases, and how this knowledge relates to evangelism and church growth.

Course Objective: That the student, utilizing the knowledge gained, will be able to ascertain basic community health problems, administer basic health care for common health problems, will know how to use community resources, and will be able to teach this basic information to other persons in the community.

Unit I: Primary Concepts of Teaching and Learning
The student should be able to:
    A. Relate and demonstrate the basic theory of teaching and learning.
    B. Identify and use the basic methods of teaching for effective learning.
Content:
    A. The Theory of Teaching and Learning
       (*Medex* 9, Unit 4, pp. 44-59)
       (*Medex* 10, Teaching plan 10, pp. 20-23)
       (*Medex* 32, Section 4, pp. 26-28, Section 5, pp. 29-33)
       Helping Health Workers Learn, Part 2, Chapter 11-19
       Where There Is No Doctor, WI-W29
    B. Basic Methods of Teaching and Learning (see above)

Unit II: The Components of Health
The student should be able to:
    A. Define health.
    B. Identify four components of health.
    C. Demonstrate healthy versus unhealthy communities.
Content:
    A. Physical Components of Health
    B. Social Components of Health
    C. Mental Components of Health
    D. Spiritual Components of Health
       Medex 32, Section I, pp. 7-23
       Working Together for Health, (Bangalore, India), Lesson I - II, pp. 4-10

Unit III: The Causes of Illness
The student should be able to:
    A. Define infection and noninfection.
    B. Name two infections and two noninfectious diseases.

C. Tell the main characteristic of a noninfectious disease.

D. Tell three characteristics of an infectious disease.

E. Identify five types of trauma.

F. Discuss spiritual health.

Content:

A. Noninfectious Diseases

(*Where There Is No Doctor*: Chapter II, p. 18)

B. Infectious Diseases

(*Where There Is No Doctor*: Chapter II, p. 19)

C. Trauma

(*Where There Is No Doctor*: Chapter X, pp. 75-106)

D. Spiritual Illness

(1 Cor. 11:27-34)

(2 Cor. 12:20-21)

Unit IV: The Identification of Disease by Symptoms

The student should be able to:

A. Identify basic symptoms of prevalent diseases in their area.

B. Use and read an oral thermometer and make correct application of findings.

C. Take a pulse in the wrist, temporal, or cardiac area and make correct application of findings.

D. Define dehydration and tell its cause.

E. Define pain and describe it by location, duration, and characteristics.

F. Identify five other symptoms of disease.

G. Relate what is meant by spiritual illness.

Content:

A. Temperature:

Where There Is No Doctor, p. 31

B. Pulse:

Where There Is No Doctor, pp. 32-33

C. Dehydration:

Medex 32, pp. 25-26

Where There Is No Doctor, pp. 151-152

D. Pain:
Where There Is No Doctor, Chapter III, p. 29
E. Others: (i.e., weakness, vomiting, diarrhea, bleeding, tumors)
Where There Is No Doctor, p. 151

Unit V: Common Health Problems of the Community
The student should be able to:
A. Define "common health problems."
B. Identify nine common health problems of their community.
C. Aid in the alleviation of common health problems of their community through teaching and example.
Content:
A. The identification and study of possible health problems of a community, such as: contaminated water, lack of adequate disposal of human and animal wastes, poor nutrition, animal and pest contamination, mosquitoes and other insects, lack of adequate trash and garbage disposal, inadequate housing, lack of education, lack of spiritual motivation for health.
B. Practical methods that can be utilized in alleviating the common health problems of a community.
Medex 10, Section 2

Unit VI: Common Diseases of the Community
The student should be able to:
A. Recognize ten common diseases of the community.
B. Survey a community and report on the common diseases found.
C. Utilize community resources in dealing with the common diseases of the community.
Content:
A. Common diseases found in rural and urban communities such as diarrhea and dehydration, malaria, hookworm, tuberculosis, leprosy, colds, pneumonia, arthritis and rheumatism, bilharzia (schistosomiasis), typhoid fever, tetanus, and measles.

B. Trauma such as fractures and broken bones, cuts (lacerations), burns, blood loss (shock).

Medex 34, *Medex* 18

Where There Is No Doctor, Chapters 13-18

Red Cross First Aid

C. How to survey and report the diseases of a community.

Medex 10, Units 1 and 2

D. How to identify and utilize common resources for common diseases in the community such as a local midwife, a local health post, a regional health unit, a regional or local hospital, or a local physician.

Unit VII: Prenatal, Natal, and Postnatal Care of the Pregnant Woman

The student should be able to:

A. Identify health problems when they occur during the prenatal, natal, and postnatal period.

B. Recognize and utilize community resources for the care of pregnant women.

C. Teach basic health care to the pregnant woman.

Content:

A. The care of a woman during the first trimester (1 to 3 months of pregnancy).

Medex 33, pp. 14-18.

B. The care of a woman during the second trimester (4 to 6 months of pregnancy).

Medex 33, pp. 19-21.

C. The care of a woman during the third trimester (7 to 9 months of pregnancy).

Medex 33, section 4, pp. 26-33.

D. Demonstration of basic material needed for a home delivery.

Medex 33, section 5, pp. 35-36.

E. The description of the newborn infant.

Where There Is No Doctor, Chapter 19, pp. 245-282.

Unit VIII: The Care of the Newborn

The student should be able to:

A. Care for a newborn infant.

B. Teach the basic health care for a newborn infant.

C. Recognize health problems in the newborn and utilize community resources to prevent and treat them.

Content:

A. The immediate care of the newborn.

Medex 33, Section 2

Where There Is No Doctor, Chapter 19, pp. 270-272.

B. The basic care of the newborn.

1. Importance of good nutrition/breast feeding.

2. Good hygiene for the newborn.

3. Significance of pure water and fresh air.

C. Possible health problems of the newborn.

Where There Is No Doctor, Chapter 19, pp. 272-275, Chapter 21, pp. 295-321.

Unit IX: The Spiritual Care of Persons with Special Health Problems

The student should be able to:

Present the gospel of Jesus Christ to persons with special health problems, whether in the hospital or in the community.

Content:

A. The dying person

1. Scripture: Psalms 23, John 11:25.

2. Prayer: For grace, forgiveness, salvation, and faith.

B. The critically ill person who may die.

1. Scripture:

a. Salvation: John 3:16, Romans 5:8, Romans 8:1,2

b. Encouragement: Psalms 23, John 10:10

c. Anxiety: 1 Peter 5:7

d. Faith: Job 42:5

2. Prayer: For recovery, trusting Christ, recommitment of life and faith.

C. The "not too ill" person.
  1. Why me? John 9:2,3
  2. Anxiety: 1 Peter 5:7
  3. Prayer: For recovery and healing, trusting Christ, rededication of life, thanksgiving for health, and faith for recovery.
D. The chronically ill person.
  1. Scripture:
    a. Faith: Matthew 7:7-14, Mark 4:40
    b. Patience: Psalm 61:2, Psalm 135:6, Hebrews 12:1
    c. Comfort: Psalm 86:11-17, Psalm 23
  2. Prayer: for faith, for patience, for seeing God through suffering, for forgiveness and salvation.
E. The "non-ill" person (family, visitors, etc.)
  1. Scripture:
    a. Purpose of life: John 10:10
    b. Purpose of illness: John 9:2
    c. Repentance and salvation: John 3:16, Romans 5:8
  2. Prayer: For comfort of ill, for God's blessing of doctors, nurses, and helpers, for acceptance of God's will, for repentance and salvation.
F. Alcoholics and drug-dependent persons.
  1. Scripture:
    a. For faith: Psalm 55:22
    b. For Encouragement: Matthew 11:28
  2. Prayer: For strength to overcome problems, for forgiveness and salvation, for faith in God to do all things.
G. For persons who attempt suicide.
  1. Scripture: Love of Life: John 10:10, Romans 8:6, Rev. 22:17
  2. Prayer: For forgiveness, for joy of life, for purpose and value of life, for salvation.

Unit X: What the Bible Teaches About Health and Illness

The student should be able to:

Describe and discuss the relationship between health, illness, and spiritual well-being as taught in the Bible.

Content:

A. Health and illness as taught in the Old Testament.

    1. Hebrew philosophy of health and prosperity equal favor from God, but illness and misfortune equal punishment from God? Deuteronomy 30:15-18.

    2. Laws and rituals of the Old Testament.

        a. Sanitation: Exodus 29:14, Deuteronomy 23:12-14

        b. Protection from contamination

            Dead animals: (Lev. 11:32-40)

            Dead persons: (Num. 19:11)

        c. Isolation and Quarantine

            Outside the camp: (Num. 5:1-4)

        d. Leprosy: (Lev. 13:14)

        e. Hygiene, diet, and rest: (Deut. 12:32; Ex. 20:11)

B. Health and illness as taught in the New Testament

    1. Why Jesus healed:

        a. To proclaim the kingdom of God. Matthew 11:1-6; Luke 4:18-21; Luke 10:9; Luke 11:20; John 9:2,3

        b. To show His concern for the well-being of people. Matthew 9:36; 14:14; 20:29-34; Mark 8:2; 1:40-41

        c. To teach the holistic concept of man. Matthew 2:1-12

    2. Jesus commissioned His disciples to heal the sick and demon-possessed. Luke 9:2-6; 10:1-9

    3. Healing in the Apostolic church. Acts 3:1-8; 5:15-16; 16:16-18

    4. Paul taught that healing is one of the gifts of the Holy Spirit. 1 Corinthians 12:9,30

    5. James combined prayer with available treatment. James 5:13-16

Notes

*UNICEF

CHAPTER 10

THE UNFINISHED TASK . . .
BEARERS OF FRUIT

"You did not choose me, but I chose you and appointed you to go and
bear fruit—fruit that will last. Then the Father will
give you whatever you ask in my name" (John 15:16 NIV).

Conclusion

After one has done all that he or she can do, the task will not be
complete. People will still be hungry. Others will continue to live in
abject poverty. War and political unrest will still cause millions to
flee from their homes and live in temporary refugee quarters.
Street children will still roam the avenues of the major cities of the
world. AIDS and other diseases will continue to ravage the bodies
of those being infected. Malnutrition will cause the death of untold
millions of children who do not have the physical strength to resist
even simple illnesses. Drought will scorch the arid plains of Africa,
menacing the lifelines of multitudes with no other recourse.
Human hurt of every variety and in every sector of the world,
especially the poorer nations of the world—will still abound.

What then shall we do? The tendency of some to this kind of prognosis is to throw up their hands and give up. Others naively presume that what they do will solve the world's worst problems. The fact is that we have not been called to solve all the world's problems, but rather to participate in the presence of Christ in the world as His agents and messengers. He is the One Who empowers and transforms, we are the instruments He has chosen to use. Our responsibility is to be found faithful!

There is another viewpoint which arises among evangelicals in particular. In essence, it declares that inasmuch as we cannot solve the physical ills of the world, let us concentrate solely on the spiritual aspects of the work. Christ is coming. We need to reach this world for Him before He returns. Without undermining the vital importance of evangelizing, we cannot afford to be like those sects who, in anticipation of Christ's imminent return, sell all and flee to the hills to await Him. As long as we are in the world, we have a responsibility to carry out both the Great Commission and the Great Commandment. Will He find us working when He comes?

While the content of this book has focused on the importance of project planning and some of the more practical aspects of responding to human needs in the context of the communities where those needs are most apparent, it should not be assumed that incarnational agents do not also have other important tasks. If the church is to deal effectively and fully with the ills of the developing nations of our world, ultimately social action must be directed toward our own governments and those policies which often direct aid funds more toward military operations than humanitarian concerns. In many cases, food has been used as a weapon to enforce political decisions rather than to alleviate human distress. .

Even though there are many countries, either because of their political ideology or religious persuasion, who stand in the way of a positive Christian witness through such ministries, we must not back down from continuing efforts to minister. Some will say that the need is justification to minister even though no witness is possible. While this may be true to some extent, we cannot forget that incarnational agents are those who embody the nature and love of Christ. Their witness cannot be confined to a silent, sentimental, do-gooder kind of humanitarianism. If it is authentically Christian and Christlike, the incarnational agent must, "Always be prepared to give an answer to everyone who asks you to give the reason for the hope that you have" (1 Peter 3:15b NIV).

It is in this respect that those of us who love the Lord Jesus and have chosen to minister to human hurt recognize that we cannot continue accepting all of our Lord's blessings without participating in that which keeps others from knowing Him or having an acceptable quality of life. We do this when we move from the qualities of life which our society may deem they have a right to enjoy, to enable others, who have so little, to transform their lives and the life of their society through Jesus Christ. If this world is ever to have a "New World Order" it will not be brought in by secular nations and physical solutions, but rather by Christ's servants who initiate the transforming process of reconciliation to God, to mankind, and to our environment.

A New World Order Must Be a Transformed World Order

As one engages in projects to provide assistance to those nations and people who have been deprived, it will not be sufficient to simply empower them to become more highly developed in the sense of having bigger and better things. Such issues as injustice and inequality cannot be changed solely by building better houses, creating more jobs, or satisfying the wants of those who look to the West as the utopia for economic and social development.

Modifying circumstances does not modify basic morality or ethical behavior. As was said in the beginning of this book, it takes transformed people to transform society. Even the well intended assistance given by those who espouse Christian motivation can create or engender further dependency and encourage class distinctions. This is especially true when whatever advantages may be provided are limited to the "Christian" community or those of the same denominational persuasion.

One of the disadvantages of using secular terminology to describe the planning processes in projects or programs to enable the less fortunate is that they often ascribe a meaning not intended by Christian practitioners. Hence, terms like contextualizing the gospel, widely used by some who are classified as being associated with liberation theology, becomes misunderstood when used as we have attempted to in this material. In the same way, the term development, as a secular term, means something quite different than that which we would want to express as the uniquely Christian approach to ministries among the less advantaged. During a meeting of evangelicals concerned with world hunger (Wheaton '83 conference), the term "transformation" was widely used and reinterpreted to convey a uniquely Christian process in ministry evangelism. Of course, this cannot take place outside of the experience of rebirth and renewal in which there is such a complete change of mind and heart that the standards of the world no longer become applicable (Rom. 12:2).

In closing, I refer to the last words in the Wheaton '83 Statement. "Finally, we confess our utter dependence on God. We affirm that transformation is, in the final analysis, His work, but work in which He engages us. To this end He has given us His Spirit, the Transformer, par excellence, to enlighten us and be our Counselor (John 16:7), to impart His many gifts to us (Rom. 12; 1 Cor. 12), to equip us to face and conquer the enemy (2 Cor. 10:3-5; Gal. 5:22-23). We are reminded that our unconfessed sins and lack of love for others grieve the Spirit (Eph. 4:30; Gal. 5:13-16). We therefore fervently pray for our sins to be pardoned, for our spirits to be renewed, and for the privilege of being enlisted in the joyous task of enabling God's Kingdom to come; the Kingdom 'of . . . justice, peace, and joy in the Holy Spirit'" (Rom. 14:17).*

Notes
*See pages 216-232 and following for the complete Wheaton '83 Statement.

APPENDIX

Rank Order Listing of World's 73 Largest Urban Agglomerations
The concept of agglomeration defines the population contained within the contours of contiguous territory inhabited at urban levels of residential density without regard to administrative boundaries.

(Population in millions)

		1990	2000			1990	2000
1.	Mexico City	20.2	25.6	8.	Buenos Aires	11.5	12.9
2.	Tokyo	18.1	19.0	9.	Bombay	11.2	15.4
3.	São Paulo	17.4	22.1	10.	Seoul	11.0	12.7
4.	New York	16.2	16.8	11.	Beijing	10.8	14.0
5.	Shanghai	13.4	17.0	12.	Rio de Janeiro	10.7	12.5
6.	Los Angeles	11.9	13.9	13.	Tianjin	9.4	12.7
7.	Calcutta	11.8	15.7	14.	Djakarta	9.3	13.7

		1990	2000			1990	2000
15.	Cairo	9.0	11.8	44.	Alexandria	3.7	5.1
16.	Delhi	8.8	13.2	45.	Detroit	3.7	3.7
17.	Metro Manila	8.5	11.8	46.	Guangzhou	3.7	4.8
18.	Osaka	8.5	8.6	47.	San Francisco	3.7	4.1
19.	Paris	8.5	8.6	48.	Ahmadabad	3.6	5.3
20.	Karachi	7.7	11.7	49.	Belo Horizonte	3.6	4.7
21.	Lagos	7.7	12.9	50.	Naples	3.6	3.6
22.	London	7.4	7.5	51.	Hyderabad, India	3.5	5.0
23.	Bangkok	7.2	10.3	52.	Kinshasa	3.5	5.5
24.	Chicago	7.0	7.3	53.	Toronto	3.5	3.9
25.	Tehran	6.8	8.5	54.	Athens	3.4	3.8
26.	Istanbul	6.7	9.5	55.	Barcelona	3.4	3.7
27.	Dacca	6.6	12.2	56.	Katowice	3.4	3.7
28.	Lima	6.2	8.2	57.	Sydney	3.4	3.7
29.	Madras	5.7	5.8	58.	Yangon, Myanmar	3.3	4.7
30.	Hong Kong	5.4	6.1	59.	Casablanca	3.2	4.6
31.	Milan	5.3	5.4	60.	Chongqing	3.2	4.2
32.	Madrid	5.2	5.9	61.	Guadalajara	3.2	4.1
33.	Leningrad	5.1	5.4	62.	Ho Chi Minh City	3.2	4.1
34.	Bangalore	5.0	8.2	63.	Pôrto Alegre	3.1	4.0
35.	Bogota	4.9	6.4	64.	Rome	3.1	3.1
36.	Shenyang	4.8	6.3	65.	Algiers	3.0	4.5
37.	Santiago, Chile	4.7	5.6	66.	Chengdu	3.0	4.1
38.	Philadelphia	4.3	4.5	67.	Harbin	3.0	3.9
39.	Caracas	4.1	5.2	68.	Houston	3.0	3.6
40.	Lahore	4.1	6.0	69.	Monterrey, Mexico	3.0	3.9
41.	Baghdad	4.0	5.1	70.	Montreal	3.0	3.1
42.	Pusan	3.9	4.3	71.	Taipei	3.0	4.2
43.	Wuhan	3.9	4.3				

World Eagle Table. Data from United Nations Urban Agglomeration Chart 1990.

Percentage of Urban Population Living in Slums and Squatter Settlements
(52 cities which head the list)

Addis Ababa, Ethiopia	90	Lusaka, Zambia	50
Yaoundé, Cameroon	90	Maracaibo, Venezuela	50
Douala, Cameroon	87	Monrovia, Liberia	50
Buenaventura, Colombia	80	Recife, Brazil	50
Mogadishu, Somalia	77	Guayaquil, Ecuador	49
Ibadan, Nigeria	75	Mexico City, Mexico	46
Lomé, Togo	75	Phnom Penh, Cambodia	46
Santo Domingo, D. R.	72	Bombay, India	45
Casablanca, Morocco	70	Colombo, Sri Lanka	44
Nairobi, Kenya	70	Tunis, Tunisia	43
Calcutta, India	67	Caracas, Venezuela	42
Chimbote, Peru	67	Barquisimeto, Venezuela	41
Mombasa, Kenya	67	Brasilia, Brazil	41
Izmir, Turkey	65	Arequipa, Peru	40
Accra, Ghana	61	Ciudad Guyana, Venezuela	40
Abidjan, Ivory Coast	60	Istanbul, Turkey	40
Agra, India	60	Lima, Peru	40
Ankara, Turkey	60	Kuala Lumpur, Malaysia	37
Bogota, Colombia	60	Delhi, India	36
Dakar, Senegal	60	Manila, Philippines	35
Kinshasa, Zaire	60	Antananarivo, Madagascar	33
Rabat, Morocco	60	Makassar, Indonesia	33
Blantyre, Malawi	56	Pusan, South Korea	31
Port Sudan, Sudan	55	Cali, Colombia	30
Ouagadougou, Burkina Faso	52	Guatemala City, Guatemala	30
Dar es Salaam, Tanzania	50	Rio de Janeiro, Brazil	30

Transformation: The Church in Response to Human Need
The Wheaton '83 Statement

Introduction

For two weeks during June 1983 we have come together from local churches and Christian missions and aid agencies at Wheaton College in the USA from 30 nations to pray about and reflect upon the church's task in response to human need. Some of us belong to churches which are situated among marginalized peoples who live in situations of poverty, powerlessness, and oppression. Others come from churches situated in affluent areas of the world. We are deeply grateful to our heavenly Father for allowing us the privilege of sharing our lives with one another, studying the Scriptures in small groups, considering papers on aspects of human development and transformation, and looking closely at the implications of case studies and histories which describe different responses to human need. Because God hears the cries of the poor, we have sought each other's help to respond (Ex. 3:7-9; James 5:1-6). We rejoice at what we believe the Holy Spirit has been teaching us concerning God's specific purpose and plans for His distressed world and the part the church has to play in them.

As we have faced the enormous challenge before God's people everywhere to alleviate suffering and, in partnership together, to eliminate its causes, we are more than ever aware of the liberating and healing power of the good news of Jesus. We gladly reaffirm, therefore, our conviction that Jesus Christ alone is the world's peace, for He alone can reconcile people to God and bring all hostilities to an end. (Eph. 2:14-17).

We acknowledge, furthermore, that only by spreading the gospel can the most basic need of human beings be met: to have fellowship with God. In what follows we do not emphasize evangelism as a separate theme, because we see it as an integral part of our total Christian response to human need (Matt. 28:18-21). In addition, it is not necessary simply to repeat what the Lausanne Covenant and the Report of the Consultation on the Relationship

Between Evangelism and Social Responsibility (CRESR, Grand Rapids, 1982) have already expressed.

What we have discovered we would like to share with our brothers and sisters throughout the world. We offer this statement, not as an attempt to produce a final word, but as a summary of our reflections.

Both Scripture and experience, informed by the Spirit, emphasize that God's people are dependent upon His wisdom in confronting human need. Local churches and missions agencies, then, should act wisely, if they are to be both pastoral and prophetic. Indeed, the whole human family with its illusions and divisions needs Christ to be its wisdom as well as its Savior and King.

Conscious of our struggle to find a biblical view of transformation that relates its working in the heart of believers to its multiplying effects in society, we pray that the Spirit will give us the discernment we need. We believe that the wisdom the Spirit inspires is practical rather than academic, and the possession of the faithful rather than the preserve of the elite. Because we write as part of a world full of conflict and a church easily torn by strife we desire that the convictions expressed in this document be further refined by God's pure and peaceable wisdom.

Some may find our words hard. We pray, however, that many will find them a help to their own thinking and an encouragement to "always give yourselves fully to the work of the Lord, because you know that your labor in the Lord is not in vain" (1 Cor. 15:58*b* NIV).

I. Christian Social Involvement

1. As Christians reflect on God's intention for the world they are often tempted to be either naively optimistic or darkly pessimistic. Some, inspired by a utopian vision seem to suggest that God's Kingdom, in all its fullness, can be built on earth. We do not subscribe to this view, since Scripture informs us of the reality and pervasiveness of both personal and societal sin (Isa. 1:10-26; Amos 2:6-8; Mic. 2:1-10; Rom. 1:28-32). Thus we recognize that utopianism is nothing but a false dream (see the CRESR Report, IV, A).

2. Other Christians become pessimistic because they are faced with the reality of increasing poverty and misery, of rampant oppression and exploitation by powers of the right and the left, of spiraling violence coupled with the threat of nuclear warfare. They are concerned, too, about the increasing possibility that planet earth will not be able to sustain its population for long because of the wanton squandering of its resources. As a result, they are tempted to turn their eyes away from this world and fix them so exclusively on the return of Christ that their involvement in the here and now is paralyzed. We do not wish to disregard or minimize the extensive contribution made by a succession of Christians who have held this view of eschatology, through more than 100 years, to medical and educational work in many countries up to the present day. Nevertheless, some of us feel that these men and women have tended to see the task of the church as merely picking up survivors from a shipwreck in a hostile sea. We do not endorse this view either, since it denies the biblical injunctions to defend the cause of the weak, maintain the right of the poor and oppressed (Psalm 82:3), and practice justice and love (Mic. 6:8).

3. We affirm, moreover, that even though we may believe that our calling is only to proclaim the gospel and not get involved in political and other actions, our very noninvolvement lends tacit support to the existing order. There is no escape; either we challenge the evil structures of society or we support them.

4. There have been many occasions in the history of the church, and some exist today, where Christians, faced with persecution and oppression, have appeared to be disengaged from society and thus to support the status quo. We suggest, however, that even under conditions of the most severe repression, such Christians may in fact be challenging society and even be transforming it, through their lifestyle, their selfless love, their quiet joy, their inner peace, and their patient suffering (1 Peter 2:21-25).

5. Christ's followers, therefore, are called, in one way or another, not to conform to the values of society but to transform them (Rom. 12:1-2; Eph. 5:8-14). This calling flows from our confession

that God loves the world and that the earth belongs to Him. It is true that Satan is active in this world, even claiming it to be his (Luke 4:5-7). He is, however, a usurper, having no property rights here. All authority in heaven and on earth has been given to Christ Jesus (Matt. 28:18; Col. 1:15-20). Although His Lordship is not yet acknowledged by all (Heb. 2:8) He is the ruler of the kings of the earth (Rev. 1:5), King of kings and Lord of lords. (Rev. 19:16). In faith we confess that the old order is passing away; the new order has already begun (2 Cor. 5:17; Eph. 2:7-10; Matt. 12:18; Luke 7:21-23).

II. Not Only Development but Transformation

6. The participants at this conference have entered into the current discussions concerning development. For many Western political and business leaders, development describes the process by which nations and peoples become part of the existing international economic order. For many people of the Two-Thirds World it is identified with an ideologically motivated process of change, called "developmentalism." This process is intrinsically related to a mechanistic pursuit of economic growth that tends to ignore the structural context of poverty and injustice and which increases dependency and inequality.

7. Some of us still believe, however, that "development," when reinterpreted in the light of the whole message of the Bible, is a concept that should be retained by Christians. Part of the reason for this choice is that the word is so widely used. A change of term, therefore, would cause unnecessary confusion.

8. Others in our consultation, because of difficulty in relating it to biblical categories of thought and its negative overtones, would like to replace "development" with another word. An alternative we suggest is "transformation," as it can be applied in different ways to every situation. Western nations, for example, who have generally assumed that development does not apply to them, are, nevertheless, in need of transformation in many areas. In particular, the unspoken assumption that societies

operate best when individuals are most free to pursue their own self-interests needs to be challenged on the basis of the biblical teaching on stewardship (Luke 12:13-21; 16:13-15; Phil. 2:1-4). People living in groups based on community solidarity may help these kinds of societies see the poverty of their existence.

9. Moreover, the term "transformation," unlike "development," does not have a suspect past. It points to a number of changes that have to take place in many societies if poor people are to enjoy their rightful heritage in creation.

10. We are concerned, however, that both the goals and the process of transformation should be seen in the light of the good news about Jesus, the Messiah. We commit ourselves and urge other Christian believers to reject the cultural and social forces of secularism which so often shape our idea of a good society. We believe that notions alien to God's plan for human living are often more powerful in forming our opinion about what is right for a nation than the message of Scripture itself.

11. According to the biblical view of human life, then, transformation is the change from a condition of human existence contrary to God's purposes to one in which people are able to enjoy fullness of life in harmony with God (John 10:10; Col. 3:8-15; Eph. 4:13). This transformation can only take place through the obedience of individuals and communities to the Gospel of Jesus Christ, whose power changes the lives of men and women by releasing them from the guilt, power, and consequences of sin, enabling them to respond with love toward God and toward others (Rom. 5:5), and making them new creatures in Christ. (2 Cor. 5:17)

12. There are a number of themes in the Bible which help us focus on the way we understand transformation. The doctrine of creation speaks of the worth of every man, woman, and child, of the responsibility of human beings to look after the resources of nature (Gen. 1:26-30) and to share them equitably with their neighbors. The doctrine of the Fall highlights the innate tendency of human beings to serve their own interests, with the consequences of greed, insecurity, violence, and the lust for power.

God's judgment rightly falls upon those who do such things. (Rom. 2:2) The doctrine of redemption proclaims God's forgiveness of sins and the freedom Christ gives for a way of life dedicated to serving others by telling them about the good news of salvation, bringing reconciliation between enemies, and losing one's life to see justice established for all exploited people.

13. We have come to see that the goal of transformation is best described by the biblical vision of the Kingdom of God. This new way of being human in submission to the Lord of all has many facets. In particular, it means striving to bring peace among individuals, races, and nations by overcoming prejudices, fears, and preconceived ideas about others. It means sharing basic resources like food, water, the means of healing, and knowledge. It also means working for a greater participation of people in the decisions which affect their lives, making possible an equal receiving from others and giving of themselves. Finally, it means growing up into Christ in all things as a body of people dependent upon the work of the Holy Spirit and upon each other.

III. The Stewardship of Creation

14. "The earth is the Lord's, and everything in it" (Psalm 24:1a NIV); "The land is mine" (Lev. 25:23b NIV). All human beings are God's creatures. As made in His image they are His representatives, given the responsibility of caring wisely for His creation. We have to confess, however, that God's people have been slow to recognize the full implications of their responsibility. As His stewards, we do not own the earth but we manage and enhance it in anticipation of Christ's return. Too often, however, we have assumed a right to use His natural resources indiscriminately. We have frequently been indifferent, or even hostile, to those committed to the conservation of nonrenewable sources of energy and minerals, of animal life in danger of extinction, and of the precarious ecological balance of many natural habitats. The earth is God's gift to all generations. An

African proverb says that parents have borrowed the present from their children. Both our present life and our children's future depend upon our wise and peaceful treatment of the whole earth.

15. We have also assumed that only a small portion of our income and wealth, the "tithe," belongs to the Lord, the rest being ours to dispose of as we like. This impoverishes other people and denies our identity and role as stewards. We believe that Christians everywhere, but especially those who are enjoying in abundance the good things of life (Luke 16:25), must faithfully obey the command to ensure that others have their basic needs met. In this way those who are poor now will also be able to enjoy the blessings of giving to others.

16. Through salvation, Jesus lifts us out of our isolation from God and other people and establishes us within the worldwide community of the Body of Christ. Belonging to the Body involves sharing all God's gifts to us, so that there might be equality among all members (2 Cor. 8:14-15). To the extent that this standard is obeyed, dire poverty will be eliminated (Acts 2:42-47).

17. When either individuals or states claim an absolute right of ownership, that is rebellion against God. The meaning of stewardship is that the poor have equal rights to God's resources (Deut. 15:8-9). The meaning of transformation is that, as stewards of God's bountiful gifts, we do justice, striving together through prayer, example, representation, and protest to have resources redistributed and the consequences of greed limited (Acts 4:32; 5:11).

18. We are perturbed by the perverse misuse of huge amounts of resources in the present arms race. While millions starve to death, resources are wasted on the research and production of increasingly sophisticated nuclear weapon systems. Moreover, the constantly escalating global trade in conventional arms accompanies the proliferation of oppressive governments which disregard people's elementary needs. As Christians we condemn these new expressions of injustice and aggression,

affirming our commitment to seek peace with justice. In the light of the issue of the stewardship of creation we have discussed here, we call on the worldwide evangelical community to make the nuclear and arms trade questions a matter of prayerful concern and to place it on their agenda for study and action.

IV. Culture and Transformation

19. Culture includes worldviews, beliefs, values, art forms, customs, laws, socioeconomic structures, social relationships, and material things shared by a population over time in a specific area or context.

20. Culture is God's gift to human beings. God has made people everywhere in His image. As Creator, He has made us creative. This creativity produces cultures. Furthermore, God has commissioned us to be stewards of His creation (Psalm 8; Heb. 2:5-11). Since every good gift is from above and since all wisdom and knowledge comes from Jesus Christ, whatever is good and beautiful in cultures may be seen as a gift of God (James 1:16-18). Moreover, where the gospel has been heard and obeyed, cultures have become further ennobled and enriched.

21. However, people have sinned by rebelling against God. Therefore the cultures we produce are infected with evil. Different aspects of our culture show plainly our separation from God. Social structures and relationships, art forms, and laws often reflect our violence, our sense of lostness, and our loss of coherent moral values. Scripture challenges us not to be conformed to this world (Rom. 12:2) insofar as it is alienated from its Creator. We need to be transformed so that cultures may display again what is good and acceptable and perfect. (Rom. 12:2)

22. Cultures, then, bear the marks of God's common grace, demonic influences, and mechanisms of human exploitation. In our cultural creativity, God and Satan clash. The Lord used the Greek culture to give us the New Testament, while at the same time He subjected that culture to the judgment of the gospel. We too should make thankful use of cultures and yet, at the same time,

examine them in the light of the gospel to expose the evil in them (1 Cor. 9:19-23).

23. Social structures that exploit and dehumanize constitute a pervasive sin which is not confronted adequately by the church. Many churches, mission societies, and Christian relief and development agencies support the sociopolitical status quo, and by silence give their tacit support.

24. Through application of the Scriptures, in the power of the Spirit, we seek to discern the true reality of all sociocultural situations. We need to learn critically from both functionalist and conflict approaches to human culture. The "functionalist socio-anthropology" approach emphasizes the harmonious aspect of different cultures and champions a tolerant attitude to the existing structures. This position is often adopted in the name of "scientific objectivity." By contrast, the "conflict" approach exposes the contradictory nature of social structures and makes us aware of the underlying conflict of interests. We must remember that both approaches come under the judgment of God.

25. Given the conflicting ethical tendencies in our nature, which find expression in our cultural systems, we must be neither naively optimistic nor wrongly judgmental. We are called to be a new community that seeks to work with God in the transformation of our societies, men and women of God in society, salt of the earth, and light of the world (Matt. 5:13-16). We seek to bring people and their cultures under the Lordship of Christ. In spite of our failure, we move toward that freedom and wholeness in a more just community that persons will enjoy when our Lord returns to consummate His Kingdom (Rev. 21:1; 22:6).

V. Social Justice and Mercy

26. Our time together enabled us to see that poverty is not a necessary evil but often the result of social, economic, political, and religious systems marked by injustice, exploitation, and oppression. Approximately 800 million people in the world are destitute, and their plight is often maintained by the rich and the powerful. Evil

is not only in the human heart but also in social structures. Because God is just and merciful, hating evil and loving righteousness, there is an urgent need for Christians in the present circumstances to commit ourselves to acting in mercy and seeking justice. The mission of the church includes both the proclamation of the gospel and its demonstration. We must therefore evangelize, respond to immediate human needs, and press for social transformation. The means we use, however, must be consistent with the end we desire.

27. As we thought of the task before us, we considered Jesus' attitude toward the power structures of His time. He was neither a zealot nor a passive spectator of the oppression of His people. Rather, moved by compassion, He identified Himself with the poor, whom He saw as "harassed and helpless, like sheep without a shepherd" (Matt. 9:36). Through His acts of mercy, teaching, and lifestyle, He exposed the injustices in society and condemned the self-righteousness of its leaders (Matt. 23:25; Luke 6:37-42). His was a prophetic compassion and it resulted in the formation of a community which accepted the values of the Kingdom of God and stood in contrast to the Roman and Jewish establishment. We were challenged to follow Jesus' footsteps, remembering that His compassion led Him to death (John 13:12-17; Phil. 2:6-8; 1 John 3:11-18).

28. We are aware that a Christlike identification with the poor, whether at home or abroad, in the North, South, East, or West, is always costly and may lead us also to persecution and even death. Therefore, we humbly ask God to make us willing to risk our comfort, even our lives, for the sake of the gospel, knowing that "everyone who wants to live a godly life in Christ Jesus will be persecuted" (2 Tim. 3:12).

29. Sometimes in our ministry among the poor we face a serious dilemma: to limit ourselves to acts of mercy to improve their lot, or to go beyond that and seek to rectify the injustice that makes such acts of mercy necessary. This step in turn may put at risk the freedom we need to continue our ministry. No rule of thumb can be given, but from a biblical perspective it is clear that justice and

mercy belong together (Isa. 11:1-5; Ps. 113:5-9). We must therefore make every possible effort to combine both in our ministry and be willing to suffer the consequences. We must also remember that acts of mercy highlight the injustices of the social, economic, and political structures and relationships; whether we like it or not, they may therefore lead us into confrontation with those who hold power (Acts 4:5-22). For the same reason, we must stand together with those who suffer for the sake of justice (Heb. 13:3).

30. Our ministry of justice and healing is not limited to fellow Christians. Our love and commitment must extend to the stranger (Matt. 5:43-48). Our involvement with strangers is not only through charity, but also through economic and political action. Justice must characterize the government's laws and policies toward the poor. Our economic and political action is inseparable from evangelism.

31. Injustice in the modern world has reached global proportions. Many of us come from countries dominated by international business corporations, and some from those whose political systems are not accountable to the people. We are witnesses to the damaging effects that these economic and political institutions are having on people, especially on the poorest of the poor. We call on our brothers and sisters in Jesus Christ to study seriously this situation and to seek ways to bring about change in favor of the oppressed. "The righteous care about justice for the poor, but the wicked have no such concern" (Prov. 29:7).

VI. The Local Church and Transformation

32. The local church is the basic unit of Christian society. The churches in the New Testament were made up of men and women who had experienced transformation through receiving Jesus Christ as Savior, acknowledging Him as Lord, and incarnating His servant ministry by demonstrating the values of the kingdom both personally and in community (Mark 10:35-45; 1 Peter 2:5; 4:10). Today similar examples of transformed lives abound in churches worldwide.

33. We recognize that across the generations local churches have been the vehicle for the transmission of the gospel of Jesus Christ, and that their primary, though not their only, role is a threefold ministry: the worship and praise of God; the proclamation in word and deed of the gospel of the grace of God; and the nurture, instruction, and discipleship of those who have received Jesus Christ into their lives. In this way transformation takes place in the lives of Christians as individuals, families, and communities; through their words and deeds they demonstrate both the need and reality of ethical, moral, and social transformation.

34. All churches are faced at times with the choice between speaking openly against social evils and not speaking out publicly. The purpose for the particular choice should be obedience to the Lord of the church to fulfill its ministry. Wisdom will be needed so that the church will neither speak rashly and make its witness ineffective nor remain silent when to do so would deny its prophetic calling (1 Peter 3:13-17). If we are sensitive to the Holy Spirit and are socially aware, we will always be ready to reassess our attitude toward social issues (Luke 18:24-30).

35. Integrity, leadership, and information are essential for the transformation of attitudes and lifestyles of members of local churches. Churches are made up of people whose lives are pressured by the way their neighbors spend their money. They are often more aware of this than of the suffering and human need in their own and other countries. Often, too, they are reluctant to expose themselves to the traumas of global need and to information which would challenge their comfort. If church leadership fails to adequately stress the social dimensions of the gospel, church members may often overlook these issues (1 Tim. 3:1-7; Heb. 13:17).

36. We should be sensitive and responsive to needs within the local church. Widows, prisoners, the poor, and strangers are people who are particularly the responsibility of the local church (Gal. 6:10). We should attempt to be well informed about local

human need and to seek God's will for us in meeting those needs. We should seek to minister to the poor in our local area who are not members of the church (James 1:27; Rom. 12:17).

37. Our churches must also address issues of evil and of social injustice in the local community and the wider society. Our methodology should involve study, earnest prayer, and action within the normative, ethical guidelines for Christian conduct set out in Scripture. Within these guidelines there are times, no matter the political system, when protest can be effective. Christians should carefully consider the issues and the manner in which they protest so that the identity and message of the church is neither blurred nor drowned.

38. The local church has, however, to be understood as being a part of the universal church. There is therefore a genuine need for help and sharing (*diakonia*) built on fellowship (*Koinonia*) between churches of different localities and contexts. In this connection we considered a model for relating churches in different areas of the world. In such "church twinnings" the relationship should be genuinely reciprocal with giving and receiving at both ends, from paternalism of any kind (Rom. 15:1-7).

39. Such reciprocal relationships in a spirit of true mutuality are particularly needed in view of the fact that every local church always lives on the edge of compromise with its context (Rom. 12:3-18). Some churches are immersed in the problems of materialism and racism, others in those of oppression and the option of violence. We may help each other by seeking to see the world through the eyes of our brothers and sisters.

40. With regard to the wider world community, Christian churches should identify and exchange people who are equipped through their personal characteristics, training, and Christian maturity to work across cultures in the name of Christ and of the sending church. These men and women would go as servants and stewards characterized by humility and meekness; and they would work together with members of the Body of Christ in the countries to which they go.

VII. Christian Aid Agencies and Transformation

41. In reflecting upon the Christian response to human need, we have recognized the central place of the local church as the vehicle for communicating the gospel of Jesus Christ both in word and deed. Churches around the world have throughout history displayed active concern for the needs around them and continue to serve the needy. We call upon the aid agencies to see their role as one of facilitating the churches in the fulfillment of their mission.

42. We recognize the progress which in recent years has been made in our understanding of the gospel and its social and political implications. We also recognize, however, the deficiencies in our witness and affirm our desire for a fuller understanding of the biblical basis for our ministry.

43. We acknowledge that the constituency of the aid agencies is generally concerned with human suffering, hunger, and need. However, we recognize that this concern is not consistently expressed with integrity. In efforts to raise funds, the plight of the poor is often exploited in order to meet donor needs and expectations. Fund-raising activities must be in accordance with the gospel. A stewardship responsibility of agencies is to reduce significantly their overheads in order to maximize the resources for the ministry.

44. We are challenged to implement in our organizations a positive transformation demonstrating the values of Christ and His Kingdom which we wish to share with others. We must, for example, avoid competition with others involved in the same ministry and a success mentality that forgets God's special concern for the weak and "unsuccessful" (Gal. 2:10; Psalm 147:6). We should continually review our actions to ensure biblical integrity and genuine partnership with churches and other agencies. Decisions on ministry policy, including how resources are to be used, need to be made in consultation with the people to be served.

45. We need to ensure that our promotional efforts describe what

we are actually doing. We accept the responsibility of educating our donors in the full implications of the way Christian transformation is experienced in the field. The Holy Spirit has led us to this ministry. In accepting the responsibility of education we recognize the process may cause some to question our approach. We will strive to educate with a sense of humility, patience, and courage.

46. In all of our programs and actions we should remember that God in His sovereignty and love is already active in the communities we seek to serve (Acts 14:17; 17:23; Rom. 2:9-15). Agencies, therefore, should give adequate priority to listening sensitively to the concerns of these communities, facilitating a two-way process in communication and local ownership of programs. The guiding principle is equitable partnership in which local people and Western agencies cooperate together. Many models for development have originated in the Two-Thirds World. Christian aid agencies should in every way encourage these local initiatives to succeed. In this way the redeemed community of the Kingdom will be able to experiment with a number of models of transformation.

47. The agencies' legitimate need for accountability to donors often results in the imposition of Western management systems on local communities. This assumes that Western planning and control systems are the only ones which can ensure accountability. Since the communities these agencies seek to serve are often part of a different culture, this imposition can restrict and inhibit the sensitive processes of social transformation. We call on development agencies to establish a dialogue with those they serve in order to permit the creation of systems of accountability with respect to both cultures. Our ministry must always reflect our mutual interdependence in the Kingdom (Rom. 14:17-18; 1 Cor. 12).

48. In focusing on the apparently conflicting requirements of our action as Christian agencies, we are conscious of our sin and compromise. In a call to repentance we include a renunciation

of inconsistency and extravagance in our personal and institutional lifestyles. We ask the Spirit of truth to lead us and make us true agents of transformation (Acts 1:8).

VIII. The Coming of the Kingdom and the Church's Mission

49. We affirm that the Kingdom of God is both present and future, both societal and individual, both physical and spiritual. If others have overemphasized the present, the societal, and the physical, we ought to confess that we have tended to neglect those dimensions of the biblical message. We, therefore, joyfully proclaim that the Kingdom has broken into human history in the resurrection of Christ. It grows like a mustard seed, both judging and transforming the present age.

50. Even if God's activity in history is focused on the church, it is not confined to the church. God's particular focus on the church, as on Israel in the Old Testament, has as its purpose the blessing of the nations (Gen. 12:1-3;15;17; Isa. 42:6). Thus the church is called to exist for the sake of its Lord and for the sake of humankind (Matt. 22:32-40).

51. The church is called to infuse the world with hope, for both this age and the next. Our hope does not flow from despair; it is not because the present is empty that we hope for a new future (Rom. 5:1-11). Rather, we hope for that future because of what God has already done and because of what He has promised yet to do. We have already been given the Holy Spirit as the guarantee of our full redemption and of the coming of the day when God will be all in all (1 Cor. 15:28). As we witness to the gospel of present salvation and future hope, we identify with the awesome birth pangs of God's new creation (Rom. 8:22). As the community of the end time anticipating the End, we prepare for the ultimate by getting involved in the penultimate (Matt. 24:36; 25:46).

52. For this reason we are challenged to commit ourselves to a truly vigorous and full-orbed mission in the world, combining explosive creativity with painstaking faithfulness in small things.

Our mission and vision are to be nurtured by the whole counsel of God (2 Tim. 3:16). A repentant, revived, and vigorous church will call people to true repentance and faith and at the same time equip them to challenge the forces of evil and injustice (2 Tim. 3:17). We thus move forward, without either relegating salvation merely to an eternal future or making it synonymous with a political or social dispensation to be achieved in the here and now. The Holy Spirit empowers us to serve and proclaim Him Who has been raised from the dead, seated at the right hand of the Father, and given to the church as Head over all things in heaven and on earth (Eph. 1:10, 20-22).

53. Finally, we confess our utter dependence on God. We affirm that transformation is, in the final analysis, His work, but work in which He engages us. To this end He has given us His Spirit, the Transformer par excellence, to enlighten us and be our Counselor (John 16:7), to impart His many gifts to us (Rom. 12; 1 Cor. 12), to equip us to face and conquer the enemy (2 Cor. 10:3-5; Gal. 5:22-23). We are reminded that our unconfessed sins and lack of love for others grieve the Spirit (Eph. 4:30; Gal. 5:13-16). We therefore fervently pray for our sins to be pardoned, for our spirit to be renewed, and for the privilege of being enlisted in the joyous task of enabling God's Kingdom to come; the Kingdom "of . . . justice, peace, and joy in the Holy Spirit" (Rom. 14:17).*

Note
*The statement may also be found in the book of conference lecture, titled, *The Church in Response to Human Need*, published by William B. Eerdmans Publishing Company, Grand Rapids, MI, 1987.

Community Survey*

Begin by making yourself known:

Hello, my name is _____. I am one of a group from _____ church which is gathering information from the people of the neighborhood. We are talking with people from all parts of this area. Your family has been chosen as one of many to represent people of this area. We would be pleased to get your thoughts. We are attempting to find ways to help your community.

Interviewer's Name:

_____ | 1 |

Place of Interview:

_____ | 2 |

Location/Village:

_____ | 3 | | 4 |

Household/Interview Number:

_____ | 5 | | 6 |

Computer ID Number:

_____

1. Age of person interviewed:
❑ 16-20   ❑ 21-30   ❑ 31-40   ❑ 41-50   ❑ 51+ | 7 |

2. Sex: ❑ male   ❑ female | 8 |

3. Marital status:
❑ Single   ❑ Married   ❑ Widowed
❑ Separated   ❑ Divorced | 9 |

4. Number of people in this house:

(indicate number, include everyone):

Age Group	Total	Males	In School
0 to 5 years	10		11
6 to 15 years	12		13
16 to 25 years	14	15	16
26 to 50 years	17	18	19
51+ years	20	21	

5. How many children have been born in your family this past year?

| 22 |

Total born in this home?

| 23 |

6. How many years have you lived in this neighborhood?

❑ less than one year ❑ 1-2 years ❑ 3-5 years

❑ 6-10 years ❑ more than 10

| 24 |

7. Place of birth:

| 25 |

If born outside of the city, ask the following questions:

8. Reason for coming to this location:

❑ work ❑ higher wage ❑ health ❑ housing

❑ education of children ❑ your own education

❑ others, explain

| 26 |

9. How many times do you visit your home area a year?
❑ more than 5 ❑ between 2 and 5 ❑ once a year
❑ less than one ❑ never

27

10. Do you plan to return home one day to reside there?
❑ yes ❑ no ❑ don't know

28

11. Do you have a farm or cows on a farm in your home area?
❑ farm only ❑ cows only
❑ cows and farm ❑ nothing

29

12. What animals do you keep in town?
Sheep/goats ❑ yes ❑ no

30

Chickens ❑ yes ❑ no

31

Cows ❑ yes ❑ no

32

13. Do you cultivate land anywhere in this area?
❑ yes ❑ no

33

14. What do you need most among these? Read choices and check only one response.
❑ Blanket ❑ School uniform ❑ Dress clothes
❑ Adults' clothes ❑ Children's clothes ❑ Other

34

15. Where do you get your clothes?
❑ Shop in town ❑ Local shop ❑ Open market
❑ Tailor ❑ Sew your own at home ❑ Other

35

16. How many times does your family eat a day?
❑ one ❑ two ❑ three ❑ more than three

36

17. How often does your family eat these foods?

	beans	fruit	eggs	meat
A few days a week				
Every day				
Once a week				
Occasionally				
	37	38	39	40

18. Which of these do you own? (Read each item and indicate with a check those owned)

❏ Bed 41

❏ Mattress 44

❏ Television 42

❏ Radio 45

❏ Bicycle 43

❏ Cassette player 46

19. Circle highest level reached in school.

Primary   0   1   2   3   4   5   6   7   8

Secondary   I   II   III   IV   V   VI

Government Secondary. (Explain)

47

20. What is the greatest difficulty in educating children in this area?

48

21. Would you like to be taught a trade or skill?

49

❏ yes   ❏ no

22. What work would you like to be taught?

_____ 50

23. Do you read a newspaper three or more times a week?
❑ yes ❑ no 51

24. What language do you prefer for reading?

_____ 52

25. What work do you do now?
❑ Carpenter ❑ Mason ❑ Student ❑ Mechanic
❑ Watchman ❑ Teacher ❑ Shopkeeper ❑ Tailor
❑ Day Labor ❑ I don't work
❑ Other

53

26. Major skill, check only one:
❑ Knitting/sewing cloth ❑ Mason ❑ Carpentry
❑ Sewing clothes ❑ Mechanic ❑ Handicrafts
❑ Hawking small items ❑ Other 54

27. What do you do in your spare time when you have no urgent activities?

_____ 55

28. How often do you listen to the radio/television?

_____ / _____ Every day

_____ / _____ Often during week

_____ / _____ Every week

_____ / _____ Less than once a week

56

_____ / _____ I don't listen to them

238

29. Where do you go to talk with others?
❏ Homes ❏ Religious buildings ❏ Market
❏ Shops ❏ Bank ❏ Club
❏ Discussion or meeting places ❏ Other places

57

30. If you could choose, which of these would you prefer in your neighborhood?
❏ Clinic ❏ Playing field ❏ Church
❏ Meeting place ❏ Library ❏ Nursery school

58

31. What two things do you use your money for most?
❏ Food ❏ Rent ❏ Kerosene ❏ Water

59

❏ Travel cost ❏ Medicine ❏ School fees ❏ Others

60

32. If you had twice the money, what would you do?

61

33. Where does the water to your household come from?
❏ Rain or snow ❏ Standpipe ❏ River or canal
❏ Well ❏ Lake or pond ❏ City system ❏ Other

62

34. How much water does your family use during a day?
❏ 3 gallons/11.35 liters ❏ 10 gallons/37.85 liters
❏ 6 gallons/22.70 liters ❏ More
❏ 9 gallons/34.5 liters ❏ Less

63

35. Do you do anything to make your water safe to drink?
❏ Yes ❏ No
If yes, explain:

64

36. How do members of your household dispose of garbage and trash?

[65]

37. How do members of your household dispose of human wastes?

Where?

[66]

38. Was someone in your family sick last month?
❏ yes ❏ no
If yes, explain:

[67]

39. One symptom:
❏ fever ❏ cough ❏ diarrhea ❏ vomiting
❏ itching ❏ pain in body ❏ weakness
❏ others (explain)

[68]

40. Where person was treated:
❏ Clinic of City Council ❏ Lions Clinic ❏ Home
❏ Hospital ❏ Not treated ❏ Other

[69]

41. Did anyone in your family die last year? ❏ Yes ❏ No
If yes, do you know why?

[70]

42. What age were those that died?

[71]

43. Who delivered the children in your household?

72

44. Were the children in your household born at home, in the health center, or in the hospital?

73

45. Have you attended any classes on nutrition?
❑ Yes   ❑ No
If no, why haven't you?

74

46. Describe what each of the following in your household eat:
Pregnant women

Infants

Children ages 1 to 5

75

47. Do mothers in your household breast-feed their babies?
❑ Yes   ❑ No
If yes, how long?

76

48. How many children are best in one family? (choose one)

    0   1   2   3   4   5

    6   7   8   9   10   or more

77

*If the respondent has children living with him/her,
ask questions 49-51. If not, go to question 52.*

49. How many of your children between two and five drink milk:
___ every day   ___ a few times a week   ___ once a week
___ occasionally   ___ don't know   `78`

50. How was your child fed the first six months?
❑ Breast ❑ Bottle ❑ Both   `79`

51. At what age was your last child first given solid food?
Month: 1 2 3 4 5 6 7 8 9   more   `80`

52. Are you using any kind of family planning?
❑ yes   ❑ no   `81`

53. If yes, what particular way?

                                                           `82`

54. If no, why not?

                                                           `83`

55. If you are given a chance of services offered to your community, which would you choose?
❑ Teaching for career and work   ❑ Nursery school
❑ Clinic   ❑ Family planning
❑ Health education   `84`

56. What worries you most? (one only)
❑ Death   ❑ Scarcity of food   ❑ Lack of work
❑ House   ❑ Education   ❑ Loss of goods
❑ Children   ❑ Lack of money
❑ Others (describe)

                                                           `85`

242

57. What do you want most in life?

❑ Money ❑ Education ❑ Children ❑ Spouse
❑ House ❑ Food ❑ Water ❑ Farm
❑ Better health ❑ Work ❑ Others

| 86 |

58. What is your religion?

❑ Christian ❑ Muslim
❑ Traditional religion ❑ Other

| 87 |

If Christian, ask:

59. Denomination:

| 88 |

60. How often do you attend worship services?

❑ Several times a week ❑ Once a week
❑ Less than once a week ❑ Never

| 89 |

61. How often do you read the Bible?

❑ Every day ❑ Many times a week ❑ Once a week
❑ Less than once a week ❑ Never

| 90 |

Ask them to complete these sentences in their own words.

62. God is like

| 91 |

63. Jesus Christ is

| 92 |

64. The only way to confirm you have a life of joy after death is

| 93 |

This completes the discussion.

Be sure that you have thanked the person for his/her time and help.

Interview completed (date):

_____

Time interview took to complete (minutes):

_____

Name of interviewer (print):

_____

Signature of interviewer:

_____

A Model Evaluation Instrument

The following is a model instrument designed to evaluate a major water supply and nutritional training project.

PART ONE: INITIAL PHASE OF THE PROJECT	Ratings	1	2	3	4	5

Mark as (1) poor (2) inadequate (3) adequate (4) good (5) excellent

A. The overall strategic purpose of the project: _____
   1. Mission's perception and understanding of the purpose of the project.
   2. Convention's perception and understanding of the purpose of the project.
   3. Communication with local station personnel, including pastors, regarding purpose of the project.
   4. Compatibility of the project to long-range mission/convention strategy.
   5. Compatibility of the project to long-range station strategy.

B. The problems to be dealt with and the needs to be met: _____
   1. Thoroughness of research (knowledge of baseline data) to determine real needs.
   2. Involvement of local people/recipients to determine problems/needs.
   3. Involvement of the recipients in determining the project objectives.
   4. Involvement/knowledge/understanding of the mission regarding problems/needs.
   5. Involvement of the convention in determining the project objectives.
   6. Agreement of the appropriate government officials with the project objectives.
   7. Agreement of local officials/leaders with the project objectives.
   8. Relative cost effectiveness in terms of total estimated cost of the project.
   9. Adequacy of initial planning to meet needs/solve basic problems creating needs.
   10. Adequacy of mission's requirements (as basis for approval) for planning processes/documents.

C. The underlying assumptions regarding the project: _____
   1. Level of opportunity/expectations for community involvement.
   2. Level of opportunity/expectations for evangelism and church planting.
   3. Degree involvement/acceptance of responsibility by community "decision-makers."
   4. Relative level of evangelistic/church planting opportunity inherent in project situation.
   5. The potential for accomplishing anticipated objectives.
                              Totals for Part One:

PART TWO: PLANNING	1	2	3	4	5

(1) none (2) inadequate (3) basic only (4) adequate (5) exceptional

A. Feasibility: _____
   1. Baseline data available prior to initiation of plans.
   2. Geological surveys, government maps, etc., gathered.
   3. Information regarding social structures of target area(s).
   4. Information regarding cultural decision-making patterns.
   5. Knowledge of physical resources (existing wells, canals, springs, water tables, etc.).
   6. Resource analysis regarding human, technical, and cultural resources available and committed.
   7. Understanding of the various religious factors and constraints likely to affect the project.
   8. Understanding of any previous attempts by other groups to do similar projects.

9. Coordination with existing government plans for the target area.
10. Level of involvement of target people in determining the actual priority needs.
11. Understanding and relationship of the cultural appropriateness of the project.
12. Understanding and inclusion of primary/secondary constraints most likely to affect success.
13. Clear definition of the scope of each phase of the project.
14. Awareness of environmental problems which may be created.
15. Plans for local maintenance, future development, and/or control following completion.

B. Scope of involvement in the actual project planning: _____
   1. Leadership of the community within the target area(s).
   2. Local pastors, local church members, convention representatives.
   3. Appropriate mission officers, committee representatives.
   4. Local government, civic leaders.
   5. Outside experts, consultants, advisors.

C. Specific objectives, goals, and action plans: _____
   1. Written objectives as initially presented to the mission.
   2. Written goals as initially presented to the mission.
   3. Written action plans as initially presented to the mission.
   4. Written details concerning logistical support as initially presented to the mission.
   5. Level of planning concerning personnel contingencies (volunteer, furlough replacement, etc.).
   6. Level of planning concerning logistical contingencies.
   7. Thoroughness of planning concerning budgetary needs.
   8. Degree to which actual planning was reflected in subsequent implementation.
   9. Clarity of time-sequence (critical path) indicators in project plans.
  10. Accuracy of baseline data in terms of actual findings.

D. Design checkpoint: The degree to which . . . _____
   1. Project provides for correlation with spiritual objectives of the mission/convention.
   2. Project provides for self-initiating activities.
   3. Project relates to the total mission/convention strategic planning.
   4. Project is in harmony with the mission/convention philosophy.
   5. Approach of the project took into consideration cultural dynamics.
   6. Local leaders were allowed to express concerns, ideas, plans.
   7. Plans provided for continuity in case of change in leadership, furloughs, etc.
   8. Budget projections agreed with actual costs.
   9. Potential problems were considered in planning stage (judge against reality).
  10. Actual practices (approaches) are in harmony with originally indicated plans.

E. The initiation of plans: _____
   1. Adequacy of logistical support.
   2. Consistency of actual functions with approved plans.
   3. Coordination of team members toward mutually acceptable objectives, goals, and plans.
   4. Adequacy of bookkeeping, records, financial systems.
   5. Accuracy of bookkeeping, records, financial expenditures.
   6. Clarity of job descriptions for all project personnel, including volunteers.
   7. Adequacy of orientation for all personnel, including volunteers, local hire, etc.
   8. Adequacy of budgetary control against approved budget.

9. Adequacy of processes for requesting personnel (allowance for lag time, job readiness upon arrival).
10. Adequacy of provision for volunteer or other personnel (housing, transport, field support).

Totals for Part Two:

PART THREE: MONITORING	1	2	3	4	5

(1) poor (2) inadequate (3) adequate (4) good (5) excellent

A. Objectives, goals, and action plans: _____

1. Amount of care taken to stay within the project's primary objectives.
2. Degree to which the project was within the framework of specific preplanned goals.
3. Degree to which specific action plans were followed.
4. Correlation between the accomplishments at midpoint and the goals listed.
5. Level of reporting to the mission, convention, or FMB as to midpoint situation assessments.
6. Quantity of work accomplished against expectations.
7. Quality of work accomplished against expectations.
8. Adequacy of modifications or adjustments against unforeseen circumstances/events/problems.
9. Adequacy of mission's monitoring of work against predetermined goals.
10. Level of local involvement in carrying out the objectives and goals.

B. Budget and utilization of funding: _____

1. Relative accuracy of the original budget estimates as approved by the area office.
2. Degree to which the project directors stayed within budgeted appropriations.
3. Degree to which project directors stayed within budget guidelines for requesting & spending funds.
4. Relative cost-effectiveness of the project in terms of the total number of people helped.
5. Adequacy of the bookkeeping procedures.
6. Adequacy of the processes of tracking, listing, and vouchering expenditures.
7. Relative efficiency of purchasing processes related to achieving the lowest and most reliable prices (considering time delays, etc.).
8. Management of equipment and stores.
9. Relative adequacy of resource inventory related to potential loss and theft.
10. Relative level of time delays, loss of work, and overruns in terms of extended costs.

C. Spiritual factors: _____

1. Degree to which evangelism and church growth goals were carried out.
2. Number of churches planted in relationship to goals.
3. Number of baptisms in relationship to project goals.
4. Correlation of evangelism and church planting with human need aspects of the project.
5. Relationship of evangelism and church planting to convention involvement.
6. Correlation of evangelism and church planting with overall mission strategies and plans.
7. Degree to which local church members in new churches have become involved in evangelism.
8. Degree of church growth as compared with other similar areas in the country.
9. Correlation of discipleship training and specific sites for projects and church planning.
10. Relative degree of involving volunteers in spiritual ministries.

Totals for Part Three:

PART FOUR: ACCOMPLISHMENT OF OBJECTIVES AND GOALS	1	2	3	4	5

(1) very poor (2) poor (3) average (4) good (5) excellent

A. Process analysis:

1. Degree to which all major objectives were met in the given time frame.
2. Degree to which all major goals were met in the given time frame.
3. Degree to which work accomplished met anticipated and planned quality standards.
4. Degree to which interrelationships of personnel involved aided the accomplishment of the work.
5. Relative quality of involvement of the target people in the accomplishment of the goals.
6. In specific aspects of the project, such as well drilling, the relative number of successful activities as compared with those which were considered unsuccessful.
7. Relative number of wells/canals/roads being maintained and operated without mission support.
8. Level to which the local people have accepted ownership/responsibility for completed projects.
9. Degree to which the project has solved/met the original need for which the project was designed.
10. Degree to which local people have initiated efforts to help themselves with similar projects.

B. Impact analysis:

1. Relative environmental impact.
2. Impact on mortality of the "under-fives."
3. Relative improvement on nutritional levels among the "under-fives."
4. Impact upon relationships between the mission/convention and the various local communities.
5. Overall "message" communicated to the recipients.
6. Local government and relations with the mission/convention.
7. Federal government and relations with the mission/convention.
8. Of volunteers as a whole upon local people.
9. Agricultural development in the area.
10. Number of reported diarrheas in the area of the projects (before and after).
11. Caloric intake of the area of the projects (before and after).
12. Relationships with Roman Catholic or other religious leadership in the area.
13. Other NGOs either in the area or in the country.
14. Relative level of dependency the people have on the mission.
15. Volunteers as they returned back to the United States.
16. Level and quantity of food supplies to the rural sections involved.
17. Baptist church growth in the area.
18. Moral/ethical values and any overtly non-Christian practices in the area.
19. Sunday School growth in the area.
20. Number of baptisms in the area.
21. Baptists in their relationship with other denominations.
22. Number of acres now under cultivation as compared with preproject.
23. Quality of produce being achieved as compared with preproject conditions.
24. Quality of drinking water now being consumed compared with the quality available prior to the initiation of the project(s).
25. "Quality of life" standard as compared with prior standard.

Totals for Part Four:

PART FIVE: GENERAL QUESTIONS

Please answer briefly in the space provided or add page as necessary.

1. How was the problem and the need originally determined? Who determined it?

2. What were the major problems encountered during the process of the project(s)?

3. What environmental problems, if any, were created as a result of the project(s)?

4. If you had to do it all over again, what would you change?

5. If the missionaries had to leave tomorrow, what parts would be sustainable/nonsustainable within the next year?

6. Describe what you feel have been the major accomplishments of the project(s):

Signed (optional)_____

Bibliography

I. General Information

Barnes, Peter., ed., *The People's Land: A Reader on Land Reform in the United States*. Emmaus, PA: Rodale Press, 1976.

Barnet, Richard J. and Ronald Muller. *Global Reach: The Power of the Multinational Corporations*. New York: Simon and Schuster, Inc., 1976.

Beckmann, David. *Hunger 1993: Uprooted People, Third Annual Report on the State of World Hunger*. Bread for the World Institute on Hunger and Development, Washington, DC, 1993.

Bentz, Thomas. *New Immigrants: Portraits in Passage*. New York: The Pilgrim Press, 1981.

Bridge, Donald and David Phypers. *Spiritual Gifts and the Church*. Downers Grove: InterVarsity Press, 1973.

Brown, Lester R. *The Twenty-Ninth Day*. New York: W. W. Norton and Company, Inc., 1978.

Cahill, Kevin M., ed. *Famine*. Maryknoll, New York: Orbis Books, 1982.

Flynn, Leslie B. *Nineteen Gifts of the Spirit*. Wheaton: Victor Books, 1974.

Freudenberger, C. Dean. *Food for Tomorrow?* Minneapolis: Augsburg Publishing House, 1984.

Gallis, Marion. *Trade for Justice: Myth or Mandate?* New York: World Council of Churches, 1972.

Gee, Donald. *Concerning Spiritual Gifts*. Springfield, MO: Gospel Publishing House, 1972.

George, Susan. *How the Other Half Dies: The Real Reason for World Hunger*. Montclair, NJ: Allenheld, Osmun and Company, 1977.

Goulet, Denis and Michael Hudson. *The Myth of Aid*. New York: IDOC/North America, 1971.

Grant, James P. *The State of the World's Children*, UNICEF, Oxford University Press, 1993.

Hancock, Robert Lincoln, ed. *The Ministry of Development in Evangelical Perspective, A Symposium on the Social and Spiritual Mandate*. William Carey Library, 1971.

Haq, Mahbub Ul. *Poverty Curtain: Choices of the Third World*. New York: Columbia University Press, 1976.

Harrington, Michael. *The Vast Majority*. New York: Simon and Schuster, Inc., 1977.

Harrison, Paul. *The Greening of Africa: Breaking Through in the Battle for Land and Food*. New York: Penguin Books, 1987.

Hayter, Teresa. *Aid As Imperialism*. New York: Penguin Books, Inc. 1971.

Jones, Brennon. "Export Cropping and Development: We Need to Know More" and "Needed: A Nutritional Impact Study." Bread for the World 6, four-page background papers, (available from Bread for the World), 1990.

Kinghorn, Kenneth Cain. *Gifts of the Spirit*. Nashville: Abingdon Press, 1976.

Lappe, Frances M. and Joseph Collins, with Cary Fowler. *Food First: Beyond the Myth of Scarcity*. Boston: Houghton Mifflin, Company, 1977.

Lingenfelter, Sherwood G. and Marvin K. Mayers. *Ministering Cross-Culturally: An International Model for Personal Relationships*. Grand Rapids: Baker Book House, 1896.

MacGorman, Jack W. *The Gifts of the Spirit*. Nashville: Broadman Press, 1974.

McRae, William J. *The Dynamics of Spiritual Gifts*. Grand Rapids: Zondervan Publishing Company, 1976.

Merrill, Richard, ed. *Radical Agriculture*. New York: Harper and Row, Publishers, 1976.

Minear, Larry. *New Hope for the Hungry? The Challenge of the World Food Crisis*. New York: Friendship Press, 1975.

Muphy, Edward F. *Spiritual Gifts and the Great Commission*. South Pasadena: Mandate Press, 1975.

Myers, Kenneth A., ed. *What Do Christians Expect From Christian Relief and Development?* Report of the National Survey of Evangelicals on Christian Relief and Development, Center for Survey Research, University of Virginia, 1992.

Myrdal, Gunnar. *The Challenge of World Poverty.* New York: Random House, Inc., 1971.

Nelson, Jack A. *Hunger for Justice: The Politics of Food and Faith.* Maryknoll, New York: Orbis Books, 1981.

Organization for Economic Cooperation and Development. *Investing in Developing Countries.* Paris, France: OECD, 1975.

Payer, Cheryl. *The Debt Trap: The IMF and the Third World.* New York: Monthly Review Press, 1975.

Prestbo, John A., ed. *This Abundant Land.* Princeton, NJ: Dow Jones Books, 1975.

Prieto, Daniel Santo., ed. *Evaluation Sourcebook: For Private and Voluntary Organizations,* New York: American Council of Voluntary Agencies.

Purkiser, W. T. *The Gifts of the Spirit.* Kansas City: Beacon Hill Press, 1975.

Schomer, Mark. "Can Food Aid and Development Aid Promote Self-Reliance?" Bread for the World four-page background paper, (available from Bread for the World), 1990.

Schumacher, E. F. *Small Is Beautiful: Economics As If People Mattered.* New York: Harper and Row, Publishers, 1975.

Sewell, John W. and the Staff of the Overseas Development Council. *The US and World Development: Agenda for Action.* New York: Praeger Publishers, 1977.

Shoemaker, Dennis E. *The Global Connection: Local Action for World Justice.* New York: Friendship Press, 1977.

Simon, Arthur. *Bread for the World.* New York: Paulist Press and William B. Eerdmans Publishing Company, 1975.

Simon, Arthur. "Let's Overhaul Development and Food Aid." Bread for the World four-page background paper, (available from Bread for the World), 1991.

Sommer, John G. *Beyond Charity: US Voluntary Aid for a Changing Third World.* Washington, DC: Overseas Development Council, 1977.

Stedman, Ray C. *Body Life.* Glendale, CA: Regal Books, 1972.

Tetsunao, Yamamori. "Toward the Symbiotic Ministry: God's Mandate for the Church Today," Food for the Hungry pamphlet, 1990.

Timberlake, Lloyd. *Africa in Crisis: The Causes, the Cures of Environmental Bankruptcy.* Washington, DC: International Institute for Environment and Development, 1985.

Toton, Suzanne. *World Hunger, The Responsibility of Christian Education.* Maryknoll, New York: Orbis Books, 1982.

US Agency for International Development. *Implementation of Recommendations of the World Food Conference, A Report to Congress.* Washington, DC: US Government Printing Office.

Withers, Leslie and Tom Peterson., eds. *Hunger Action Handbook: What You Can Do and How to Do It.* Decatur, Georgia: *Seeds* Magazine, 1987.

World Bank. *World Development Report.* Washington, DC: The International Bank for Reconstruction and Development/The World Bank, 1993.

Yohn, Rick. *Discover Your Spiritual Gift and Use It.* Wheaton: Tyndale House Publishers, 1974.

II. Theological Reflection

Cassidy, Richard J. *Jesus, Politics and Society: A Study of Luke's Gospel.* Maryknoll, New York: Orbis Books, 1978.

Dunn, James E., et al. *Endangered Species.* Nashville: Broadman Press, 1976.

Freudenberger, C. Dean and Paul M. Minus, Jr. *A Christian Responsibility in a Hungry World.* Nashville: Abingdon Press, 1976.

Hellwig, Monika K. *The Eucharist and the Hunger of the World.* New York: Paulist Press, 1976.

Hessel, Dieter T., ed. *Beyond Survival: Bread and Justice in Christian Perspective.* New York: Friendship Press, 1977.

Jegen, Mary Evelyn and Bruno V. Manno., eds. *The Earth Is the Lord's.* New York: Paulist Press, 1978.

Parham, Robert. *What Shall We Do in a Hungry World?* Birmingham, Alabama: New Hope Press, 1988.

Samuel, Vinay and Chris Sugden. *The Church in Response to Human Need*. Grand Rapids, Michigan: William B. Eerdmans Publishing Company, 1987.

Scanlon, A. Clark. "Bold Mission Thrust Update," March 1987.

Sider, Ronald J., ed. *Cry Justice: The Bible Speaks on Hunger and Poverty*. New York: Paulist Press, 1977.

Song, C. S. *The Compassionate God*. Maryknoll, New York: Orbis Books, 1982.

_____. *Rich Christians in an Age of Hunger: A Biblical Study*. New York: Paulist Press, 1977.

Tamez, Elsa. *Bible of the Oppressed*. Maryknoll, New York: Orbis Books, 1982.

Tolstoy, Leo. *The Kingdom of God Is Within You*.

Tolstoy, Leo. *Resurrection*.

Wagner, C. Peter. *Church Growth and the Whole Gospel: A Biblical Mandate*. San Francisco: Harper and Row, Publishers, 1981.

III. Nutrition and Health Care

Cameron, M. and Y. Yofvander. *Manual on Feeding Infants and Young Children*. Calorie Advisory Group, Room A-555, United Nations, New York, NY 10017, 1976.

Ghosh, S. *The Feeding and Care of Infants and Young Children*, Voluntary Health Association of India, New Delhi, 1976.

Jelliffee, D. *Child Nutrition in Developing Countries*. USAID, Office of Nutrition, Washington, DC 20523, 1969.

Jones, E. (and others). *A Field Guide for Evaluation of Nutrition Education: An Experimental Approach to Determination of Effects on Food Behavior in Lesser Developed Countries*. Allison Park, PA: Synectices Corporation, 1975.

King, M. (and others). *Nutrition for Developing Countries*. 30 Guilford Street, London, WC1N 1EH, England: TALC, 1973.

Koppert, J. *Nutrition Rehabilitation: Its Practical Approach*. 30 Guilford Street, London, WC1N 1EH, England: TALC, 1977.

IV. Agriculture and Community Development

Chrispeels, M. and D. Sadava. *Plants, Food and People*. W. H. Freeman Company, 660 Market Street, San Francisco, CA 94104, 1977.

Darrow, K. and R. Pam. *Appropriate Technology Sourcebook*. 30 Guilford Street, London WC1N 1EH, England: TALC, 1976.

Hopfen, H. *Farm Implements for Arid and Tropical Regions, Food and Agricultural Organization, Distribution and Sales Section*. Via delle Termi de Caracalla, 00100 Rome, Italy, 1976.

Lindblad, C. and L. Druben. *Small Farm Grain Storage*. 3706 Rhode Island Avenue, Mount Ranier, MD 20822: VITA, 1976. (Note: VITA has a whole series of "Small" books relating to various types of agricultural projects. Ask for the "Small" series.)

Masefield, G. *A Handbook of Tropical Agriculture*, Masefield, England: Oxford Press, 1976.

Sanders, D. *Visual Communication Handbook*. 30 Guilford Street, London, WC1N 1EH, England: TALC, 1977.

Village Technology Handbook. VITA, (as above), 1977.

V. Various Periodicals

The following magazines and newsletters are available several times a year. They cover a variety of subjects related to community development and health care. Some of these references also have lists of helpful new books, posters, and filmstrips that can be ordered.

Appropriate Technology (Energy, farming, health, water)
Available from:
  Intermediate Technology Publishers, Ltd.
  9 King Street (Covent Garden)
  London, WC2E 8HN, England

Assignment Children (Development, health, nutrition, water)
Available from:
  UNICEF, Palais Wilson
  Case postale 11
  CH-1211 Geneva 14
  Switzerland

Cajanus (Health, marketing, nutrition), Available from:
  Caribbean Food and Nutrition Institute
  P. O. Box 140
  Kingston 7 Jamaica

CERES (Development, farming, nutrition)
Available from:
  Food and Agricultural Organization
  Distribution and Sales Section
  Via delle Terme di Caracalla
  00100 Rome, Italy
  New York, NY 10003

Children in the Tropics (Health, nutrition)
Available from:
  International Children's Center
  Chateau de Longchamp
  Bois de Boulogne
  75016 Paris, France

Rural Development Network Bulletin (Development, farming)
Available from:
  Overseas Liaison Committee
  11 Dupont Circle
  Washington, DC 20036

Salubritas (Health, nutrition, training)
Available from:
American Public Health Association
Division of International Health Programs
1015 Eighteenth Street, NW
Washington, DC 20036

Soundings (Farming, health, nutrition, water)
Available from:
World Neighbors
5116 N Portland
Oklahoma City, OK 73112
(Note: World Neighbors produces a large amount of materials in several languages on filmstrip and other media. Ask for a catalog.)

TAICH News (Development, family planning, farming, health)
Available from:
Technical Assistance Information Clearing House
200 Park Avenue South

World Health (Health, nutrition, development)
Available from:
World Health Organization
1211 Geneva 27
Switzerland

VI. Domestic Hunger
"Citizens' Board of Inquiry into Hunger and Malnutrition in the US" Hunger USA., Boston: Beacon Press, 1968. (pamphlet)
Ending Hunger: An Idea Whose Time Has Come, Praeger, NY, 1985.
Howell, Barbara. "Hunger in the US" BFW four-page background paper. (Available from Bread for the World with self-addressed/stamped envelope or $4.00.)
Kotz, Nick. *Let Them Eat Promises: The Politics of Hunger in America*. New York: Doubleday and Company, 1971.

Mayer, Jean., ed. *US Nutrition Policies in the Seventies*. San Francisco: W. H. Freeman and Company, 1971.

Perella, Frederick J. and Mariellen Procopio. *Poverty Profile*. New York: Paulist Press, 1976.

Piven, Frances F. and Richard A. Cloward. *Regulating the Poor: The Functions of Public Relief*. New York: Random House, Inc., 1972.

The Global 2000 Report to the President. Council on Environmental Quality and the Department of State, 1981.

The State of the World's Children. UNICEF, 1985.

VII. Other Sources of Information

American Farm Bureau Federation
425 13th Street, NW
Washington, DC 20006

Children's Foundation
1028 Connecticut Avenue, NW, #1112
Washington, DC 20036

Community Nutrition Institute
1146 19th Street, NW
Washington, DC 20036

Food Research and Action Center
2011 I Street, NW
Washington, DC 20006

House Agriculture Committee
Subcommittee on Domestic Marketing
Consumer Relations and Nutrition
1301 Longworth House Office Building
Washington, DC 20515

Interfaith Center on Corporate Responsibility
475 Riverside Drive, Room 566
New York, NY 10027

International Bank for Reconstruction
Development (World Bank)
1818 H Street, NW
Washington, DC 20433

National Catholic Rural Life Conference
3801 Grand Avenue
Des Moines, IA 50312

National Farmer's Union
1012 14th Street, NW
Washington, DC 20005

Overseas Development Council
717 Massachusetts Avenue, NW
Washington, DC 20036

Rural America
1346 Connecticut Avenue, NW
Dupont Circle Building
Washington, DC 20036

Senate Agriculture Committee
Subcommittee on Nutrition
322 Russell Senate Office Building
Washington, DC 20510

UNCTAD, United Nations
New York, NY 10017

UN Center on Transnationals
605 Third Avenue
New York, NY 10016

UN Food and Agriculture Organization (FAO)
1776 F Street, NW
Washington, DC 20437

US Agency for International Development (AID)
Department of State
320 21st Street, NW
Washington, DC 20523

US Department of Agriculture
Washington, DC 20250